The Ci
and
the Square

Jack Gale

www.capallbann.co.uk

The Circle and the Square

©1997 Jack Gale

ISBN 1 86163 013 1

Cover design by Paul Mason
Internal photographs by Liz Gale

Published by:

Capall Bann Publishing
Freshfields
Chieveley
Berks
RG20 8TF

Dedication

This book is dedicated to the return of the spirit of Mary Magdalene, estranged bride, lover, healer and Goddess of vines, gardens and good times. May the Lady in Blue bring wholeness, healing, balance and fun.

Acknowledgments

The author wishes to sincerely thank the following psychics and research colleagues for their invaluable contributions over the years: Carole Young, Jo Shrimpton, Tony Lee, Doreen Lee, Jenni Stather, Fay Cockell, Jackie Huxter-Freer, David Aylward, Ian Wicks and Nick Ashron. Thanks, also, modern-day Avalonians Paul Weston (a true quester) and Chandira for their interest and encouragement and to Denise Stobie of the wonderful Library of Avalon at Glastonbury for sharing information and for providing the library as a venue for my talks. The author is grateful to Geoffrey Ashe for showing him round Dion Fortune's one-time residence, Chalice Orchard, Father Geoffrey Scott for permission to reproduce the Douai Abbey portrait of John Thorne, Father Damien of Prinknash Abbey for generous provision of information, Father Ian Dickie for provision of access to the beatification papers of the Glastonbury Three at Westminster Cathedral archives office and Ann Wain, manageress of the *George and Pilgrims Hotel* for kindly showing him round the *George*'s cellar. The author also wishes to thank Ian Freer for using his astrological expertise in order to draw up a horoscope of the Three's execution day, Andrew Collins for all that he has done for psychic questing and for the opportunity to speak at several Psychic Questing Conferences, the Rev. James Turnbull for sharing his thoughts on the long-term effects of the 1539 events and Liz Gale for doing a nice job (again!) with the photographic illustrations. Last but not least, affectionate mention MUST be made of that intrepid band of magicians and brothers from the secret Glastonbury order who withdrew to the inner planes in 1539 but never stopped working and also Madeleine; priestess and friend, then and now. Cheers!

Contents

Glastonbury Tor, evening

Introduction

This book may raise a few eyebrows. I make no apologies for the strange, bizarre and almost unbelievable nature of the events chronicled in the following pages, having simply endeavoured to report experiences and discoveries as honestly and as faithfully as I felt to be possible. Some of the related material may be potentially quite controversial. My aim has not been to give offence but, as stated above, to simply report the findings of my questing colleagues and myself. Whatever else I intend, it is certainly no slur upon the memory of the three brave men who died on Glastonbury Tor on 15th November, 1539. The Glastonbury Three were all Benedictine monks from one of the last great abbeys to fall before Henry VIII's Dissolution programme ran out of steam following the execution of Thomas Cromwell; ironically himself the driving force behind the tragic events which took place on the Isle of Avalon in the late Autumn of 1539. Many have commented upon the oddly ritualistic nature of the three executions; the method of implementation of which may strike us today as highly contrary to common sense. If an example were to be made would not Glastonbury town or Wells have been a better bet? In order to enact this hideous echo of a mediaeval passion play, it would have been necessary to drive heavy horses dragging wooden hurdles upon which the condemned were stretched (a favoured pre-execution treatment of Reformation victims) up the steep, slippery slopes of the Tor in a screaming, pitiless wind on a cold November day, as Geoffrey Ashe has pointed out in his book *King Arthur's Avalon*. At the summit the three were unbound, then hung, drawn and quartered; bodily parts being subsequently displayed in neighbouring Somerset towns as a deterrent to those who might dare to oppose the royal will. At the last minute the trumped-up charge of treason was changed to one of "robbery" which, in effect, meant that efforts had been made to conceal certain sacred treasures from the greedy hands of Thomas Cromwell and his commissioners. This is the picture of the executions with which popular history provides us.

Archival study (correspondence between Cromwell in London and his commissioners in Somerset) has revealed that two other hangings took place the same day at nearby Wearyall Hill, while psychic communication has also brought to light the existence of a covert "hit list" which was ruthlessly worked through in the days following the executions of Abbot Richard

1

Whiting, Treasurer John Thorne (taken name Arthur) and Under-Treasurer Roger Wilfred. The main body of the Benedictine brothers of Glastonbury was sent out into the world following the closure of its parent institution. Things were not as bad as they might have been; each brother was provided with the kind of pension which would have enabled a single man to live a careful, unspectacular life-style without excessive hardship. For a few others however, whose names the authorities carefully left unrecorded, it seems to have been a very different story. Psychically-received information indicates that a small group were regarded as a serious threat. One of my highly-gifted psychic colleagues, with no prompting from myself, has seen them being cunningly poisoned and flushed-out of the underground meeting places to which they had retreated at the end via the use of large dogs and fire in a manner reminiscent of events which took place at the culmination of the Warsaw Ghetto uprising during World War II. The magical skills of one of their number were considered to be so threatening that he spent his last hours in a dank, filthy cell so securely chained that he was not even able to trace sigils on the dirt floor using a fingertip. Why? This book endeavours to provide some answers.

It should not be assumed that this volume merely constitutes a study of a particularly bloody chapter in English history. My investigations revealed much that was weird, fascinating and inspiring. Other writers have guardedly hinted at the existence of a secret Gnostic/alchemical mystery school once located within the abbey's walls; a small band of initiates daring enough to risk their reputations (and lives) as a result of their dedication to the pursuit of hidden knowledge and, once attained, the use of that knowledge in practical magical work. Many alchemists of the late Middle Ages carried out their researches and rituals behind the walls of monastic institutions; it was not uncommon. Perhaps a supreme example can be found in the mysterious Sir George Ripley, the Canon of Bridlington, whose legacy and influence played a major part in the strange and secret drama which came to a violent end in the Autumn of 1539. Ripley was the sort of person who was possessed of sufficient nerve and audacity to enable him to execute with style and flourish the kind of feats not "normally" associated with the monastic life. Early on in his career, he received complaints from the brothers with whom he was lodged regarding the strange smells which issued from his quarters; complaints which do not seem to have deterred him in any way. When dedicating his book *The Compound of Alchemy* to Edward IV, Ripley saw fit to advise the hell-raising veteran of the Wars of the Roses to cut down his alcohol consumption; advice which took him several pages to deliver!

"Working the system", Ripley obtained a Papal dispensation which absolved him of all duties with regard to the usual monastic observances, enabling him to pursue his alchemical studies twenty-four hours a day if he so desired. Not being a man to keep his head down despite the nature of his activities, Ripley casually collected a knighthood in the course of his wanderings through life. During his residence at Rhodes, he is reputed to have studied occult sciences with the Knights of St. John. Deliberately obscure and baffling in his literary style (at times reminiscent of that of Aleister Crowley) he admitted that he wrote to confound "the owls and the bats" and to enlighten the few. He even died with style; remains resting in a tomb decorated with sculpted alchemical devices which were eventually removed by a frowning, uneasy 18th Century cleric! Ripley's mandala diagram, *The Wheel*, certainly provided the inspiration for the "Great Rite" (of which more later) in which Christ was equated with the sacrificed Solar God; a ubiquitous and universal archetype found in many pagan pantheons and also equated with the alchemists' King Sol, while Mary Magdalene, his bride, was equated with Queen Luna. This rite, as we shall see, took place upstairs at a well-known Glastonbury drinking place. Given that monastic alchemists were not that uncommon, it seems that, by 1539, at any rate, the covert Avalonian variety were going somewhat further than most. The activities of the "Priesthood" (as one of Frederick Bligh Bond's Otherworldly communicators called it in the early years of the century when he made a brief, "throwaway" reference to this highly secret group) form the main focus of this book; activities which ceased on the physical plane when the Reformation holocaust descended upon Glastonbury Abbey in 1539. These activities also form a context for the strange and terrible nature of the executions when three men faced their deaths with a much-admired courage and quiet dignity; one of whom at least was a key Priesthood activist.

A holistic combination of psychic work and "feet on the ground" archival research has revealed the Priesthood's concern with a potent form of sacred alchemical geomancy and its use of a methodology which reflected an eclectic blend of mystery tradition techniques which was utilised in the manipulation of terrestrial subtle energy currents of unimaginable power. If this book's heart is to be found anywhere then it is deep in the Isle of Avalon's sacred soil; the earth through which the Michael and Mary currents found by Hamish Miller and Paul Broadhurst follow their snaking, serpentine course; currents of vital relevance to this book.

The Circle and the Square is written neither from the perspective of the university academic nor the "New Ager". Rather, its subject matter is seen from the viewpoint of a practising occultist of pagan persuasion who has, for many years, approached various historical mysteries and mysteries of the Sacred Land using a fusion of hard-graft reference research and psychically-received input. Despite the many articles and books published over the years on the subject of "strange" Glastonbury my colleagues and myself have found many secrets embedded in this mysterious terrain; matters puzzling, profound and wonderful which, for various reasons, seem to have been overlooked until now, among them, the return of Glastonbury's forgotten saint, Mary Magdalene. Phases, fads and fancies swim in and out of favour with a high turnover rate in Glastonbury, now a real hotbed of New Age activism. While much of this may be well-intentioned, one sometimes feels that some of those involved pay little or no attention to the ensouling spirit of the ground beneath their feet, concerned, as they are, with imprinting their own mark upon it regardless of its actual needs, of which they are probably quite ignorant because they have not bothered to ask any questions in this respect. As we near the Millennium there seems to be ever more need for LISTENING to Albion's sacred sites to find out what they wish to tell us, even if it may be merely the unpalatable cry of "Leave me alone".

In this volume emphasis is placed upon the strange life and activities of John Thorne (monastic taken name Arthur), the chairmaker, ostensibly the abbey's treasurer and a historical figure with whom I have a particularly intimate association. Beatified along with the two companions executed with him and with a host of other Catholic Reformation martyrs by Pope Leo in the late 19th Century, John's life as revealed by documentary research and by input from a number of totally independent psychics with whom I have been fortunate enough to work was weirder than the wildest imaginings of occult fiction. In addition to holding the treasurer's post (and thereby being a prime Reformation agents' target) John was a covert alchemist and occultist whose work incorporated an eclectic range of influences, reflecting the powerful Gnostic tradition which is occasionally tantalisingly glimpsed but more usually hidden behind the facade of a well-visited West country tourist centre. John LIVED his magic to the extent that he gave his body and earthly life to the "Great Work" to which he dedicated himself. For those with eyes to see, well-camouflaged signs of his double life may be seen in the decorations on the famous "Glastonbury Chairs" which he designed and built in his spare time; copies of which may be seen in Glastonbury and other locations. The man's varied magical activities perhaps bear comparison with episodes from the lives of Aleister Crowley, Dion Fortune, Austin Osman Spare, John Dee (with whom he had a connection) and other colourful figures from the pages of British occult history. His secret and sacred alchemical marriage to his French priestess resulted in the creation of an awesomely powerful energy form which was left to incubate beneath Glastonbury High Street for four and a half centuries, until the next phase in this aspect of "The Work" could be accomplished in the 1990's; John's life having been disrupted by his execution and leaving a work in progress awaiting completion. His creation of site guardian entities (often in the form of dragons or griffins) to watch over concealed sacred treasures, his ritualised and sacrificial death, enacted at a geomantically precise location at a time when the Sun's position in the heavens was almost identical to that which it occupied at the assassination of John F. Kennedy 424 years later; these are indeed the stuff of legend.

It was the researcher and author Andrew Collins who coined the term "Psychic Questing". This is a useful label for an activity which he does not claim to have invented. Many exponents arise as one flips back through history's pages, among them Wellesley Tudor Pole and Frederick Bligh Bond; our spiritual ancestors who blazed the Glastonbury questing trail in the early 20th Century and whose work carried out at that time is so relevant to that of my colleagues and myself today. For me, psychic questing involves the cross-referencing of material received psychically with the results of long hours of documentary research in an effort to throw light upon mysteries concerning historical events and sacred places. The archival research component is vital, for without it one is merely presenting more "channelled" information. It also helps to keep the quester firmly grounded and obviously lends credibility to reported findings. This book contains a reported summary of several years which I spent following a trail which led me from Greenwich to Glastonbury. I hope that the reader will find the following account stimulating, thought-provoking and entertaining. Yes, much of the material contained within these pages IS fantastic, to put it mildly. As I stated at the start of this introduction, I make no apologies. I simply leave readers to judge for themselves.

Chapter 1

The Path to Avalon

6th July, 1991. Well, it seems a reasonable starting place. Having visited my parents at Peyton Place, Greenwich (yes, there really IS a street bearing the name of the now half-forgotten "soap" of yesteryear) I discovered a psychic fayre to be taking place in the nearby Borough Halls and popped in to check things out. The coolness of the hall's dimly lit, cavernous interior provided a marked contrast to the hot Summer afternoon outside. I found the usual array of Tarot readers, palmists, etc, plus a few stalls selling the predictable array of crystals and divination sets. Continually-tinkling New Age music produced a vaguely sleep-inducing audial backdrop. After an initial wander I found myself seated across the table from a reader called Molly. Among many of the quite apt things which she told me was the statement that I had, in a past life, been a member of a religious order at the time of Henry VIII. The remark interested me, although its effect could not really have been described as profound. It made a change from remarks such as "You'll be a healer dearie", or "You were a witch in a past life", which one often encounters in such a context, at least. Filing the past-life comment away for possible future reference as the quester must habitually do (NO psychically-received material, however seemingly inconsequential, should be consigned to the bin), I gave the matter no further thought for nearly a year.

It was not until March 1992, when I received an abrupt Otherworldly communication during a seemingly routine telephone chat with my valued friend and psychic collaborator Jo Shrimpton that Molly's remark came back to me. There is something oddly magical about telephones. Perhaps this is because they focus receptivity; a context in which most other distractions are cut out. In my earlier questing years, a considerable volume of the most valuable psychically-received material "came through" during "ordinary" telephone conversations with psychics such as Jo, Carole Young and Tony Lee. In fact, the frequency with which this tended to happen became something of an "in" joke between my psychic colleagues and myself. In the midst of a quite mundane natter about family affairs, Jo suddenly paused and

I knew from past experience that "something" was getting through. "Hang on Jack", Jo said. "This is for you. . . roses. . . a red rose and a white rose. I can see Henry VIII and I can see his royal seal on some document. " A pause followed. "Now I can see a monk in a habit. It's you. . . . I'm sure it's you. . . in a past life. You've got bare feet and sandals. You're carrying a huge bunch of keys. . . . That's it. "

Information had now come through two totally independent psychics. The "up front" presence of the formidable Tudor monarch and the manner in which his seal was stamped upon something seemed to indicate that his reason for being shown to us at all constituted something more than a mere chronological reference point. It seemed more likely that he had some kind of direct or indirect involvement in whatever it was that happened to me four centuries ago, assuming for a moment that we WERE dealing with past-life "stuff". A few weeks later I started leading my Sacred Greenwich walking tours on Saturday mornings, which were to continue sporadically for the next four years. Concerns regarding the release of my first published book *Other Meridians, Another Greenwich*, further Greenwich questing work and the preparation of talks which I would soon begin to deliver on the London occult/pagan circuit left little space for possible further deliberation on the subject of supposed Tudor past-lives. For a while, the whole matter was put "on hold".

In late August, 1993, my wife Liz and I made a long-promised visit to Glastonbury. As Companions of Chalice Well we were able to stay in the Little St. Michael retreat house at the rear of the Chalice Well gardens. I found the three days quite magical. Lounging up on the lower slopes of Chalice Hill as the sun dropped below the horizon on the last evening, I felt as if I had entered an enchanted realm. Stretching out on a comfortable bed under a low, 17th Century ceiling on warm, late-Summer nights and hearing, through the open window, the ceaseless tumbling of the Red Spring's sacred waters had been idyllic to say the least. This, of course, was a classic case of seeing Glastonbury through rose-coloured spectacles; the reality being frequently rather less romantic due to the complex dynamics of this mysterious place.

Dion Fortune called Glastonbury a "spiritual volcano" and the energies found there can certainly be volcanic at times. For those living permanently in Glastonbury and surviving this experience there must surely be some requisite mechanism for "doing a deal" with the powerful place spirit, if only on a subconscious level. In practise, this COULD involve being totally unaware of the"energies" (as they say), the thinness of the local inter-dimensional veil and the Otherworldly presences which are often so conspicuous, in which case it then becomes just another small Somerset town. Let us face fact; "ordinary" people were living "ordinary" lives in Glastonbury long before the great upsurge of Avalonianism in the early 20th Century which threw up names like Frederick Bligh Bond, Alice Buckton and Dion Fortune, to name a few. (Dion coined her own reference terms in this context; she called the then-newly resident followers of Glastonbury's spiritual impulse Avalonians and the folk whose ancestors had dwelt upon this sacred earth for centuries, living the kind of rural existence which could be encountered anywhere else in Somerset, Glastonburians.) When the great burst of spiritual and creative activity so wonderfully documented in Patrick Benham's book *The Avalonians* subsided, the "everyday" side of Glastonbury's existence continued as indeed it does to this day; the area again becoming a focus of spiritual activity in the rather different climate of the late 1960's. Articles by visionaries such as the one and only John Michell appeared in magazines and newspapers born of the "Underground" cultural explosion whose perhaps best-remembered public manifestation was the 1967 "Summer of Love".

Despite the current trend towards remembering them with cynicism, the events of that era seemed highly radical at the time; revolutionary, in fact. In London itself, the outward signs of the flowers and love trend appeared to be relatively short-lived, having given way, by the Autumn of 1968, to events such as the occupation of the *London School of Economics* and the demonstration against the Vietnam War in Grosvenor Square; a more hard-core, left-influenced, politicised outlook replacing the pop mysticism. Much of what was said and done during the "hippy" era was, admittedly, naive in the extreme.

Reading some of the old Underground papers now, one may well squirm with embarrassment at the seemingly half-baked, immature, superficial idealism. Much of the literature may now strike one as painfully unliberated despite its pretensions to the contrary. The public face of the radical feminist movement, for instance, was still in the process of surfacing; women often being portrayed in Underground magazine illustrations (obviously intended to be shockingly radical) as mere sex objects no different to images to be found at that time in any top-shelf "men's mag". Many who wore flowers in their hair and kaftans draped around their bodies when they went to "love-ins" and "happenings" at that time are now hardworking middle-aged citizens with families and mortgages. So much for revolution. But. . .

On a macrocosmic level, the "revolution" of the late '60's may seem to have been somewhat ineffectual in broad cultural terms. Microcosmically, however, I believe the tale to have been a little different. When all is said and done, it does seem that there WAS a shift in consciousness, the effects of which were both long-lasting and profound. Take, for example, the renaissance of interest in Earth Mysteries and "Leys" (to use Alfred Watkins' much-abused and misused term). Publically, the Herefordshire miller, magistrate and innovative spare-time photographer never claimed that the landscape alignments which he discovered were anything more than trade routes. However, in the late '60's, linking with UFO research, "Leylines" (the term is a '60's-ism never used by Watkins himself, who just called them leys) came under the microscope again. This time, the more occult aspects received consideration. (Not that this was actually anything new, as Dion Fortune had written about these "lines of force" in her 1930's novel *The Goatfoot God*.) Twenty-odd years after the '60's ley renaissance Hamish Miller and Paul Broadhurst released their book *The Sun and the Serpent*; a ground-breaking and profoundly important study of the English St. Michael alignment; of which much more later in this volume. One wonders if this meticulously-researched. soberly-conceived, modestly-couched volume would ever have seen the light of day had it been deprived of the metamorphosis in ideas which preceded its appearance by some twenty years.

Back in that heady era, periodicals like *International Times*, *Frendz* and *Gandalph's Garden* featured articles on mystic places which placed particular emphasis on Glastonbury. The result, for the place itself, was the influx of a whole new wave of mainly young people bent on searching. . . for something. On a more mundane level in Glastonbury, not all of the more lasting effects were positive. Some members of the invading army of seekers, it was reported, exhibited a lack of sensitivity and consideration towards the people whose families had lived in the area for generations. The inevitable counter-reaction followed and "No Hippies" signs began to appear in pubs, shops and cafes. Tom Graves' excellent book *Needles of Stone* (for my money still the best book around dealing with the now-controversial area known as Earth Energies) makes some astute comments on this era. Although he lived in nearby Street at the time of writing, Graves states that he has never been able to stay in Glastonbury for any length of time unless doing so within a carefully prepared pilgrimage context. He remarks upon the reciprocal nature of "tuning in" to place spirits which, if one focuses one's attention upon them, will sooner or later respond in no uncertain terms. Years of experience of such work have convinced me of just how "spot on" Graves is in this context.

Present-day Glastonbury is still a small country town where folk go about their businesses. Bakeries and grocery shops nestle alongside sales outlets for all manner of New Age trinkets. One could pretend that all in the local spiritual garden is lovely, but to do so would be naive, dishonest or both. Huge numbers of followers of varied spiritual paths descend upon the place each year, coming for a variety of purposes. A highly-charged atmosphere can quickly develop as a result of the interaction of powerful place energies and a mixed bag of human emotions. "Negative stuff" (using pop psychological jargon) which may be downloaded and, if not "earthed", may go zooming around the psychic airwaves amplified and propelled by the local energy matrix; woe betide the unprotected person with whom it collides. Keeping one's psychic protection well up whilst in Glastonbury smacks of sound practise.

In questing terms, little that was profound occurred during my August 1993 visit, but then it was not conceived as a questing trip, just a few days' break in an interesting place. However, it was during a stroll around the Abbey ruins that I began to feel things "churning" psychically. The reputed site of Arthur's grave made a strong impression upon me. I thought about the ornate, black marble tomb situated here in pre-Reformation times; recorded descriptions oddly resembling just such another tomb seen psychically by my friend and colleague Fay Cockell three months previously during a session psychometrising Roman coins found at the Dianic Temple site in Greenwich Park; a marble tomb accompanied by a vision of a short sword with a gleaming, oiled blade. For the record, the reputed remains of Arthur and his queen were found by monks south of the Lady Chapel in 1191 as a result of the appearance at the Abbey of a mysterious visiting brother who told them where to dig in a manner highly reminiscent of modern psychic questing. In 1278 the bodies were transferred to the elaborate marble shrine in the choir, where they remained until the Reformation.

Liz and I were both aware of psychic energy radiating from the marked grave site as we approached it. After calibrating my pendulum I found that the surrounding energies exhibited a negative polarity which became a positive one once inside the grave's boundary markers; the pendulum's gyrations becoming so powerful that the divining instrument went berserk in my hand, causing some amusement to Abbey visitors. Identical polarity responses subsequently registered during visits in the company of David Aylward, Fay Cockell and Jenni Stather. As we wandered around the grounds, I experienced a curious feeling that the place had some sort of ill-defined link with my native Greenwich, particularly with Inigo Jones' Queen' House. (See my 1996 book *Goddesses, Guardians and Groves* for information regarding the psychic aspects of this remarkable building.) I regretfully left Glastonbury, aware that I would be back in the not too distant future. The intriguing question of a possible Greenwich link and my personal connections with the place in respect of a possible past-life as a Reformation period monk hovered at the back of my mind. My curiosity had been well and truly aroused!

Chapter 2

The Black Monks

It would seem that many people are unaware of the fact that the Manor of Greenwich was controlled by the monks of the Benedictine Order (who also ruled Glastonbury) for 500 years and that the landmark widely known as Greenwich Church (St. Alphege's) was controlled by a Benedictine prior until the Order's expulsion from the area in 1414. This provides us with an interesting link with Glastonbury and its great Benedictine Abbey. The relevance really lies in the siting of the early Stuart Queen's House at Greenwich, for it appears that one of the Benedictine Order's own buildings was previously located upon the ground now occupied by Inigo Jones' architectural gem.

In 918 Count Baldwin of Flanders, husband of Elstrudis, daughter of King Alfred, died in Ghent. Although arranged for political reasons, the marriage had been a happy one. Certainly, Elstrudis was a popular figure in Flanders. In her husband's memory she gave the manorial rights of Greenwich, Lewisham and Woolwich in what is now South London to the Benedictine abbey of St. Peter's at Ghent. Manorial rights did not amount to total land ownership, but involved the right to the collection of tithes, toll fines, etc. The monastic staff stationed at Greenwich seems to have been a small one. There is no record of anything like an abbey although a priory existed close to the Thames at East Greenwich, possibly on the site of the present power station.

A Benedictine's presence was not always popular with the locals and in the 13th Century the Abbot came over from Flanders to sort out a few problems. A stepping-up of measures to curb the power and influence of alien priories on English soil culminated, during the reign of Henry V, with the bill of 1414 which removed the holdings of such institutions at the stroke of a pen. Apart from local resentment, this measure was taken because the expanding French-speaking presence in Greenwich (and some other places) was seen as a growing security risk. The Abbey of St. Peter's, of course, was less than impressed and three centuries later it was still lamenting its losses at the hands of "the heretics".

In previous works I have discussed the importance of the geomantic setting of the Queen's House at Greenwich. As we shall see, the historically-possessed Benedictine expertise in exploiting covert geomantic knowledge is reasonably well-known. In June 1396 one Giles Delaporte, a Flemish agent, was sent to record the holdings of the Abbey of St. Peter's in South London. Delaporte's report, still housed among the Ghent archives, mentions a tiled gatehouse which faced the fields; the latter being equatable with the flat ground to the immediate South of the Queen's House, in what is now Greenwich Park. Wyngaerde's panoramic prospect of Greenwich from what is now Observatory Hill, executed in 1558, shows one such gatehouse situated in a position which tallies with that described by Delaporte, coinciding with the later siting of the Queen's House by Inigo Jones. The existence of the gatehouse was referred to on odd occasions throughout the 15th and 16th Centuries and it may be seen in a 1620's painting by an unknown artist showing the view from One Tree Hill, now on view to the public in the Queen's House. It served, at one time, as an outbuilding of Greenwich Palace. Wyngaerde's depiction shows it to have been a quite substantial, two-storey building. Those unaware of Delaporte's survey usually assume that it was erected by Humphrey, Duke of Gloucester, whose manor house Belacourt became Margaret of Anjou's palace when she seized it following the Duke's mysterious death. Henry VII razed this building to the ground before erecting in its place the Greenwich Palace so loved by the monarchs of the Tudor dynasty. However, he did not touch the gatehouse.

The famous "ghost" photograph taken by chance in 1966 by a visiting retired Canadian clergyman with no interest in psychic matters MAY have served as a kind of atmospheric "tape recording" which shows one of the Benedictine personnel, if the spectre's attire is anything to go by. The photograph was taken on the mysterious tulip staircase in the Queen's House. In May 1991, my psychic colleague Jo Shrimpton made a psychometric reading of the Motherstone fountain site in Greenwich Park. She was aware of (among other things) a small group of brown or black-robed monks processing down past the ancient Queen Elizabeth's Oak. Whether these men were Flemish Benedictines of pre-1414 or part of the local early Tudor community of Observant Friars (who also came to horrific ends during the Reformation) we do not, as yet, know.

The life of St. Benedict himself has been so well documented in the past that I shall not dwell upon the founder of the Order of Black Monks in great detail here, although a little general information could be helpful. He was born towards the end of the 5th Century in Umbria, Central Italy; later studying at Rome. Around the year 500 he joined a community but soon afterwards left for Subiaco, where he lived as a hermit. Here, he built up a following of disciples and an organisation consisting of twelve small monasteries. Local animosity is believed to have led to an attempt on Benedict's life and around 530 he left for Monte Cassino near Naples, where he composed the final version of his famous monastic rule. Here he remained until his death and founded a great abbey, which was carefully situated upon a hilltop geomantic power spot. Gregory's dialogues tell us that Benedict was gifted with second sight and also able to work miracles. Monte Cassino witnessed one of the most ferocious battles of the Second World War and for a study of the occult aspects of this conflict the reader is referred to Nigel Pennick's book *Hitler's Secret Sciences*.

Benedict is often pictured with a broken chalice said to contain poison and a raven who is said to have removed the chalice at the saint's command. He is probably most famous for his "Holy Rule" which became a conduct model for European monastic communities. The rod which he is sometimes shown holding has been interpreted as a corporal punishment device. The Benedictine nuns were founded by Benedict with his sister Scholastica. At one time, a community of Anglican Benedictine nuns existed at Baltonsborough; birthplace of St. Dunstan near Glastonbury. Bodies found by monks during an excavation following the great battle of World War II were assumed to be those of the brother and sister. Benedict's rule was a workable blueprint for an essentially community-based life combining religious devotion and manual labour. The saint's life provides little hint of the massively powerful order which was eventually to grow out of the humble foundation at Subiaco.

Nigel Pennick and Sig Lonegren have both written about the Benedictines' ability to find geomantic power sites upon which to build their monasteries, thus gaining subtle control of surrounding area. In his book *Spiritual Dowsing*, Lonegren draws our attention to the fact that the 6th Century Pope Gregory, himself a Benedictine, urged missionaries to build places of worship at sites of already recognised sanctity. Given the order's track record it seems that there was more to this piece of advice than the potential for hijacking existing congregations of pagans and modifying their religious institutions! All over Europe, Abbeys sprouted at selected geomantic power sites: Monte Cassino in Italy, Monserrat in Spain, Fulda in Germany, Glastonbury in Britain, etc. The word control seems to have loomed large on the Benedictine hidden agenda. Pennick's book *Sacred Geometry* discusses the theories of Louis Charpentier and Kurt Gerlach regarding the order's exploitation of power sites and the knowledge of subtle energy manipulation. Charpentier suggests that geometrical properties were combined with sound; specifically Gregorian chants, in order to amplify existing forces and to produce altered states of consciousness. Gerlach discovered the non-random manner in which Benedictine monasteries were sited in Bohemia. A geometrical arrangement was apparent as was the use of the ancient Ruste unit of measurement.

An idea of the great extent of the Benedictine sphere of influence is given by a glance at its British holdings at the time of the Reformation. Here, in addition to a staggering number of abbeys and monasteries, there were cathedral priories whose abbots were also their bishops and other major priories independent of abbeys or cathedrals. Many abbeys and cathedrals boasted satellite priories often located far from the parent institution and frequently found at geomantic places of power such as Kilpeck in Herefordshire. The order's influences stretched across the country like a vast web; an appropriate simile in geomantic terms. Power exerted by the Black Monks went beyond the purely religious, into the political arena. At Glastonbury it verged on the absolute, applying pressure where even a monarch might fear to tread. As this chapter draws to a close we return to the tiled gatehouse at Greenwich, located with customary geomantic precision by the Benedictines. It seems that a sacred artifact of great power was once buried beneath its flooring and it is upon this artifact that we are about to focus our attention, for its link with the great Abbey of Glastonbury was both strong and intimate.

Chapter 3

Beneath the House of Delight

Ostensibly, Inigo Jones' Queen's House at Greenwich was intended to be a cosy bolt-hole for a queen who needed to have such a place to which she could withdraw in order to rest from the pressures of court life. However, as explained at length in my previous book *Goddesses, Guardians and Groves*, research and psychic work indicate that there was a little more to it than this, hinting at historical usage for magical and ceremonial purposes by, among others, Templars and Masons; also revealing the building to be placed in a geomantically key position. The building is sited upon the "Greenwich Line"; a major surface alignment/subtle energy band which, to the North, passes through Hawksmoor's Church of St. Ann at Limehouse and, to the South, through various ecclesiastical landmarks and an ancient subterranean complex in North Kent. Geomantic factors may have been behind the seemingly odd choice of site; the house having been built straddling what was then the main Woolwich Road, its North and South blocks on opposing sides of this busy, muddy highway linked by a central first-floor bridge room.

The building was commissioned by James I, who wanted it as a gift for his queen, Ann of Denmark. It seems that the old Black Monks' gatehouse was demolished in order to make room for it. Ann's premature death caused her husband to halt the work but it was eventually completed by his son, Charles I, for HIS queen, Henrietta Maria. Queen Henrietta's use of the House of Delights as it was affectionately called was short-lived, due to the outbreak of the English Civil War. (Interestingly, in September 1993, my wife Liz psychically "tuned-in" to an elevational drawing of the Queen's House. As well as becoming aware, as Carole also did, of its Sacred Kingship function, she also received the words "Box of Delights" and it is important to stress that, at this point, she was unaware of the royal nickname which it had once sported.) Inigo Jones is an obscure figure. While much is known of his work, little is known of his personal life but we do know that he visited Stonehenge for surveying purposes and was very interested in the work of the Roman mathematician Vitruvius; one of whose concerns was the practical use of proportions found in nature. Both of the above aspects would "fit in" with a person whom, one senses, had somewhat covert esoteric inclinations. His early work as a theatrical costume and set designer led to his being "noticed" and eventually serving as court architect.

A number of straight surface "leys" or terrestrial subtle energy bands pass through the building. In Needles of Stone, Tom Graves described several independent dowsing surveys which indicated that two such bands actually intersect and form a right angle. Psychic work by independent researchers indicates this site to have been a recognised place of power and sanctity even before the arrival of the Romans, who dedicated it to Apollo. (Diana, his sister, was also awarded a hilltop shrine close by; still a powerful site.) An ancient Henge was psychically glimpsed here by quester Alex Langstone in 1993. Certainly, the veil is thin at the site, as evidenced by the Rev. Hardy's "ghost" photograph of 1966. The energies on the Tulip Staircase, where it was taken, can make one feel almost dizzy at times. As Graves has pointed out, the building's layout is geomantically interesting, consisting of a multiplicity of cubes. In some rooms, geometrical designs on floors and ceilings seem to amplify and concentrate the subtle energies.

The first strong indications of the building's link with Albion's destiny came when I visited the site on a hot Sunday afternoon in August 1993 in the company of psychics Carole Young and Alex Langstone. Carole at once sensed the entire building being covered by an immense crown, accompanied by a magnificent white horse standing in front of the Queen's House and facing up the Greenwich Line in a Southerly direction. She felt the beast to be Albion's totem animal and she felt the huge crown to be a sovereignty symbol: "The Sacred Crown of Britain". The word "Kingship" was very recurrent. "The horse is STILL very active" Carole told me, and we were informed via the Otherworld that kingship, the horse and the Arthurian mythos all link at the site, whose current importance to Britain's subtle energy matrix was forcefully stressed. The Arthurian connection was further emphasised by Carole being shown a sword whose blade was embedded in a block of stone, standing on the dry, parched grass in front of the Queen's House. When we returned the following December it was cold, wet and windy; two days prior to the Winter Solstice. On this occasion we intended to enter the building, which the constraints imposed by time had not allowed us to do in August. As we wandered round to the building's Thames-facing North side, Carole briefly saw Queen Henrietta waving to us from a first-floor window. I had previously sensed that the little flight of curving steps above the North basement door was an important part of the overall "hidden" configuration, having seen spirit lights hovering above them when studying large-scale architectural plans and having sensed strong attendant energies during on-site dowsing surveys. By the steps, Carole sensed the energy of a huge, Sacred jewel which pointed again to Sovereignty. The jewel was a sapphire, relating to the initiation of a line of Sacred kings. She felt that death and rebirth-aspected initiation rites had been carried out on this spot which marked an "initiatory arch" over a huge time-span which included pagan Saxons (a cemetery used by them has been found close by), Templars and Masons.

Perhaps most intriguing of all was news of a "great book" which had once been buried, presumably in some sort of casket, on the Northern side of what is now the Queen's House. This book, we were told, was a *Book of the Laws of the Sovereignty of Britain*". At some point, the volume had been unearthed, something had been added to the text and the artifact had then journeyed to a new resting place at Glastonbury. From what we know of Humphrey, Duke of Gloucester, brother to Henry V, soldier, scholar, academic, philanthropist and covert occultist, the book may well have been HIS work, particularly in view of his one-time custodianship of the tiled gatehouse which once stood upon the present Queen's House site, beneath or close to which the book would have been buried. A quite detailed account of the Duke's remarkable life is given in my book *Goddesses, Guardians and Groves*. Like some other historical personages featuring in the present volume, he died under mysterious circumstances, in his case in 1447 on the day before his trial on a manufactured treason charge.

The Benedictines enter our story again, for the Duke's best friend was Abbot Wheathampstead of St. Albans; a figure whose occult interests and activities were widely known. In 1907, Vickers, Humphrey's biographer, wrote to the effect that the St. Alban's monks were ". . . *famous for the study of occult sciences*". Before we entered the Queen's House on that cold, dull Winter afternoon, some further information snippets were imparted with regard to the book. The great volume, Carole was told, had been taken to Glastonbury and concealed near the Tor. It seems likely that it was hidden along with other precious artifacts before the Reformation holocaust descended upon the Abbey. Due to its presumed importance it may well have been concealed in a place even more secret and inaccessible than those where other objects were sheltered from the King's vandals. On 28th September, 1539, after the arrests of the Glastonbury Three (Abbot Richard Whiting, Treasurer John Thorne/Arthur and Roger Wilfred /James, the Assistant Treasurer) Reformation agents Pollard, Moyle and Layton wrote to the Vicar General Thomas Cromwell describing the search for and discovery of *"money and plate hid in the wall vaults and other secret places"*. They explained that in addition to Whiting, who was later confined for a spell in the Tower, they had also seized the two treasurers on a charge of "arrant robbery" for ". . . *the Abbot and monks had embezzled and stolen as much plate and ornaments as could have sufficed for a new abbey. . .* " But had the agents found ALL the hidden treasure? It seems that they thought not. On 16th November, the day after the hangings, Pollard told Cromwell (by letter) that Whiting would give no further information regarding names of *"accomplices"* or locations of further concealed Sacred artifacts ". . . *nor he would confer more gold nor silver nor any other thing more than he did before your lordship in the Tower. . .* " Pollard added: "*The other monks. . . took their deaths very patiently, whose souls God pardon. . .* ".

As John Michell and others have suggested, who knows what precious objects may one day be discovered on the Isle of Avalon? In 1586 the chronicler Weston wrote of his meeting with an elderly monk who had been on the Abbey staff in 1539 and who, when interviewed, lived near Wearyall Hill. The old man claimed to own a cross which encased a nail from the crucifixion and he stated that a number of other artifacts had been successfully hidden by his colleagues. Like John Thorne, Duke Humphrey, nearly a century previously, must have felt a conspiratorial net tightening around him. If he had, for its safe-keeping, "exhumed" the book and secretly handed it to the Abbot of St. Alban's, then once secure within the great but doomed Benedictine organisation in Britain, it must have found its way to the famed library at Glastonbury; a legendary book collection which, going by the records, seems to have displayed something of an esoteric side, entry being only permitted to certain monks. Such a precious artifact would surely have been hidden in a highly-secret place as soon as warning bells rang, particularly in view of the fate suffered by other libraries if dissolved monasteries. (Pages from books plundered from the Glastonbury library ended up as shopkeepers' parcel wrappings.) Material psychically received by West London pagan medium Tony Lee indicates that the book's content is concerned with Albion's continuing sovereignty and that it exhibits a strong link with the Arthurian mythos. Tony psychically "saw" Duke Humphrey handing the book, in secret, to a Benedictine monk. Other information received by Tony implies that the book's subject matter is so ancient as to verge on the timeless and that many centuries passed before this sacred material was committed to paper, probably by Humphrey, whose book collection, including tomes of an occult nature, was famed throughout Europe.

Although it was the psychic discovery of the "great book" which steered me (with little prompting) on a questing course which led to Glastonbury, it now seems, in retrospect, to have been almost like a bait (or carrot); the quest to find it diminishing in profile when other, equally fantastic matters came to light. Perhaps this was its function and, despite the initial impression, it is not yet time for its finding. We were given but a vague guide to its place of concealment, "somewhere near the Tor". One pictures a bewildering web of inter-connecting passages below Glastonbury; some legendary, some concrete, some shadowy and uncertain, all dominated by the mythical and inaccessible Crystal Cave beneath the Tor still spoken of locally and written of by Ross Nichols.

The Glastonburian subterranean complex seems to exhibit a quality not unlike that possessed by a similar configuration at Greenwich in the vicinity of the Dianic Temple; a weird amalgam of physical reality, myth and legend, where dividing lines are hazy at best and where the tangible and concrete appear to warp into something existing more on other planes. As we shall see, the Tudor monk psychically sensed by mediums Jo, Molly, Carole, Tony, Muriel and Ian (all independently) to have been myself in a past life was soon to be identified as one Brother John of Glastonbury; a man who, according to Jo, used a huge bunch of keys in the course of his day to day work which, as treasurer, he would have done. This being the case, it was more than likely that he would have been involved in the concealment of the book and other artifacts. Whatever the case, a return trip to Glastonbury seemed to be on the cards!

Chapter 4

Symbols, Swords and Boots

Information received by Carole Young on that December afternoon at the Queen's House soon fell into context in the light of a transmission which had been received and relayed by Jo Shrimpton during a telephone chat a month previously. (It is vital to stress that Carole knew nothing of this.) During a quite mundane conversation, Jo abruptly experienced a vision of a monk who, she told me, was Brother John. She felt that this character was the same person as that whom she had glimpsed clutching his hefty bunch of keys a year and a half previously. This time, there was a strong sense of fear; fear of discovery by a tyrannous authority.

John and his colleagues were feverishly working to hide some artifact at the bottom of a dene hole or shaft. Very precious objects, it seemed, were being concealed in barrels. (The barrel figures quite strongly in our quest. Jenni Stather, a psychic colleague from East London, drew my attention to the curious significance of these receptacles due to material psychically received by her in 1995. The barrel was used in the form of a pictorial device as the rebus of Richard Bere, the Abbey's penultimate Abbot and, seemingly, a close friend (unofficially) of Brother John Thorne/Arthur. A rebus is a kind of symbolic visual representation of a person's name which involves the use of a pictorial play on words, or visual pun. A sculpted stone version of Bere's rebus may still be seen among the Abbey ruins at Glastonbury. His ill-fated successor, Richard Whiting, adopted an image of the fish of the same name for his device, linking curiously with an old prophecy passed down to us from Avalonian folklore to the effect that a disaster would follow the occasion when a whiting swam on the Tor's summit.) Jo sensed a West Country location. She saw a scroll, then monks writing in a large book. There was a renewed sense of persecution and fear of discovery. She then went quiet. "You O. K. Jo?" I asked. Sounding shaken, Jo explained that she had just witnessed John's execution -by hanging! She was further shown poison

Stonework in the Abbey ruins showing Abbot Bere's barrel rebus

pellets being furtively dropped into goblets, followed by the death agonies of the unwitting drinkers. It seemed that following John's death, a group of people were being covertly wiped-out as a "hit list" was ruthlessly worked-through. And that was it; surely enough for anyone in one sitting; certainly enough for Jo who, reeling with the impact of this grim action re-play headed into her kitchen for a much-needed cup of coffee. As she later told me, something a bit stronger could have been more appropriate!

On the evening of 30th December I spoke again to Jo, via the telephone. During our conversation she was suddenly psychically shown "a cave full of crystal". (She was, it must be added, unaware that the legendary cavity within the Tor has been historically referred to as The Crystal Cave.) When I announced my plan to return to Glastonbury in the near future, Jo was told that it was vital for her to advise me to first buy a pair of "good strong boots with grip soles". When I went I was to go equipped with a length of stout rope and a flask containing a hot drink. "Do NOT attempt any physically risky bits alone even if they look O. K. " I was instructed. Weird stuff -it seemed that an Otherworldly contact expected me to home in on some concealed Sacred artifact as soon as I reached Glastonbury. Would it really work THAT fast? It seemed unlikely but much past experience had repeatedly proved the validity of Jo's psychic material. The boots message was puzzling indeed, but due to the "no nonsense" tone of this instruction I felt inclined to play it safe and do as I was told. The whole idea seemed so bizarre that it surely must have some validity. Who after all, would make up such a curious directive? Certainly not Jo. In any case, my black Dr. Marten's were wearing out and it was a good excuse to get a new pair of boots.

I retired to bed that night around 11 p.m., from which time until 3 a.m. I was bombarded with a succession of images seen behind closed eyelids; impressions of the type usually labelled as hypnogogic, experienced in the borderland state between sleeping and waking when psychic material often comes through. The first vision showed what I took to be a couple of Otherworldly guardians watching over concealed treasure; one of them being distinctly frog-like. Intuitively, I had the feeling that they were artificial elementals, created by a magician for a specific purpose. I was twice shown the Sowhilo/Sigil/Sol rune; one of victory and Solar-based power which was used by the Nazis to emblazon the collar badges of the SS, at a time when it was already an ancient symbol. One image dominated the rest, occurring countless times for hours on end: a classically-formed, Excalibur-type sword. In gloomy half-light, at around 2 a.m., I was shown a chalice. The seemingly golden vessel glowed darkly; an ornate drinking vessel emblazoned with an equal-armed cross which suddenly changed into the rose-type device which I had seen repeatedly carved on the Abbey's stonework the previous August. As the long image sequence neared its end I was shown a mixture of staring, elemental, non-human faces which I again took to be guardians. The psychic pictures faded at last and I fell into a dreamless sleep.

The following morning I telephoned the Chalice Well Trust and booked a short stay at Little St. Michael retreat house two weeks later. A brief lull followed. On 7th January, I met Jenni Stather, a friend and colleague from my former teaching days in East London who is also a gifted psychic. The plan was to have a drink and catch up on gossip. We made for the Royal Festival Hall; as good a place as any at which to mellow-out and hear each other's news. After a sandwich, we adjourned to the bar. Having consumed a few pints I began to feel quite laid-back and certainly not anticipating the receipt of questing messages from the Otherworld. The denizens of the Otherworld, however, are well aware that such times present them with the ideal opportunity to zoom in with information which they wish to impart, as little resistance (possibly in the form of mental tension) is likely to be encountered. So it was on this particular evening. As we chatted and drank the hall's long bar buzzed with a babble of conversation as concert goers milled around, keen to grab a last drink before getting to their seats for the start of the performance.

Out of the blue, Jenni abruptly changed tack conversationally, telling me that it was imperative for me to visit an old hotel/pub in Glastonbury High Street when I made the then-impending visit. After some mental effort she recalled the name of the hostelry: The *George and Pilgrims Hotel*. Some years previously, as a trainee teacher, Jenni had been assigned to a Glastonbury school for one of her teaching practices. Having long been a natural psychic, she recalled strange sensations experienced whilst sitting in the broad bay window looking out onto the High Street. Further, she told me that I MUST sit in the window myself. When pressed, she could only tell me that she had absolutely no idea as to what was special about this particular spot in the bar of a hotel which obviously went a long way back in time. It was a case of trusting intuition; something which the quester must learn to do, be it her or his own or someone else's. There was SOMETHING special about it, and that was that.

Nothing else very revelatory emerged from the evening's conversation. I was puzzled by the remark about odd feelings having been experienced in this old West Country drinking place. On the strength of the emphatic manner in which the information was relayed to me it would have seemed unwise not to check it out. In retrospect, the comment was absolutely "spot-on" and a good example of the bizarre workings of synchronicity. There was indeed something special about the area inside the bay window and, as I later discovered, something a lot more special about what lay hidden almost directly below it; a force whose radiations could be felt up in the bar; left snug and concealed to incubate over the centuries. To have said that it was important for me to visit the *George* was surely the understatement of all time!

Chapter 5

At the Chalice Well

At 1.30 p.m. on Tuesday 11th January, 1994, the Badgerline bus from Bristol pulled up at the top of Glastonbury High Street. Walking along Chilkwell Street to Chalice Well gardens, I booked in with the volunteer worker selling tickets at the gate. I had already been informed that I would have the retreat house entirely to myself; even Leonard and Willa, the wardens at that time who lived next door in Vine Cottage, being away until the next day. I quickly established a "base" in Little St. Michael's cosy kitchen, unloading good supplies of tea making materials and having an initial brew-up (always a priority) before launching into the afternoon's activities.

My first call was upon the Arthurian scholar Geoffrey Ashe. Having long been interested in the life and work of the great early 20th Century occultist Dion Fortune (Violet Firth) I had been intrigued, during my previous visit, to have come upon what I assumed must be her one-time temporary dwelling place on the Tor's lower slopes. This quite unique building is still known as Chalice Orchard. As it happened I was also familiar with Mr. Ashe's own works and had sent him a complimentary copy of my book *Other Meridians, Another Greenwich*, which I thought might be of interest to him. In the accompanying letter I had asked him if it would be possible for me to look around the gardens at Chalice Orchard in the light of the Dion Fortune connection and my interest therein. Mr. Ashe responded with a friendly invitation to pop in for a cup of tea and, as one might imagine, the prospect of meeting this knowledgeable man in the setting of Dion's former home, where he had lived for some years, was an appealing one indeed. Of the more recent writers who have focussed upon the bizarre and tragic events of November, 1539, Geoffrey Ashe seems, to me at any rate, to be by far the most perceptive. (Perhaps it has something to do with living almost on top of the execution site!) In his book *King Arthur's Avalon* he hints at an intuitive feeling that there was more to the curious manner in which the Tor executions were carried out than immediately meets the eye, pointing to an element of what almost seems to have amounted to ritual sacrifice. As well as being a lively and very interesting conversationalist, I found Chalice Orchard's occupant to exhibit a warm, friendly personality which caused me to feel at home and relaxed very quickly.

During a fascinating tour I was shown Dion Fortune's original fireplace and the two porthole-like windows which she had cut in the walls, providing a wonderful view of St. Michael's tower up on the summit. Over the years, the World War 1 army surplus hut about which Dion wrote in *Avalon of the Heart* had suffered a strange metamorphosis, growing into a bungalow equipped with a spacious verandah. A small cluster of buildings, basically chalets which had also undergone a metamorphosis process, nestled nearby; once the temporary dwellings of those who came for the meetings of Dion's Chalice Orchard Club, which was an esoteric group built around a Western Tradition backbone. Dion's writing hints at a tension which existed in her life between the pagan and Christian currents; both of which she seems to have needed. Given the highly Gnostic nature of Glastonbury's hidden side (one of this book's main themes) one is led to feel that she was uniquely suited to living there although she never did so on a permanent basis, alternating Avalonian stays with periods spent in London. She saw the Abbey as essentially Christian and the Tor as indisputably pagan. It is worth noting that she chose to reside at the latter location when in the area. Despite the esoteric Christian tone of many of her volumes of instruction papers and purpose-written manuals such as *Psychic Self-Defence*, her novels which many believe incorporated much hard-core occult teaching under a fictional cover label, are glorious works of paganism, perhaps revealing that aspect of herself which was influenced by the potent place energies running under Chalice Orchard, nestling close to the reputed home of the Celtic Underworld God Gwynn ap Nudd, on an island which was also the legendary home of the enchantress Morgan le Fay, who featured in much of her fictional writing in various guises.

During a conversation over tea and biscuits, Mr. Ashe mentioned the pioneering research of Geoffrey Russel in respect of the Tor maze, quoting Russel's view that it went underground for the last stretch close to the Bur Stone, high on the South-Eastern slopes. As I left the bungalow, I paused on the verandah. A brief break in the almost incessant rain and a temporary clearing of the Western sky revealed a dazzling sunset; the deep-red Solar globe sinking in all its majesty behind the drenched Somerset Levels; a panoramic prospect of which was afforded by our perch on the Tor. I drank in the sight of that Avalonian skyline which was to call me back time and time again. Having said "Goodbye" I made my way down the wooden steps and quickly discovered the reason for Jo's odd received message about the need for a new pair of boots.

The classic black lace-up Dr. Marten's boots had become my habitual footwear. Despite their ruggedness, these boots are essentially for the urbanite, being quite unsuitable for wear in slippery terrain except the variant which sports deeper soles. Once worn down, the soles become glass-smooth as I had found to my cost three years previously when trying to descend the unexpectedly difficult Black Hill on the Wales/Herefordshire border wearing a pair of rather ancient DM's. The soaking woodwork of Chalice Orchard's steps had become treacherous after so much rain and I suddenly found myself slipping. My right foot reached the edge of a step and then halted, ridged sole gripping wet timber. Teetering momentarily, I quickly regained my balance. Clad in the usual DM's I would almost certainly have gone down. At best it could have been an undignified tumble with a few bruises, at worst, a spinal injury. Whatever the result might have been, I was grateful for the practical character of one of my Otherworldly contacts!

I made for the town, intent on buying some food. The short Winter day was all but spent when I reached the shops. Night was approaching already. Equipped with a bag of fish and chips I returned to Chilkwell Street, torrential rain now falling with renewed vigour and an Odinic wind howling. The streets were deserted; a marked contrast to the crowded urban scene to which I was accustomed. Upon reaching the warmth and comfort of Little St. Michael I downed the evening meal seated at the kitchen table and then had the inevitable brew-up. Thus fortified I rang Jenni Stather on the retreat house's coin box telephone, as I had arranged to maintain contact with her during my visit in case anything psychically turned up at her end, which, as it happens, it did. "Well, have you been to the *George and Pilgrims* yet?" she asked. "Bet you haven't. " I admitted that I had not so far reached the *George*. However, I planned to return that evening. Remember me mentioning it in the Festival Hall?" Jenni asked. "I'm getting the feeling that you going there is really imperative. Make sure that you sit in the bay window overlooking the High Street; or as near to it as you can reasonably get. " Marching orders received, I locked the retreat house and headed back to town, bound for the *George*. What the hell was it about this place that was SO important? I had to find out.

At that time I knew nothing of the *George*'s history, unaware of its great significance to my quest. I found the bar to be friendly, relaxing and warm; an advantage on such a January night. Much old woodwork had survived and it seemed that the place could not really have changed that much since those far-off days when Brother John was the Abbey's treasurer. Sitting alone with a pint at a long wooden table close to the bay, as instructed, I began to get odd feelings. My left hand (the "receiving" hand which always registers psychic activity or sacred site energies) tingled madly as I studied the worn stonework around the mullioned bay window. (As it happened, I was seated almost directly above the tunnel entrance in the cellar rediscovered by Bligh Bond, of which much more later.) It was at this point that I began to sense vague, ill-defined links with my supposed previous life incarnation as Brother John.

Subsequently chatting to hotel staff at the reception desk I learned that the building was erected by Abbot Selwood in the late 15th Century as a pilgrims' rest house. Further, it was said to be "haunted" by the ghost of monk, believed by some to be one of the Glastonbury Three! (Dion Fortune's 1934 *Avalon of the Heart* briefly mentions such a spectre.) As is so often the case, my informants could not name any people of whom they knew who had personally experienced the ghost, although in one instance professional integrity stood in the way here, as apparently quite recently a male resident at the hotel had suffered a traumatic experience in the "haunted room" upstairs and it would have been quite out of order for the staff to name him or give details from the viewpoint of a confidence breach and I did not ask them to do this. The room in which the ghostly presence tended to be encountered was, appropriately named The Monk's Cell.

The following day I was kindly given a brief glimpse of the room, which certainly exhibited a strong psychic atmosphere. O.K., so suppose this "ghost" turned out to be Brother John; would this totally negate the possibility of my being a reincarnation of the man? I think not, for to assume that this would be the case would surely constitute a gross over-simplification of the situation. (Nearly two years later I was to witness an unspectacular manifestation of the "ghost" myself, in the bar.) Apart from other considerations such a spectre could be the result of some sort of atmospheric tape recording being occasionally replayed through time, called a "Stone Tape" by some after Nigel Kneale's play about such a phenomenon. There are many recorded phenomena which fit such a suggested explanation, such as the Roman legion seen marching through a cellar in York and the priestesses seen at the pagan Saxon burial ground at Greenwich. Personally, I suspect the case at Glastonbury to be rather more complicated, however. In the book *Ancient Magicks for a New Age* (unpromising title, great book) which he co-wrote with Geoff Hughes, Alan Richardson discusses the notion of reincarnation in respect of Colonel Charles Seymour; a contemporary of Dion Fortune. He suggests that Seymour would have inclined to the view that only part of the Higher Self of a person reincarnates at one time, the remainder staying on as a "watcher"; a model which seems oddly appropriate to the case of Brother John and his colleagues.

I eventually returned to base feeling relaxed and mellow after a few pints and some laughs exchanged with a team of Anglican clergy who were attending a conference at Abbey House. They had invaded the bar "in civvies" intent on unwinding after the day's rigours. Yet, as folk inevitably will in such circumstances, they spent the whole evening talking "shop", trying to outdo each other with hair-raising tales of bizarre parish visiting experiences. After more tea I tackled the library of local interest books which is tucked away behind a screen in Little St. Michael's lounge. Sleep seemed an ill-affordable luxury in the face of the staggering array of potential questing information paraded before me on the shelves. As I worked the wind screamed relentlessly round the little cottage; rain hammering on the windows. In an eerily synchronous manner, book after book came off the shelves and dropped open at exactly the right place. I was not "spooked" by this experience as I had encountered it before during my Greenwich work.

I soon fleshed-out the historical background to Abbot Selwood's pilgrim house, where I had been drinking earlier that evening and was intrigued to discover the existence of a tunnel running from its cellars to the abbey's gatehouse via a passage under the High Street. The veteran psychic quester and inspired archaeologist Frederick Bligh Bond had excavated the passage, finding its way to be terminated only 20 feet from the cellar as a result of sewer construction. A highly resourceful local woman, Mrs. Bilborough, explored the tunnel in 1918 and wrote vividly about the exhausting effects of her subterranean crawl along a passage only three feet in height, also describing "steep steps down" which may have been a reference to the wonderful old stone spiral staircase, or newell stair, which takes one down to the *George*'s cellar. We shall encounter this tunnel again, in much greater detail. One of Little St. Michael's books contained some information about other tunnels in the area, including one found as recently as 1974 beneath the Abbey Barn, seeming to lead in the direction of the Tor. This subterranean working was discovered as a result of a subsidence and filled-in via the pumping of concrete. The next volume to be opened took me straight back to the Pilgrims' House. The book in question, by an anonymous author and simply named *Glastonbury*, mentioned a now-vanished statue of an "initiate craftsman" which had once stood on the building's battlements and stated that the *George* had once been a meeting place for "masonic guilds". A reference to Collinson's *History and Antiquities of Somerset* quoted an account of the cellar tunnel which had featured in this 18th Century work, describing the many turnings located if one had negotiated the passage in the days prior to the construction of the sewer under the High Street. I subsequently tracked-down Collinson's book in the *British Library* where I was able to read his account for myself, finding it to be suggestive of a description based on much earlier accounts.

Many more fragments of highly relevant material fell into my hands during that wild January night. I encountered Hamish Miller and Paul Broadhurst's groundbreaking research on the passage of the Michael and Mary bands of subtle Earth energy and the amazing phallus and chalice configuration which they create on the Tor, also the Jesuit Weston's account of his meeting with an elderly monk who claimed to be one of the last survivors of the holocaust which descended on the Abbey in 1539. Retrospectively, it seemed as if the questing stage was being set for me as these very pertinent snippets of information presented themselves. At 5 a.m. I called it a day and snatched a few hours' sleep. Although, at that time, I had little idea of how they fitted together, I had the feeling that I had been presented with pieces of a jigsaw puzzle which, when correctly assembled, would lead me to discover something which, in nature, was more than a little profound.

Chapter 6

Secrets of Stone Down

"There's some bloke I'm getting -a portly gentleman. I think maybe he liked
a drink. I get the feeling that he was a monk. . . Ouch. . . (clutching stomach).
. . this is heavy stuff, isn't it? All I can say is I'm glad steel's smoother now
than it was then. Bit of a lad wasn't he? A real geezer. Had a twinkle in his
eye, knew how to enjoy himself. Bit unusual for a monk and yet he was just
as spiritual as any of the others even if he was a bit different. Watching this
bloke's back would have been a full-time job, I reckon. He was always near
the firing line. Yes, his death was horrible and yet in a funny sort of way. . .
spiritually, it was sort of necessary. Can't explain that. He's offering you a
chalice of mead. A man who liked a drink. . . but what a scholar! He just
never stopped questing for knowledge, right up to the end. Not everyone
liked him. I get the feeling that there were some other monks who'd have
given anything NOT to have him around. . . "

The above comments were made by a psychic named Ian Wicks a few
moments after meeting me in August 1996, with absolutely no prompting
from myself. As we shall see, they form quite an accurate description of
Brother John Thorne/Arthur, Treasurer of Glastonbury Abbey and Tor
hanging victim of 1539. As I climbed the Tor on that blustery but bright
January morning in 1994, my mind repeatedly returned to the mysterious
figure who met his death at the summit of this awesome sacred hill four and a
half centuries previously and I found myself pondering on the question of
"What was he REALLY like?"

Upon reaching the summit I discovered that a large chunk of the Somerset
Levels surrounding Glastonbury had become submerged as a result of the
recent heavy rainfall and a man I met under the shadow of St. Michael's
tower who had climbed the Tor in order to blow a conch shell (a not
extraordinary type of activity at this location and very well he did it too)
ventured the opinion that the Isle of Avalon would be well and truly living up
to its name if much more rain fell. After scanning the horizon, my attention

focussed upon Stone Down. There is something just a little bit special about Stonedown Hill, with its shadowy evidence of the one-time presence of megaliths. The special quality, however, does not come from anything to do with archival study, fascinating and utterly vital though it is, but from one's direct experience of interaction with the landscape. One needs to BE at the place to grasp this and to realise that those who think that they have "done" Glastonbury when they have but visited Chalice Well, climbed the Tor and forked out a small fortune on esoteric trinkets in the High Street are seriously missing out.

Ross Nichol's consistently amazing work *The Book of Druidry* touches on this intriguing area located to the immediate North-East of the Tor. Miller and Broadhurst's *The Sun and the Serpent* does too; the authors informing us that the serpentine Michael band, never far from key spots on the Avalonian landscape, it seems, winds its way down Stonedown Hill en route for the magnificent Gogmagog Oaks at Paradise. In the section of his book dealing with the mysteries of Glastonbury, the late Mr. Nichols produced some gem-like snippets of information not to be found elsewhere. A friend who knew him personally is of the opinion that these were actually psychically received. Nichols believed that part of the power channelled into the Tor was drawn from the Stonedown area. He saw the North-East as a "channelling-down way"; the power being channelled coming directly from the Sun at the Summer Solstice or from "other forces" which he did not care to name in print. Nichols refers to the three standing stones found on old maps of the locality, feeling that they may have exhibited some sort of astronomical function. (Prof. Alexander Thom, whose groundbreaking researches based on years of measurement in the field demonstrated the megalithic culture's knowledge of a sophisticated Pythagorean-type geometry long before Pythagoras was born, has also written regarding the possible astronomical significance of these stones.)

Today, if one walks down Stonedown Lane and then turns left along the little trackway at the bottom, crossing the aptly-named Paradise Lane in order to reach the ancient Gogmagog Oaks, one enters an enchanted and magical realm. Walking back up Paradise Lane one feels that one is treading a very old, well-worn processional route to the Tor. On a "good day", too, one can sometimes sense that one is very far from being alone here, surrounded by a throng of invisible presences. For a long time I thought that this was "just me" until I met other, independent folk who had received the same impression from the place. Some readers may be already familiar with the concept of the St. Michael Line, brought to public consciousness by that great Earth Mysteries visionary John Michell. Aligned with the Beltane sunrise (1st May) and also with sunrise on the old festival of Lughnasad (or Lammas) on 1st August as well as being aligned with the sunsets of the festivals of Imbolc (1st February) and Samhain (31st October) the line passes across the country in a roughly East-North-Easterly direction, going through many hilltop sites dedicated to St. Michael (including the Tor) in the process, also a number of other key sites which include Avebury. It runs into the sea at Hopton, East Anglia, doing the same on the opposite side of the country at St. Michael's Mount, where it intersects a similar alignment passing through many key European sites at which Michael shrines are located and where classic visions of St. Michael have been historically experienced.

Twelve Tribe Nations, by John Michell and Christine Rhone, gives detailed information about the latter alignment, as does Jean Richer's *Sacred Geography of the Ancient Greeks*, which Christine Rhone has translated from the original French. Our knowledge of the English Michael alignment took a huge step forward with the publication of *The Sun and the Serpent*; a groundbreaking and truly inspirational book by Hamish Miller and Paul Broadhurst. These gifted dowsers tracked the course of the Michael Line from the West to East coasts, discovering that, caduceus-like, two subtle energy bands of opposing polarities which they named Michael and Mary carve out a sinuous, serpentine path as they wind themselves around the central alignment's straight spine. As we shall see later, the Michael and Mary bands were found to be of major importance to the quest focussed upon in this volume. On that brisk January morning I was aware, for the first time, of actually standing on the spot where masculine Michael mates with feminine Mary at a place of death and rebirth.

I faced North-East from the tower and studied a 1974 Ordnance Survey map which, mysteriously, showed one of the old stones to be standing in a field near Stonedown Lane at a position actually intersected by the straight spine of the Michael alignment. I looked at the map again, then back at the landscape. No, surely this just did NOT make sense. There, standing in the field exactly where it was supposed to have once been, was the stone. I blinked. Yes, it was STILL there! Had someone found the bloody thing and put it back? Oh come on. . . . But there it was; a standing stone about four feet in height, looking as if it had never been taken away. "Let's go for it", I thought, and began to scramble down the Tor. Checking field boundaries repeatedly, I soon found myself standing close to the relevant field, just off

Stonedown Lane, puzzled by the fact that the stone so clearly glimpsed from the Tor had vanished into thin air!

Vanishing megalithic stones are part and parcel of our Earth Mysteries heritage; that I knew. My adopted Aunt Beatrice, a true daughter of the red sandstone earth of Herefordshire upon which Alfred Watkins walked, has told me old tales of the Wirgin Stone; a single, phallic-looking menhir standing in a field near the Wirgin bridge over the River Lugg at a location believed by some to not be its original home. According to local lore (and within my aunt's own memory) the stone vanishes every now and then; historically on the eve of a great national disaster. (The disappearance which she remembers took place in the late 1930's!) Aunt Beatrice remarked that to move the thing would have taken several men and a tractor. It seems that it mysteriously returned several days after it had vanished. I make no apology to readers for this weird tale of a menhir at Stonedown which briefly appeared and then vanished; she or he is free to take it on board or dismiss it. I am simply reporting what happened. A time warp? Who knows. Perhaps this odd experience marked my first encounter with the psychic joker; a Loki-like entity which I would certainly meet again in the course of the quest.

Later, at the Abbey Barn, I dowsed the location of the tunnel found in 1974 which appeared to lead in the direction of the Tor. In-filling with concrete may seem like a vandalistic act but a subsidence HAD taken place which obviously called for safety measures. As my speleologist friend Clive Gardiner pointed out, concrete pumped in at the point of the subsidence was unlikely to fill the entire tunnel. An account written at the time of discovery referred to the tunnel as spacious and some dowsing on my part concurred with this view; the tunnel width at the rear of the barn registering three and a half of my paces when projected up to the surface. The barn had been a place of importance to John Thorne and others involved with the risky business of concealing sacred artifacts, as future psychic work would reveal.

In September 1995 I was to be afforded a glimpse back in time which revealed a sackful of treasure temporarily dumped out of the way atop a hay bale stack, just beneath the barn's high rafters. (Historical records confirm such a stacking process, as does the presence of high ventilation holes in the barn walls which helped the drying-out process.) On another occasion in 1996, I would make an astral journey along the tunnel, but more of that later. The barn, it seems, had afforded lighter moments for John too. During the

Summer of 1996, I had a split-second "recall" vision of an ecstatic good time experienced by the treasurer and covert occultist and his French priestess/lover; seeing the high, narrow windows set in that dark wall from the floor. I subsequently amused myself by wondering what he would have said if one of the other brothers had happened to wander in while things were happening. Living up to the "geezer" image sensed by psychic Ian Wicks, I suspect that following a lightning rearrangement of clothing, this cool character would have said something like "This is a visitor from France -I'm showing her round. She's a bit tired at the moment so she's resting on the hay. She's a good Catholic; not like those awful heretics they have out there in the South. " (The lady in question actually came from Provence and was a covert priestess of Mary Magdalene, but we will learn more of her later.) Should the brother have seemed a little unconvinced, John would probably have quickly employed a diversionary tactic, coming out with something like "I'm glad I bumped into you. Father Abbot was talking to me this morning. He's rather concerned about the state of the barn at the moment. . . " As Ian Wicks remarked, watching this man's back could have been a full-time occupation, for it seems that much of his life was spent sailing close to the wind.

Upon entering the Abbey gates, I was surprised to see an anonymous-looking chunk of masonry standing close to the wall, decorated with the familiar "World Tree" version of the Algiz/Elhaz rune. I questioned a passing member of the Abbey staff, who knew nothing of the runically-derived sigils and was a little dismissive. The finding of runic symbology carved upon the abbey's stonework, however, seemed significant as far as I was concerned, even if not THAT out of the ordinary as the runic alphabet definitely survived the Christianisation of this island. Two years later I would experience use, by former monks now working on the inner planes, of Anglo-Saxon runes as psychic information microchips, as we shall see.

After leaving the Abbey I wandered up the High Street and was intrigued to find a shop which sold replicas of the famous "Glastonbury" chairs which were originally made, as history records, by Brother John, who signed them with a Latinised version of his own name, using Arthur rather than Thorne. I was told by the shop's staff that an original chair (or so it was believed) could be seen in the Bishop's Palace at Wells along with Abbot Whiting's own chair, and that one of the Glastonbury chairs in nearby St. John's Church was also suspected of being an original. (During the following two years I researched the chairs in some detail and found, studying the work of experts such as museum curators, that the actual positive identification of an "original" is an almost impossible task from the orthodox antiquarian's viewpoint.) The man who took the name of the legendary king rather than one of the more usual saints' names when he became a monk was, it seems, a gifted amateur cabinet maker. Until 1525 the local abbacy had been held by Richard Bere, the penultimate abbot before the Reformation. Bere was a close friend of Cardinal Wolsey, who was to be faced with the job of appointing Bere's successor as no internal agreement could be reached at Glastonbury; frail old Richard Whiting, then the Abbey Chamberlain responsible for the smooth running of the institution's toilets, wardrobe, dormitories and pilgrims' inn being selected for the post. During his abbacy, Bere had journeyed to Rome as emissary of Henry VII. (His dynamic personality, natural charm and powerful intellect made him ideally suited to such tasks.)

Bere had been impressed by the chairs which he had seen supporting the bodies of higher-ranking Italian monks and expressed the desire to have something of the kind at Glastonbury in place of the austere, none too comfortable forms which were standard issue at that time. The Glastonbury chair was the result. How much its overall design resulted from Italian influence (as some suppose) and how much it resulted from John's own inventiveness I do not know, but it does seem that the decoration must surely have been highly personal as far as he was concerned. Symbology involved, which included the secret symbol of a highly covert magical order which existed within the Abbey's walls until the members were unofficially wiped-out in 1539 and also included a squared circle alchemical device encapsulating the notion of the reconciliation of polar opposites also recognised by John Michell as the New Jerusalem diagram will be discussed later in this volume. John's name appears on a document relating to the election of Bere's successor signed by various monks in 1525 and it seems likely that he was into middle age by the time of the Tor executions. The shop selling the replicas also provided a leaflet in which their maker gave his own interpretation of the decorative designs, stressing that he was open to the views of others on the subject and in fact actively welcomed them. He referred the symbols as "astro-masonic". A glance at the chairs will at once indicate to anyone vaguely "in the know" that their maker was involved with a little more than orthodox Christianity.

Back at Chalice Well, I did some last minute dowsing in the gardens. As I worked, one of the then-wardens approached and gave me a little dowsing exercise. This was to see if I could ascertain the point at which the serpentine

Michael energy band enters the part of the garden known as Arthur's Court. At that point I was utterly unaware of the extreme relevance of this task to my quest. It almost seemed intrusive, but in order to humour the person who had asked me to see if my pendulum could find Michael's entry point I went along with it. I reached the Court's peaceful haven feeling quite detached about the task in hand, seeing it as an academic exercise, which, in reality, it was far from being, had I but known. Perhaps due to this state of mind, I unwittingly achieved the right brain/left brain balance state needed for reliable dowsing; the lack of emotional attachment and pre-conceived ideas about the result presumably proving to be beneficial. The Court was calm and quiet and standing there in that tranquil atmosphere I soon found the point at which the Southerly edge of the band came through the wall, close to the end of the bench. The warden concerned then confirmed that I had found the right spot, but still supplied no reason for asking me to carry out this exercise in the first place. In retrospect the whole affair was very synchronous, for two and a half years later, at midday on the Summer Solstice, I would be reaching the climax of an hour-long "virtual magic" ritual in Arthur's Court, carrying out a working in which the intersecting Michael and Mary bands played a major part; a working which signalled the completion of the first phase of an operation which had commenced four and a half centuries previously.

During a conversation with the warden I mentioned the fact that I hoped to visit St. John's Church (if open) to view a John Thorne chair said by some to be an original. I then learned that Little St. Michael boasted its own Glastonbury chairs, up in the top-floor meditation sanctuary known as the Upper Room, which I at once visited. As its name implies, the sanctuary is strongly linked to a vision of the room in which Christ and his disciples celebrated the last supper. The Chalice Well Trust, which administers the gardens and the retreat house, had been the brainchild of the pioneering Christian esotericist and psychic Wellesley Tudor Pole. Visiting the Chalice Well site as a boy in 1907, Tudor Pole was at once aware of its power and ancient sanctity. He also visited the Abbey ruins, where he experienced a strong intuitive feeling that he had spent a past life as a monk at this location. In 1958 his long-cherished dream became a reality and the Chalice Well Trust was founded.

Whether or not one agrees with Tudor Pole's own religious viewpoint is perhaps only important to the fundamentalist, be she/he pagan or Christian. His act of faith (putting his money where his mouth was and securing a large and necessary bank loan) in founding the Trust did the Chalice Well site, Glastonbury and spiritual seekers all over the world an immense service. In many ways he was a very "ordinary" man (whatever that is); a merchant and man of affairs as well as being a mystic and a gifted psychic. To Tudor Pole, spirituality was worthless if it was divorced from or irrelevant to everyday life. His involvement with the discovery of the blue glass bowl, an artifact of great spiritual power, will be detailed later in this volume. Despite his feelings for the place he never lived in Glastonbury, not even, like Dion Fortune, on a part-time basis. Although ostensibly a Christian, his brand of religion was far from orthodox and even in his early teens he was taken to task by his school teachers who were unimpressed by his divergent beliefs. Reincarnation, for instance, seemed as a living reality to him. Although broadly speaking one could find some parallels between his spirituality and that of Rudolph Steiner, there does not seem to have been a direct influence as in the case of the late Sir George Trevelyan, who was also influenced by Tudor Pole.

In his books *The Silent Road* and *A Man Seen From Afar* Tudor Pole gave matter of fact, unspectacular but meticulously detailed descriptions of events from the life of Jesus Christ in a manner which implied some sort of psychic vision, although he never precisely stated that they were the result of such a process. To him, Christ was a human being born into the world via the same physiological mechanics as the rest of us, although he was nevertheless a channel of divine energy. An aspect of Pole's view which the rigidly orthodox or fundamentalist might find shocking or heretical may be found in his attitude to Christ's mission, for he believed that Christ's "lower self" or everyday personality did not always comprehend the manner in which his "higher self" had to implement directives from the divine source. Such a view sympathises with sentiments expressed in some of Dion Fortune's works, notably *The Training and Work of an Initiate* and *Esoteric Orders and their Work*. In her writings, she discusses such hypothetical cases as a person voluntarily sacrificing her/his own life because the higher self deems it to be spiritually necessary while the lower self may be distinctly unaware of such a situation.

Wellesley Tudor Pole's writings exhibit a clear vision of what the upper room of the last supper looked like, even down to details of furnishings and food. In his book *Writing on the Ground* he describes the realisation of his desire to turn this vision into a concrete, physical reality, which he eventually did on the top floor of Little St. Michael, using psychic intuition to help him to find the appropriate items of furniture, etc. For him, however, supper was not the whole story, for he saw the breakfast of a new day to follow and it was his intention, so far unrealised, that the Wellhouse Lane end of the room would one day be equipped with the accessories needed for the consumption of such a breakfast; a table to be lit by the rays of a Sun rising from behind the Tor and orchards. Today, half of the Upper Room is still set out with the tables, chairs and eating and drinking accessories of the last supper vision; the other half acting as a straightforward meditation sanctuary. Until quite recently the "Last Supper" section of the room was divided from the rest of it by a veil-like curtain but this has now been removed as this was deemed to be more fitting for the present time; a move which I, personally, felt to be a very positive one.

Perhaps a contemporary parallel to Tudor Pole's physical manifestation of his last supper vision may be seen in the Avalon Foundation's desire to build the physical counterpart of a Glastonbury Temple which Kathy Jones and Barry Taylor have already glimpsed as existing on the etheric; a temple exhibiting some intriguing links with the "Egg Stone" discovered buried among the Abbey ruins by Frederick Bligh Bond in the early 20th Century.

I looked around the peaceful Upper Room and there was the chair -a real beauty! I have to confess to experiencing a sense of some pride as I studied this lovely piece of antique woodwork. Whether it was actually "an original" suddenly seemed unimportant. Even if not made with John's own hands it nevertheless magically carried the essence of his mysterious designs. "Well, if I REALLY was him I didn't make a bad job of it" I thought. My attention was soon grabbed by a companion chair standing nearby. Although of identical shape this item did not exhibit the characteristic circle and square (John Michell's New Jerusalem diagram) on the back support, decorated instead with an intriguing double arch design set below two strange winged creatures a little like griffins placed on either side of a curiously-angled shield sporting a cross reminiscent of the insignia of the Knights of St. John. I left the Upper Room fully aware that both chairs would receive a lot more attention from me in the future.

With many of the roads between Glastonbury and Bristol in a semi-flooded state I wondered if the bus would reach its destination, but it did, with luck. Once aboard the Inter-city train, I mellowed-out with a cup of tea and a cigarette; mentally chewing-over the happenings of the past twenty-four hours. I knew that I had been provided with a number of quest building blocks and jigsaw puzzle pieces. Exactly HOW they went together I did not know at that point. I finished the tea, wrote-up my experiences in a coherent form and then caught up on some sleep as the train swept through the dark, rain-washed countryside, carrying me back to Paddington. It had certainly been worth the trip!

Chapter 7

Vision of Arthur

Returning home late in the evening, I rang Jo Shrimpton for a psychic update. She had, as it happened, been aware of "things happening" while I was in Glastonbury. As we talked, she was shown a deep shaft lined with what she took to be granite. At the bottom was the spreadeagled skeleton of someone who had either fallen or been pushed centuries ago. Jo was aware of a complex of subterranean chambers; some interconnecting. Her attention was then switched to John Thorne's chairs. "Some interesting carving, including a secret symbol on the back. . . " The imagery then abruptly changed to Mallory-type impressions of Arthur. Given that Arthur was also John's monastic taken name, it was reasonable to assume that the once and future king must be involved somewhere along the line. Jo went on: "A king with a goatee beard wearing a crown and a purple cloak, holding up a sword so that it points down towards the earth. Although his head is held high his eyes stare down at the ground. It's a long, strong sword with a jewelled handle. The king's followers wear chain mail. One says the word "quest". A name: James. A scroll, recently unrolled and bearing a seal. A skeleton at the bottom of a shaft again and the name Jonathan."

I had been getting vague glimmerings regarding some sort of secret activity which once went on in the cellars of the pilgrims' house, connected to the Abbey via the tunnel explored by Bligh Bond and Mrs. Bilborough in 1918. There was the feeling of a covert society, to which John seemed to have belonged. The old book which I had found at Little St. Michael had referred to a statue of an initiate craftsman said to have once been positioned upon the building's battlements and to meetings of the masonic guilds. I have never come across any references to the statue or the meetings elsewhere. I feel that the anonymous author used the term masonic guilds rather loosely. Our knowledge of Freemasonry is shadowy, to say the least, before the 17th Century. However, I feel that he or she was unquestionably on the right track and that meetings of some kind of secret society of a not unrelated nature

DID take place at what is now the *George and Pilgrims Hotel*. At this point, Jo was taken to that very place. She went on: "A name. . . Marigold. A landlord -paid in kind to keep quiet and say nothing about what was going on. (I was later to find out that John had some very good reasons for "keeping in" with this particular landlord who was probably a lay person employed and housed by the Abbey. Not ALL of John's activities, I subsequently learned, took place downstairs.) Flagstones. . . an old inn. Pewter mugs, beer barrels, the smell of ale. Stools. . . a dog. . . a fireplace. Steps which lead down. Cold. . . dark. . . the sound of running water. (Bligh Bond mentioned water seeping into the cellar from under the High Street.) A hidden doorway concealed by old sacking. Panic. A young woman at the inn. Entering the tunnel. . . have to crawl. (The accuracy of this description of the tunnel was impressive indeed, particularly as Jo had no idea as to the location and had read nothing of the research material.) A heap of precious coins hidden in the tunnel. (This image seems to have been symbolic imagery, as something precious WAS concealed in the tunnel, as we shall see. The "young woman" was also very relevant in this respect.) Very unpleasant. Can't go any further." The focus of the transmission returned to chairs. "The chair. . . look under the seat. (This remark spurred David Aylward, Fay Cockell, Jenni Stather and myself, during the following weeks, to overturn every "John" chair upon which we could lay our hands!) There could be a hollow leg on one chair which contains something. Five pills in a metal box.... NOT medicine. (Alchemical supplies?) The box and the chairs are linked. All tunnels under Glastonbury lead to one large chamber. (A real gobsmacker!) I can see a cavern made of. . . crystal; yes, like crystal. Linking tunnel points on a map make a pentagrammic shape with the big chamber at the centre. That's it, I think."

Ross Nichols' *The Book of Druidry*, a collection of papers outlining much of the "meat" of Druidic practice and belief was published fourteen years after his death as a result of the efforts of Philip Carr-Gomm, present Chosen Chief of The Order of Bards, Ovates and Druids. In a section of the book dealing with the Druidic calendric eight-fold division of the year (a schema also followed by Wiccans and other pagans) Nichols gave the complete text of the O. B. O. D. Beltane ritual which once took place on Glastonbury Tor. The closing of the ceremony refers to the sleeping King Arthur and describes a trinity comprising the Tor, the well and the cave; the latter containing both the dragon and the treasure, being entered ritually between two pillars (the Michael tower -air, and the Chalice Well -water). A following note outlines the Glastonbury Pentagram Scheme. An accompanying diagram shows an irregular but symmetrical, foreshortened pentagram centred upon the Tor. Nichols obviously saw the cave as a key feature of the Glastonbury ritual landscape. Certainly, Jo's transmission provided much food for thought.

On January 20th, David Aylward called round with a small glass artifact which he had found in Greenwich Park, where some turf had been laid back close to the Dianic Temple site. A curator at the local Borough Museum subsequently identified it as an 18th Century scent bottle. Fay Cockell dropped in by chance (?) about ten minutes after David's arrival and it seemed an excellent opportunity to apply her formidable psychometrist's skills to the "find" to see if it had anything to tell us, which it did. Fay's reading began with a very peculiar statement: "Speak of riches to whom they pretend and you will find the end." Such remarks are not rare within the context of psychic sessions. They may strike one as mock-profound, over-generalised or downright meaningless. The quester, however, while not getting excited, files them away for future reference as, in my experience at least, today's garbage can sometimes turn out to be tomorrow's gold. A French female name followed, Geraldine or Genevieve, then the words "Glastonbury Jew". These words were accompanied by a vision of a Gothic window, probably in a church, with a large chest located immediately below it, a little to the left. Visiting St. John's Church in Glastonbury ten days later, Fay was staggered to find this very window and chest. In the position where she had seen what she took to be a chest, she found the reputed tomb of Joseph of Arimathea; the "Glastonbury Jew"! As if that were not enough the tomb was topped with fabric reputed to be the cope once worn by one of the Glastonbury Three: Abbot Richard Whiting. Fay was told "A lot more tunnels. Go down one and turn left" and was shown the diamond shape with which I was to become familiar during the coming two years; the secret symbol of the Abbey's covert magical order.

Not much, maybe, but enough to whet appetites and the three of us decided there and then that we would go to Glastonbury together as soon as possible. By the time that David and Fay left, the date was set and rooms had been booked. We had little more than a week to wait and somehow, I felt that our trip was likely to prove eventful to say the least. . .

Chapter 8

Three go Weird in Avalon

The Sun was setting on Friday, 28th January 1994 when David Aylward arrived at my home, driving a car which he had hired for the journey. At 10.00 p.m., we came to a halt at Stonehenge. With full moon just past and the Fire Festival of Imbolc but four days away, the site's energies were at a high. Even at this time of night the security in operation was suggestive of that at a missile base. The guards, although quite friendly, kept a close eye on us and seemed relieved when we drove away. In terms of observable psychic activity the Henge was certainly a lively place. Lights flickered around the stones while shadowy, ill-defined figures appeared to be performing a wild, circular dance in the centre. At one point I observed a great flame shooting high into the sky. After relieving ourselves we moved on, reaching our guest house by 11.30 after having initially called at the wrong one, unwittingly causing a sleeping landlady to rise from her bed for nothing! The place was nicely situated, perched on the lower slopes of the Tor close to the old hamlet of Edgarley. After a quick cup of tea we retired to our respective rooms. My room was a tiny single with a large window set into the roof which afforded an excellent view of the starry sky. If I stood on tiptoe I could just see the streetlights burning down in the town.

Not feeling quite ready for sleep, I propped myself up in bed and then slipped a cassette into my personal stereo; a tape recorded live at Fairport Convention's 1992 25th anniversary festival at Cropredy, at which I had been present. Pertinently, the first song to which I listened was Richard Thompson's *Poor Will and the Jolly Hangman*. The aptness of this stark ballad was hardly lost on me, with its chorus offering a toast to the Jolly Hangman who'll "hang you the best that he can". Yes, here I was about to settle down to sleep on the same hill as that upon which I had been executed 450 years previously! Sweet dreams!

The little room seemed to be very "vibed-up", just as Stonehenge had been, but I was almost too tired to notice. After a few songs I removed my

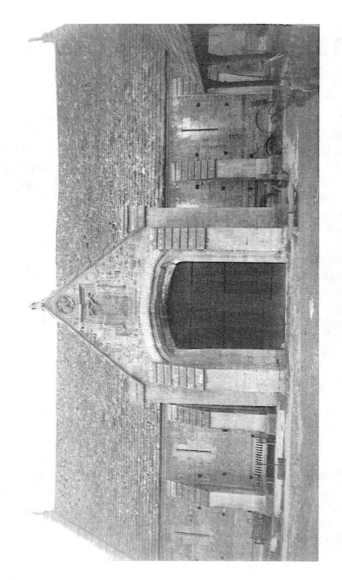

The Abbey Barn

headphones and drifted into a hypnogogic state. An inner voice suddenly announced "Your life was given as a sacrifice". I was then shown a huge X-shaped Gebo/Giffu rune, filled with rippling silver-blue light waves. I had been shown this rune repeatedly since Imbolc 1992 and at that time even wore it engraved upon a silver ring. It is a rune of partnership and energy exchange, particularly with the Otherworld. I was suddenly aware of the howling of the Tor wind, seeming to have blown up from nowhere and now shaking the building. Opening my eyes, I saw a dark-blue glow in the corner of the room, which I at once recognised as being an indication of the presence of the Northern deity Woden/Odin. I was reminded of his role in Viking times as gallows God, his own sacrifice on the World Tree Yggdrasil, rewarded by knowledge of the runes and of his other role as deity of the fury of the storm. (The rune Ansuz, sacred to Woden/Odin, is both a rune of poetic inspiration and a force which sweeps away blocks in the mind with its hurricane-like force rather in the manner in which the Eastern deity Ganesha performs a similar function in certain circumstances.) The wind and psychic activity finally abated around 3 a.m., when I fell asleep.

In the morning David and myself found that the batteries which powered our personal stereos were dead. Dave was puzzled, as the batteries in his machine were almost new. Fay's watch battery, too, ran out the next day, just as mine had done on the occasion of my last Tor visit. In *The Book of Druidry* Ross Nichols commented upon the curious electrical properties of the Glastonbury earth, recounting an occasion back in the old "Avalonian" days when, as a boy, he had slept on the ground beside the Abbey Barn, sensing "electrical vibrations" on his body upon waking. In some odd way the Tor seems to suck power from small batteries. This weird phenomenon could possibly relate in some way to the presence of the great Celtic Underworld Goddess Ceridwen, who in my experience and that of others, particularly the Bardic revivalist Gwdihw, finds electrical equipment fascinating. (Her cauldron of inspiration was in many ways a forerunner of the Holy Grail.) Whilst staging dramatic presentations involving the old tales of this Goddess, Gwdihw has often found pieces of electrical equipment to inexplicably fail; working perfectly again after the completion of the event. On one occasion I presented Ceridwen with some brand new batteries as an offering in the course of a working from which I hoped to gain inspiration; one of her cauldron's gifts. Some electrical resistivity testing carried out in Chalice Well gardens in March 1994 with electronics genius Rodney Hale produced some baffling and quite unexpected results. Glastonbury has a few surprises up its sleeve where electricity is concerned. True, the sudden bursts of anomalous activity

The Lady Chapel

registered by the instrumentation operated by Rodney and myself COULD have been due to the distant functioning of farm machinery, but. . .

Breakfast over, we made for the town. Our first call was at the shop selling the replica "John" chairs. When we went in the proprietor kindly allowed us to sit in them. David and Fay both remarked upon a sense of "balance" experienced while doing this. We then dropped in at the *George*, where a helpful member of staff took us up to the "haunted" Monk's Cell bedroom. I took some quick rubbings from an old and oddly interesting-looking chest which caught my attention. These later provided Carole Young with the material for psychometric work which proved to be quite a revelation. The patterns carved upon the wood were also of considerable interest (we later found them to be duplicated on an ancient chest in St. John's church; a piece of composite furniture possibly cobbled together -according to one of the clergy to whom we spoke -using timber salvaged from the Abbey) and seemed to echo the circular motifs characteristic of the Dutch-American "Hex" magic tradition. They will be discussed at greater length in a subsequent chapter. Psychic concentration was rendered difficult by time constraints and, of course, the need to socialise with the lady who had been kind enough to take us into the room. I was, however, certainly aware of the room being highly active from the psychic viewpoint. This, in retrospect, was hardly surprising given the nature of events which I later learned had taken place on the *George's* upper storeys.

At the Abbey we studied the curious stone slab emblazoned with the "World Tree" variant of the Elhaz/Algiz rune, also very similar and in part identical to the bindrune which at that time had recently been adopted by the eco-magical organisation Dragon. David suddenly received a psychic instruction which told him to pull the slab away from the wall. He did, to find an identical rune carved on the other side! Fay was vaguely aware of some feint echoes of the troubled events of 1539, particularly when touching the old timber door which had captured my attention during my August 1993 visit. She recoiled with distaste, muttering the word "horrible". Intrigued as to what was horrible, I too "tuned-in" psychically to the door. I was at once engulfed by a suffocating wave of mixed negative emotions; a brief but intense sense of pain, fear and paranoia which had somehow been preserved within the door's fabric since the end of the Glastonbury Three. I quickly made for the fresh air outside, gasping for breath. This was the one and only time that I have experienced this kind of negative "action replay" for my inner plane contacts have repeatedly told me that there is no point in

Abbot Bere's crypt; St. Joseph's cult centre

wallowing in a remembrance of this gory stuff for its own sake; a self-indulgent and masochistic exercise. It is NOW that matters, they tell me; what is being done NOW to continue and complete magical work commenced in the 1530's and disrupted by events which were recorded in the history books.

Recovered, we made for the crypt below the Lady Chapel; the cult shrine of Joseph of Arimathea. Abbot Bere, the Abbey's penultimate head, had masterminded its construction in 1500; very difficult too, due to the substantial building already standing above it whose floor had to be raised in order to accommodate a crypt not entirely below ground level. David found the atmosphere dark and oppressive on that chilly Winter morning, although St. Joseph's Well tucked away in its little alcove felt like an oasis of calm and healing. We had a similarly "good" feeling about the enclosed rectangle marking the supposed site of Arthur's grave. As we stood there, David Aylward psychically received the strange comment "To help prove the existence of Arthur".

Leaving the Abbey, we walked along Chilkwell Street to Chalice Well gardens. As she stared down into the Well's dark waters, Fay experienced a sudden vision of St. Michael's tower on the Tor and heard the words "Tower of Doom". (Really encouraging!) Across Wellhouse Lane, we entered the austere Victorian reservoir building, now a cafe and shop. Stepping over the White Spring we browsed among items for sale located in the far depths of the enclosure; the shop area giving the impression of being housed in what was once a cave. Tunnels, I knew, had once been constructed behind the reservoir; these leading on to natural cavities which might well have taken one into the fabled Crystal Cave beneath the Tor but for a series of cave-ins reported by explorers.

In *The Book of Druidry*, Ross Nichols puts forward the view that anyone entering the Crystal Cave now (presumably astrally, as all physical entrances seem to be securely blocked) would need to be well experienced in occult matters and particularly in the area of psychic protection, given that this cavity has not been entered for a long time and the psychic atmosphere may well be somewhat stale. At the shop proprietor's invitation, David, Fay and myself were allowed into a small, pitch-dark cavity adjacent to the shop. This place, one felt, really had some potential and one found oneself wondering what it would be like to spend twenty-four hours alone in here. Would one suffer the apparent insanity which overtook a group of monks who, according to local legend, ventured into a passage they discovered which seemed to lead under the Tor.

Nicholas Mann has made some extremely interesting and quite provocative observations with regard to the White Spring; not only about the Victorian vandalisation of the picturesque, sacred combe from which it gently flowed but also in respect of the general "playing down" of its very existence since then which he feels almost amounts to a conspiracy. Mann rightly sees the fusion of the waters of the Tor's White Spring with those of the Blood Spring issuing from softly-rounded Chalice Hill as constituting a profound sacred and alchemical symbolism, which will be dealt with at length in this volume a little later. Suffice it to say for the present that the waters of both springs once mingled freely; Hamish Miller and Paul Broadhurst speculating that this may actually have happened at the place now known as Arthur's Court which, pertinently, is also an intersection point of the Michael and Mary bands. See Nicholas Mann's splendid book *The Isle of Avalon* for his highly original thoughts on the subject. Emerging from the White Spring area, the Tor's windswept heights seemed like a logical next stop. David and Fay ascended at great speed, feeling as if some Otherworldly force propelled them to the summit at the double. It was our intention to dowse the nodal point of the Michael and Mary bands; the exact point of intersection not being outlined in *The Sun and the Serpent*. My pendulum started to behave in a very odd manner, which, if one took its findings at surface value, seemed to indicate that the nodal point was continually shifting its position. Yes, the good old psychic joker was making her/his presence felt. As I stood there in the half-light, bewildered by the behaviour of my manic dowsing tool, Fay suddenly psychically received an abrupt message which gave us "notice to quit" in no uncertain terms, ordering us off the Tor. Given that any result obtained would be of highly dubious reliability we called it a day as far as dowsing was concerned, but unanimously decided to settle for compromise as far as the received message was concerned, heading for the Bur Stone on the Tor's Southern slope.

Although apparently naturally formed from the Midford Sandstone which geologically forms the Tor's cap, the Bur Stone is a near-perfect sphere and is obviously the focus of much attention. The nodal point of Michael and Mary is not far away and it was also at this point that Geoffrey Russel suggested that the Tor maze went underground for the last stretch of its journey. Darkness fell as we carried out the simplest of rituals, adding our offerings to those of other pilgrims who had dressed the little hawthorn beside the stone with coloured strips of rag which cracked and rattled in the pitiless, relentless Tor wind. After consuming some apple juice and pouring some upon the earth as an offering, I played some slow Celtic airs on my tin whistle before we carefully made our way down to the guest house for a rest break; the plan being to follow this with a return to the town for an evening meal at the George. The joker still seemed to be in evidence; on several occasions I nearly missed my footing on the way from the Bur Stone to the path, at one point plunging an ungloved hand into a bed of stinging nettles as I struggled to steady myself. ("That'll teach you. . . ")

The next morning we left the guest house a good hour later than planned. As we had found the church to be locked so far, there seemed little chance of gaining entry; morning services presumably ended by now. However, something guided us to St. John's, where we met a clergyman who was just leaving. (Synchronicity literally to the second!) Obligingly, he unlocked the building and allowed us in for a quick look round. After initial amazement at seeing the high Gothic window and Joseph of Arimathea's tomb EXACTLY as Fay had glimpsed them during our psychic session back at Greenwich, we concentrated on examining the possibly "original" Glastonbury chair; its cylindrical understrut noticeably different to those sported by other chairs in the church, which took the form of elongated hexagonal prisms. We were also fascinated by a great wooden chest located close to the entrance. According to Miller and Broadhurst, the Michael band radically changes its course beneath this item of furniture. It seemed a good idea to take some rubbings of the chest's carved decoration, some of which resembled that seen the previous day in the Monk's Cell. As stated previously, our helpful host told us that there was a possibility that the item was a composite structure built from timbers rescued from the dismantled Abbey.

Across the road, we wandered round the little complex of shops, etc, clustered around a courtyard known as the Glastonbury Experience. Eventually, we found ourselves in the non-denominational Chapel of Brigid where, two years later, I was to be briefly reunited with Abbot Richard Bere; my past-life boss and good friend. In the chapel we found yet another John-style chair. The back panel looked much like those found upon others which we had seen from the front, with the familiar squared circle motif. The back, however, was a quite different story. The linear figure which we found appeared to be indisputably runic in origin! The design took the form of an X-shaped diagonal equal-armed cross with two branches at the extremities of each arm. Initially I took these for Elhaz/Algiz runes, but a closer look convinced me that they were in fact four Tyr/Tiewaz runes pointing inwards. To be precise, the figure appeared to be a bindrune combining the X-shaped Gebo rune seen in my bedroom two nights previously with a Tyr/Tiewaz rune quartet. The Tyr rune is, of course, named after the Northern deity of justice and war; not a God of mindless Martian violence and head-smashing but one who represents combat deemed to be in a cause both just and honourable. In her article *The Glyph of Spider Woman* in the April 1992 issue of *Pagan News*, Chrys Livings shows exactly such a bindrune, explaining that the four Tyr runes are pointing in the direction of the glyph's heart or centre, pushing energy towards a target or goal. (The figure was shown as part of a glyph sequence for use in magical workings of empowerment, etc.)

After making a rubbing from the chair we returned to Chalice Well, where a helpful gardener took us up for a quick look at the chairs which I had previously found in Tudor Pole's Upper Room. Both of my friends were fascinated by the chair emblazoned with the double arc and shield motifs. Time was marching on and it was now time to think about our return to London, which we decided to accomplish via a quick stop-off at Avebury. The sun was dropping behind the Western hills as we pulled up at the Sanctuary, and night had fallen by the time that we reached Avebury village. It had been the most glorious sunset imaginable. There was not a whisper of wind as we strolled among the great old stones. Avebury was still, cool and bathed in a radiant afterglow; its healing calmness a strong contrast to Glastonbury's volcanic energies. That silence reigned which seems so peculiar to this wonderful place, punctuated only by the occasional unearthly, echoing calls of the resident peacocks. We wandered down to the end of the High Street, turned and started to walk back up again. Suddenly David, speechless, pointed to a lighted ground-floor window which we were passing. Glancing quickly in I saw a cosy living room equipped with yet ANOTHER John Thorne chair! My mind at once went back to something temporarily forgotten on a conscious level. Jenni Stather had recently told me that she had received psychic information to the effect that a Glastonbury chair could be found somewhere in Avebury! Well, she certainly got that one right! As we headed back towards London, none of us felt that any grounds for complaint existed with regard to the volume of "stuff" seen and experienced during that memorable weekend.

Chapter 9

The Dancing Wheels

One of my first tasks, upon returning to London, was to see what I could dig out about the mysterious wheel-like designs which I had found carved upon the chest in the *George*'s Monk's Cell and also upon the compositely-constructed chest in St. John's Church. At that time I found relatively little, but the subject abruptly returned to me a couple of years later whilst seated in the *British Library*, thumbing through a copy of Nigel Pennick's 1982 book *Hitler's Secret Sciences*. My attention was caught by a reproduced photograph showing a "swastika stone" found in Spain by members of the Nazi Ahnenebe. This "ancestral heritage" institution was charged with the task of using historical research material in order to demonstrate the ancient pedigree of the party in racial/mystical terms. The swastika, as readers will know, was a very old Indo-Germanic symbol which the Nazis adopted. The photograph which Pennick reproduces originated in an Ahnenerbe publication. A grid of small squares (10 x 12) flanked by what look like Sig runes is surmounted by two facing swastikas, one deosil (clockwise) and one Widdershins (anti-clockwise). Above the swastikas is placed a fascinating mandala. At the centre we find what looks like a whirling turbine; actually 24 overlapping crescents which "rotate" in a Widdershins direction. A concentric circular band beyond the circle of crescents contains 11 small circles, each divided into 6 equal parts via "flower petals" simply made by dividing the circumference into 6 by stepping off the radius of the given circle and then drawing an internal arc centred upon each of the circumferential points thus derived, which most of us did in primary school geometry. So what?

The reason as to why this picture grabbed my attention is quickly explained: I had seen just such configurations in Glastonbury on the chests in the *George* and St. John's Church; both, as a matter of interest, situated on the Michael band. (According to Miller and Broadhurst it runs across the cobbles at the immediate rear of the *George*. When I personally dowsed it, it was of such width as to enter the building and to pass through what is now the restaurant area; its size, of course, being variable according to a number of factors.) The designs also, as stated previously, resemble those used in German/American Hex Magic. Little in print on this obscure aspect of practical occultism is currently available. The American writer Silver Raven Wolf wrote a book on the subject published in 1995 and available in the U.K. entitled *Hex Craft*. Otherwise, the interested reader is referred to Edred Thorsson's splendid book *Northern Magic*, which provides a concise outline of Hex procedures.

Briefly, this magical system was taken to America by German immigrants who travelled there from the 17th Century onwards, settling mainly in Pennsylvania, New York, Maryland, Virginia and New Jersey. They were referred to as Dutch not because they came from Holland but due to the name which they gave themselves: "Deutch" or "Deitch". Often settling in remote rural areas these folk managed to maintain their practises until the advent of the social changes wrought by the Great Depression and the Second World War. Unlike runes, Hex magic symbols are all inscribed within a circle, giving a mandala-like appearance as opposed to the angular quality of the runes. In contrast to runic clinical starkness, Hex symbols are often decorative; a "prettiness" hiding their true purpose. In common with rune magic, however, Hex magic requires meticulous physical execution of the symbol used plus a spoken incantation.

According to Thorsson, the entire disc represents the complete universe. It may be internally divided into zones via concentric circles. A disc divided into three parts would comprise (in order from circumference to centre) the outer or objective universe, the subjective universe or inner world of the occultist and the core self of the magician/universe core intelligence. Hex signs vary however, and not all are thus divided. If Hex magic principles are applied to the Nazis' swastika stone we would have a division between objective and subjective universes separating inner and outer worlds.

Thorsson describes the traditional six-fold pattern identical to the circles found on the swastika stone and also to those found on the Glastonbury chests as being the eldest and most frequently used design. A sixfold sign, he tells us, can interact with forces creating form using energy as a raw material, which surely accounts for its popularity in workings aimed at changing existing conditions. Six relates to the hexagon, from which a hexagram, or six-pointed star can be created. In Western occultism this sign, which consists of two superimposed equilateral triangles, is sometimes seen as representing the union of the Lower and Higher Selves; the goal of the ceremonial magician in some schools. It is also often seen as a masculine, Solar symbol, which may be of relevance here given the presence of the Michael band.

Silver Raven Wolf's book shows a hex design which incorporates four widdershins-rotating crescents. She interprets this symbolism as a reference to the Lunar aspect of the Goddess; the apparent movement indicating the dance of the seasons. The 24 rotating crescents in the Spanish stone seem to buzz with energy, even in a photograph. Looking at them is an experience akin to looking at a 1966 "Op Art" painting. In my book *Goddesses, Guardians and Groves* I wrote about the strange energy vortices created by the design properties of certain floor patterns in the ante-rooms of the Queen's House at Greenwich. I still incline towards the view that patterns like these and those on the Spanish stone actually do generate energy. Looking at the latter it is difficult to determine whether one is observing a mere optical illusion, psychic energy or both.

On the chest in St. John's Church several quite different motifs nestle side by side. Examining rubbings which I had made, something struck me. The widdershins crescent mandalas, which seem to wizz round as one looks at them, actually contain 11 crescents, whereas the deosil ones contain 12. Possibly the widdershins variety represent a waning moon whereas the deosil type signify a waxing Lunar condition. In the Western tradition 11 is the number associated with the averse, or "shadow" sephira; the "dark" aspect of the Qabalistic Tree of Life; the number of the Qliphoth, or "evil demons" of unbalanced force. (For a penetrating study of the difficult subject of the reverse side of the Tree, whose spheres are linked by the Tunnels of Set, see Kenneth Grant's book *Nightside of Eden*.) The waning period tends, too, to be associated with the darker aspects of the Goddess in pagan tradition. As part of a cycle it is every bit as vital as its opposite number, by its very existence creating a state of equilibrium.

The various mandalas were juxtaposed on the St. John's chest in a variety of combinations; widdershins and deosil crescents being sometimes found beside Solar, 6-petalled designs (which would indicate a pairing of Solar and Lunar energies which echoes the powers of the Michael and Mary bands and the alchemical reconciliation of opposites) and sometimes beside a curious wheel divided into eight equal parts by four straight lines drawn through the centre from the circumference, reflecting both the eightfold division of the wheel of the year now used by Wiccans and Druids and the 8-rayed Star of Chaos used by magicians of a Chaosist persuasion at the present time.

Perhaps all this stuff was pretty decoration. . . and perhaps it was something more.

Chapter 10

Joker in the Pack

Following the return of Fay, David and myself from Glastonbury at the end of January 1994, Jenni Stather began to take an increasingly active part in the quest. I had known Jenni as a colleague during my teaching days in East London, and had always respected her very considerable psychic skills. Since my departure from the teaching scene for health reasons we had kept in touch, and Jenni had followed my Glastonbury work with mounting interest, frequently receiving profound snippets of psychic information during telephone conversations in a manner to which I had become accustomed already as a result of experiences which took place when talking to Carole and Jo in the same circumstances.

The morning of Thursday, 24th February 1994 found Jenni and myself speeding down the motorway en route for Avebury, where we planned to break our journey before continuing on to Glastonbury. Our purpose in stopping at Avebury was not at all complicated; it would give Jenni a rest from the rigours of driving and allow us time to visit some favoured stones, browse in the shops and grab a quick sandwich in the *Red Lion*. Avebury was chill and gloomy; a great contrast to the atmosphere on the occasion of my previous visit.

Reaching Glastonbury in the mid-afternoon, we dropped our bags at the guest house (the same one as that at which I had stayed with Fay and David) and then wandered around the town for a while. After a cup of tea we made for St. John's Church, where, once again, we just happened to meet a clergyman who was about to lock up. Displaying the same friendly and helpful nature as that previously exhibited by his colleague he delayed closing the building until we had examined the possibly "original" chair and also looked at Abbot Whiting's cope. This done, we drove to Wells where Jenni hoped to look up an old chorister friend. When we reached the town the February cold had intensified and an icy wind blew through the quiet, lamplit streets. The choristers were in the process of disrobing following a service and after hanging around for a while, we met Alec; the gentleman in question, who invited us in to have a cup of tea in his intriguing Cathedral Close residence.

As we discussed the Glastonbury Three, Alec, a history graduate who had specialised in the Tudor period, reminded me that they had been tried at Wells on the day prior to their executions. As he talked I was aware of strong psychic energy building in the cosy little living room and Jenni sensed a spirit figure lurking in a shadowy corner by the bookshelves. Upon returning to Glastonbury, we decided to eat our evening meal in the restaurant of the *George and Pilgrims Hotel*. Jenni was aware of a psychic "tingle" when standing directly above the cellars and, oddly, extreme cold at the entrance to the toilets, which I also felt. After eating we moved into the bar, where the atmosphere was just as strong as on previous occasions. For some reason, Jenni felt a sudden urge to conduct an impromptu "seance" there and then, right in the middle of the Thursday evening drinkers. "Tuning in", she asked me to slowly repeat the names of the three hanged men, which I did. She soon became aware of a male spirit presence seated on the opposite side of our heavy old oaken table. My hands, also, tingled madly. Back at the guest house, she did a further "tune in", this time using a pendulum as an aid; receiving John Thorne/Arthur as the name of the monk who "haunts" the *George*! She could see no contradiction implied by my now growing conviction that I was, in fact, John's reincarnation; feeling that the 1539 traumas has caused me to shed something; some part of my subtle self, which had remained in the *George*'s spiritual atmosphere for centuries. (Again, one is reminded of Col. Seymour's comments about part of a person reincarnating and part remaining behind as a "watcher".) Alone in her room that night, Jenni saw the familiar diamond motif featured on the chair backs hanging on the wall by the window, radiating a warm, golden light. It apparently remained there until she fell asleep. My own night, too, was not uneventful, as I dreamed of a coat of arms-like picture of Henry VIII with a framed image of a red lion below it. The lion suddenly bounded out of the frame and vanished! It seems likely (in fact, almost certain) that John would have met Henry face to face on at least one occasion, for it is on record that the King was lodged at the Abbey for a few days when he visited a few years before the fury of the Reformation was vented upon the institution.

Earlier that evening, the psychic joker had been in evidence again. As we left the *George*, Jenni was dismayed to find that her car keys were missing from her right-hand jacket pocket; their customary place of storage when not in

60

use. So, where WERE they? Taking out my pendulum, I stood in the freezing wind in the deserted High Street, endeavouring to find the answer. I was repeatedly told that they were to be found in Jenni's bag. A subsequent search revealed this to be a classic case of "dowser's wind-up", or duff information! Eventually, they were discovered zipped securely into her LEFT-hand jacket pocket, a place in which she NEVER puts them! In my own experience (for what it may be worth) it is extremely difficult to get a reliable response when dowsing for an object which one has lost and wishes to find again as quickly as possible. That tightrope-like balance between analysis and intuition, between the two brain hemispheres, is hard to maintain when emotions begin to run high and objectivity is undermined by awkward to dispel preconceived ideas about where the mislaid object just might be, or, rather, where it OUGHT to be.

The following morning, we chatted to a woman who managed one of the town's many esoteric bookshops. When I gave her some idea as to the scope of my research, she told me that many locals see the 1539 events as Glastonbury's unresolved karmic blot! She further told me about a local retired clergyman who was passionately interested in the whole issue and we decided to look in on him that evening. In the afternoon, we visited the Abbey. Jenni felt little until we reached the 16th Century Chapel of St. Patrick, where we both became abruptly aware of a suffocating smell which suggested putrefaction. The aroma was quite overpowering and we both felt an urge to vomit. When we came out for some welcome fresh air, Jenni received some psychic information and steeled herself to return in order to "check it out". She later told me that she had received the impression that the dismembered remains of The Glastonbury Three were brought back here before being sent off for display in the neighbouring towns. (History records that they were boiled in pitch.) Questioning Abbey staff about the smell we were met with blank incomprehension; one person even saying that the place normally has quite a pleasant aroma which, in fact, it does! Jenni was fairly shaken by the experience. Back in the car, she sprayed herself with Aura-cleanse and resorted to the use of Aura Soma, which seemed to do the trick. She soon felt much better although a slight sense of nausea lingered and she was somewhat puzzled by my laid-back and jokey attitude to it all; actually a coping strategy resulting from what was actually an intense personal involvement.

At 5.30 p.m. Jenni announced a desire to visit Cheddar. I was slightly dubious but finally agreed and we set off. We had nearly reached the Gorge when, for some reason, I asked her how our petrol state was faring. (Jenni is normally a meticulously careful person when it comes to the state of her fuel tank.) Was the joker around again? Maybe. Our tank, as it turned out, was almost empty! With no immediate memory of passing a service station recently we decided to carry on and to hope. Winding our way through the majestic, mist-shrouded gorge was an undoubtedly dramatic experience given an edge by the rapidly-dropping fuel level. As we reached the moorland beyond visibility came down to near-zero and everything became enveloped by a thick, milk-white mist. Tension rose as we drove on through seemingly endless wild, uninhabited terrain, with not the ghost of a petrol pump in sight. After an eternity we reached a cluster of dwellings at a crossroads. We pulled up and I hunted for other human beings; relieved to find one who directed us to a nearby service station that "might still be open" at Chewton Mendip -fortunately downhill all the way! I have seen some welcome garages but this was surely the loveliest ever. In the nick of time, we refuelled, snatched a quick drink at the local and then returned to Glastonbury via Wells, leaving the fog behind in the process.

Before consuming our evening meal we hunted down the retired cleric to whom I had been referred by the bookshop owner with whom I had chatted that morning. He did not seem to be at all surprised by the bearded quester's sudden appearance (Jenni waited in the car) and welcomed me into his home with the warmest of hospitality. In the course of our conversation he casually informed me that Arthur IS returning. He then painted a picture, in words, of one religious sect oppressing another over the centuries and the cumulative heritage of unhealed wounds and curse-like effects, whose spiritual consequences continue to be felt. He felt that the nature-based Celtic Christian Church survived covertly until Norman times but was finally squashed by the paranoid Roman desire for absolute supremacy; this being the beginning of a series of such scenarios; a wounded atmosphere and seething sense of outrage still hanging over the Abbey like a dark cloud waiting to be cleared. He was sure that the "curse" resulting from events such as the 1539 executions still manifests itself; on occasions physically. He talked enthusiastically about a prophecy of Glastonbury one day becoming a vibrant spiritual community again, citing Geoffrey Ashe as a latter-day prime-mover.

The clergyman felt that there was need for healing via a heart-type reconciliation at a deep, Jungian level. A good start, he felt, would be the establishment of a Christian healing ministry followed by a new ecumenism on the level of genuine reconciliation which should include the growing pagan community. When I asked him if he believed in pagan/Christian co-operation he replied in the positive, stressing the need for a non-judgmental viewpoint on both sides, hand in hand with mutual respect. I certainly could not argue with that.

Reeling as I tried to digest the considerable volume of profound comments with which I had been bombarded over the last half-hour, I took my leave, thanking this remarkable visionary for his time and hospitality. We then enjoyed a pleasantly uneventful evening meal back at the George, with no "ghosts", lost keys or freezing loos! It was a relaxing end to another eventful chapter in the story of my quest.

Chapter 11

The Cardinal

As 1994 wore on I became increasingly preoccupied with the writing of my book *Goddesses, Guardians and Groves*; a work which in many ways represented the culmination of all that I had worked for on the "Sacred Greenwich" front since 1978. This activity, together with giving talks, continuing to lead my Saturday morning Sacred Greenwich walking tours and producing the odd booklet and related artwork soon left little space for the Avalonian quest. However, I knew, at the back of my mind, that it would only be a matter of time before it all bubbled up again. Sporadic quest messages continued to come through via psychics who only had to be in my company for a minute in order to have the requisite mechanism activated without any prompting from myself. When I allowed myself the luxury of a spell of open meditation, the quest would erupt into my consciousness like a volcano. All communications received during this period were fully recorded and filed away for future reference. With *Goddesses, Guardians and Groves* accepted for publication by Capall Bann and finally typed up, I could return to the quest with a clear conscience and really get back "into things". During the Autumn of 1994 and the following Winter, Spring and Summer, I haunted the reading rooms at the *British Library* and other research institutions, plunging myself into the documentary research component which is so vital to effective questing. This would seem a logical point at which to pause in the narrative of my strange experiences on the Isle of Avalon (I did not return again until March 1995) in order to look a little more closely at the research material related to the various component parts of the quest. Oddly enough, my researches led me back to another Tudor-associated location which has fascinated me throughout my life: Hampton Court.

Time and again I have felt drawn to Hampton for a reason which never really made itself clear. Even as a child I used to experience an odd sense of deja vu, particularly when passing through the private apartments of Cardinal Wolsey. Walking around Hampton Court Park among the deer on a sunny Summer morning, one feels a sense of timelessness, as if the Cardinal or

Henry VIII himself could step out from behind a tree at any moment. By an odd twist of fate or whatever, a woman close to me holds a strong belief that she was Anne Boleyn in a past life. (I am not very interested in the tired old arguments so often trotted out in objection to the holding of such convictions, raising the tired old point that folk who get some inkling of a past life always find that they were "someone famous". The lady in question also had a past life as a village wisewoman, or witch, who was brutally murdered by the ecclesiastical authorities and whose name is probably quite unremembered by history, also one as an Anasazi indian shaman in the South-Western desert of what is now the United States; another life undocumented and unrecorded.)

Did John Thorne/Arthur and Anne Boleyn ever meet? The answer is yes, they almost certainly did, for it is on record that Henry VIII visited Glastonbury before that lady fell from favour with him. John probably knew that the writing was on the wall, as it were, when the somewhat unwelcome visit took place, but at least it gave him a chance to size-up the opposition. As we shall see, John was not blind to the charms of attractive women and was also not a person whom people tended to overlook even if he was not always popular. One suspects that there may have been a degree of eye contact between the covert occultist who was also the Abbey's treasurer when he found time and the lively young queen. The woman who senses her past-life as the latter has a vague recollection of John, during one of his probably few spells alone with her, strolling around the Abbey grounds in her company and, upon leaving her to walk through an arch, pausing to turn back and enigmatically suddenly advising her to "take care" and "beware" as if he had some premonition of her impending doom at the hands of the man who was to be indirectly responsible for his own spectacularly hideous death.

Returning to Hampton on Good Friday 1994 I found that the old magic was still there. There was the same feeling of familiarity and timelessness in the Wolsey apartments and in the courtyard outside Henry's Great Hall and also the stirrings of an odd conviction that the cardinal had at least some connection with the more covert activities which went on at Glastonbury. The location of Hampton Court Palace itself is more than a little interesting. When Wolsey leased it the site was occupied by a manor house belonging to the Knights Hospitalers or Knights of St. John. Readers will know that this was a brother order of the Knights Templars; many of whose properties eventually passed into the Hospitalers' hands following the Templar order's destruction in the 14th Century. This does not seem to have been the case with Hampton, however, as site occupation by the Hospitalers dates back to the 12th Century, when agricultural produce from the manor was sold in order to increase the Hospitalers' funds. The buildings were extended during the 15th Century and were visited by Henry VII in 1503. Two years later Hampton was leased to Lord Daubney, Chamberlain to Henry VII, who lived there until his death in 1508. In 1514 Cardinal Thomas Wolsey, Henry VIII's powerful chief minister, took over the lease. To attract such a figure in the first place the dwelling at Hampton must have been already one of some grandeur or at least must have exhibited some kind of recognisable potential.

A look at Hampton's siting and its links with the Knights of St. John reveals some familiar threads. Shirley Newton is the only writer who, to my knowledge, has focussed upon Hampton's esoteric aspects which she did in an article in the August/September 1993 issue of *New Age* magazine; an otherwise (for me, at any rate) unremarkable periodical. She later amplified points raised in her article in a talk delivered to the London Earth Mysteries Circle. Ms. Newton points out that in place names "ton" can refer to a high place where Druidic meetings took place and also mentions the close proximity of Kingston, where Anglo-Saxon monarchs were crowned on the Kings' Stone, of great antiquity.

The visionary and gifted researcher Mary Caine has discovered a terrestrial zodiac at Kingston similar to the great zodiac at Glastonbury if less well-known. Here is not the place to get into a deep discussion about the pros and cons of terrestrial zodiacs. No, maybe their existence cannot be proved via orthodox research, but the fact remains that they have a powerful etheric existence which one plugs into when working with them magically, often with profound results as we shall see later on in this book. Hampton occupies a fairly central position in the Kingston Zodiac, immediately in front of the hooves of Taurus the bull. Ms. Caine speculates that Hampton may have boasted a maze before those planted by Henry VIII and William III, linking it with the speculated maze on the slopes of the Tor and with bull-related mythology. She points out also that the area where the maze is located has traditionally been known as The Wilderness.

Shirley Newton takes up the maze theme, referring to the tale of Theseus and Ariadne and, in passing, advocating a simple method of "threading" the Hampton Court maze. Ms. Newton also states that Hampton is felt by some to represent the thirteenth sign at the Kingston Zodiac's centre. This is of note as the thirteenth sign is sometimes allocated to Arachne or Auriga. (Not

66

being an astrologer I have no intention of expressing an uneducated view as to the pros and cons of the nature of the thirteenth sign; occasionally a cause of some controversy.) One of Britain's largest spiders is, as it happens, a native of Hampton Court: the aptly-named Cardinal Spider; a specimen of which may be seen in the arachnid room at the *British Museum* of Natural History. According to the folklore of Hampton, Wolsey issued a decree protecting the Cardinals from extermination on the grounds that they possessed divinatory powers. If we are considering possible links between the "Cardinal of Ipswich" and the covert occultists of Glastonbury this may well be relevant as, according to psychically-received information, the group's totemic animal was the spider!

Cardinal Thomas Wolsey was clearly a remarkable man as his meteoric rise from Ipswich butcher's son to the most powerful man in England clearly demonstrates. After obtaining the Hampton lease in 1514, he set about erecting new buildings on the site, first building Base Court, with forty-four guest lodgings on two storeys then a second court with a three-storey range of lodgings for the King and Queen. By 1525 this building phase was completed and Henry stayed at the palace, as it had become. The construction of a long gallery and a chapel followed. By 1528 Wolsey's popularity with his monarch had dropped like a stone and Henry took Hampton for himself, soon adding new and even more magnificent buildings. By 1514 Wolsey had been made Archbishop of York and was elevated to the College of Cardinals by Pope Leo X in 1515. His influence upon Henry had been considerable. He had, in effect, taken over the monarch's decision-making duties in order to leave young Henry more space for sporting pursuits and socialising and his involvement with national foreign policy had also demonstrated a high profile. As quickly as he had risen, however, he fell.

Although a churchman Wolsey loved material comforts and was not averse to fleshly pleasures, fathering some illegitimate children. His sumptuous lifestyle and the extravagance of his Hampton entertaining became a legend. But WAS there a more esoteric side to him? When walking alone in Hampton Court Park he always insisted on remaining totally unobserved; completely out of sight. One wonders WHAT he was doing and WHY such secrecy was so vital to him. Then there is the Glastonbury connection. Wolsey was a good friend of penultimate abbot Richard Bere and responsible for the choice of the ill-fated Richard Whiting as Bere's successor. Henry himself could hold his own when discussing matters astrological and astronomical. John Robyns, Fellow of All Souls' Oxford in 1520 and later

Henry's chaplain discussed the subject of comets with the king in 1532 and was impressed by Henry's grasp of mathematics.

Shirley Newton has found what she sees as a chakric groundplan at Hampton which, if accepted, constitutes a macrocosmic terrestrial version of the human chakric system if one uses the Tantrically-originating model of the bodily energy centres as a reference frame. She also has a sharp eye for detail, quickly spotting the Hospitaler connection and also a Masonic one. Apart from Wren's contribution (Sir Christopher is believed by some to have been involved in Masonic-type activities) our attention is drawn to a plaque on the right-hand side of the entrance facing the Palace. The plaque states that the "Toy Inn" once stood on this spot, built in 1650 for the New Model Army's soldiers. Rebuilt in 1740, it was demolished a century later. The plaque also tells us that Thomas Dunkerley had a "Masonic House of Harmony 255" on this spot. Ms. Newton mentions the significant number of "ghost" stories and legends attached to the palace. Towards the end of her article she returns to the subjects of the 13th Zodiac sign and mazes. She points out that two great works of art hang in the Queen's Drawing Room, one portraying Europa's love match with the bull and the other Ariadne drawing back the veil (or web) to reveal truth. We are reminded that bulls and mazes are important parts of the Western Mystery Tradition and that Ariadne of the Cretan maze is also Arachne or Auriga; Spider Woman. (The reader is referred to Chrys Livings' excellent article in *Pagan News*, April, 1992 for an original study of the Spider Woman theme.)

Shirley Newton refers to one of the radial avenues of Hampton Court Park which aligns with Kingston church as being a "ley". I was keen to discover any properties exhibited by this avenue and on the cold, windy afternoon of Good Friday, 1994, I checked it out with my pendulum. I discovered a straight surface subtle energy band twenty-one of my own paces wide on that day; its width exactly corresponding with the distance between the trees on each side. I felt a strong "buzz" as I wandered around Wolsey's rooms, which have always possessed an odd familiarity for me. In the Tudor apartments I found an interesting piece of graffiti etched into the stone windowsills: a six-petalled flower in circle mandala echoing the designs which I had found carved upon the chests at Glastonbury.

Wolsey fell from power eleven years before the Tor executions. There are definitely some curious links between aspects of Hampton Court lore and the activities of the inner group which flourished in Glastonbury Abbey until

1539. Wolsey's friendship with the dynamic Bere seems to be highly pertinent. Information psychically received in 1996 suggested that John Thorne/Arthur was very much "Bere's man" and that the charismatic abbot may, unlike his successor, have been involved in the covert group's activities, if not their leader. As we shall see, the group possessed connections which reached way beyond the confines of the abbey, beyond Somerset and even beyond British shores. This being the case, Wolsey himself may well have been involved, particularly in view of the group's totemic animal having such a high profile at Hampton; a species actually being named after the Cardinal, who is said, according to folklore, to have believed that it possessed secret wisdom and the powers of healing and divination. Perhaps one day a clearer picture will develop. . .

Chapter 12

A Questing Martyr

Even today, the mere mention of the name Frederick Bligh Bond can provoke an surprising emotional reaction. As Andrew Collins rightly pointed out in the introduction to his book *The Seventh Sword*, Bond was a key pioneer figure as far as psychic questing (as we now call it) is concerned. His tale is that of a frustrated genius and also that of a man most intimately connected with the threads of the quest under discussion in this book.

Frederick Bligh Bond was born on 30th June, 1864; the son of an Anglican clergyman who was also headmaster of Marlborough Royal Free Grammar School. A small, frail boy, he spent much of his childhood "daydreaming"; demonstrating what seems to have been a natural psychic ability; a faculty also possessed by his daughter Mary. Undergoing architectural training in London (Bond did not boast a university education -a fact to be later seized upon by his enemies), he obtained his FRIBA and took up a practice in Bristol, also becoming known as a self-taught authority on pre-Reformation ecclesiastical furniture and architecture. His first book on the subject, *Roodscreens and Roodlofts*, was co-written with Dom Bede Camm (a Benedictine monk) in 1909. A keen member of the Somerset Archeological and Natural History Society, he led guided walks around places of historical interest in his spare time. Although Bond had an orthodox Anglican upbringing his inclination towards the "unseen" manifested at an early age; an inclination later destined to bring both exhilaration and heartbreak.

It was perfectly natural for Bond to wish to combine two passions in his life: archaeology and psychical research. Unfortunately, those who held the power did not see it thus. Possessed of a strong inner conviction that largely forgotten chapel foundations lay beneath the green turf of the Abbey ruins, chapels whose dimensions, when added to those of the existing remains yielded up numbers of esoteric significance, he set about his work. Frederick Bligh Bond did not receive psychically-transmitted information himself. He was a quester who, like myself, worked with a number of psychics, the first being Capt. John Allan Bartlett, a West Country man who had discovered that he possessed automatic writing skills almost by "chance". Although the messages purported to come from individuals once involved with the Abbey, Bond maintained an open mind, also speculating that they MAY have been derived via reading from a kind of collective memory like the "Akashic" records often referred to by occultists. He also referred to a group of souls who remained concerned about the state of Glastonbury and its heritage, sometimes called the Company of Avalon, or The Watchers.

The first sitting with Bartlett took place in 1907; the year in which the Abbey came up for sale and was bought by Ernest Jardine, a Northern industrialist. By 1908 it had passed into the hands of the Church of England. The Abbey site came under the control of the Diocesan Trust, whose chairman was the Archbishop of Canterbury. This body, in turn, appointed trustees to control the excavations due to take place. In May 1908 Bond became Director of Excavations, representing the Somerset Archeological and Natural History Society. His brief was purely that of excavation, restoration being left to William Caroe, the Church Commissioners' Architectural Advisor. In 1909 Bond took the paid position of Diocesan Architect; an appointment at which his tireless critic, the Bishop of Bath and Wells, was far from happy. In those snobbery-ridden times the appointment of a mere self-taught ex-grammar school boy lacking an education at an acceptable university to such a responsible post was generally considered to be rather dubious. By 1912 concern was already being expressed at his careless attitude to the general appearance of the Abbey site whilst work was in progress. Why was he not more concerned with clearing away the unsightly spoil heaps? In 1913 he lost the post of Diocesan Architect to William Caroe. Six years after the start of his work at the Abbey and the receipt of the first psychic message things were becoming very rocky; a situation not helped by Bond's stormy and difficult relationship with his estranged wife.

The storm broke with all its fury with the publication of Bond's book *The Gate of Remembrance* in 1918; a book in which he suddenly announced that some excavations had been guided by psychically-received material.

Unease about Bond's possible spiritual direction had already been growing in the Diocesan ranks as a result of his 1916 lecture on the subject of Gematria; the esoteric system in which secret numerical values are encoded in the Hebrew alphabet. As it happened, Dean Armitage Robinson, a man with more than a little influence upon the course of Bond's destiny, had been present and, like Queen Victoria, had NOT been amused. *The Gate of Remembrance* was just too much for the church to handle; sadly, to the amazement of Bond, who sincerely believed that the ecclesiastical authorities would actually be interested to learn of his sources. By 1921 he was allowed to do very little at the Abbey site, and in 1924 he was made to surrender his key to the ruins and had to pay to come in like an ordinary punter. For a while, he clung to his beloved Glastonbury, unsuccessfully trying to run a boarding house close to the Abbey. He also lived in a small, red-brick house which is still standing at Edgarley, under the shadow of the Tor on the Shepton Mallet road. Here, his daughter Mary executed some amazing murals depicting weird denizens of the astral plane which must have rivalled the work of the great Austin Osman Spare. As Dion Fortune tells us in *Avalon of the Heart*, the dwelling's next occupant quickly "exorcised" the psychically-inspired paintings with whitewash.

Also in 1924, Bond received psychic information regarding Abbey treasures buried in the grounds by the monks in 1539. As Treasurer, John would certainly have been involved. Cross-referencing the given locations with dowsing, Bond asked the authorities for digging permission, which was refused without any reason being supplied. Bond's contact with Sir Arthur Conan Doyle at the College of Psychic Studies in London had led to the latter suggesting an American lecture tour, to which Bond agreed. In 1936 he was filled with despair when he returned to Glastonbury. As he had been accused of falsifying the foundations of the Edgar Chapel apse, the remains of the latter had been removed and the area covered with soil. A broken man, Bond returned to Wales, dying at Dolgellau in 1945.

Received messages purported to come from several historical periods, but most relevant to our study are those dictated by Tudor Benedictine monk Johannes Bryant. Bryant told Bond's psychic that he had "died" in 1533 and so mercifully missed the holocaust of six years later. His meticulously detailed accounts of Abbey life, including a visit by Henry VIII, are therefore of considerable interest. A warm, emotional, life-loving personality comes over; his accounts being conveyed with much humanity. We have a further link with the early Tudor period and with Abbot Whiting himself in events which followed the arrival of Dom Aelred Carlyle in Glastonbury in the Summer of 1910. Benjamin Fearnley Carlyle was Abbot of a community of Anglican Benedictine monks on Caldey Island, off the Welsh coast. He occasionally came to Glastonbury when visiting a small community of Anglican Benedictine nuns at Baltonsborough. In 1910, he decided to drop in on Bligh Bond before returning to Caldey. Carlyle was a controversial figure in church circles, rather a law unto himself, "doing his own thing" on Caldey with no expense spared. His extravagant life style often provoked criticism, as did the manner in which Caldey's financial affairs were conducted. In 1910 he presented a larger than life persona; he and Bond presumably making an intriguing combination.

On December 5th, 1908, during a sitting, Bond had asked Johannes if he had any knowledge of parts of a skeleton which had recently been unearthed behind the reredos wall. The monk replied that they were Whiting's, having been secretly reclaimed by the "faithful" from Bath and Taunton where the Abbot's pitch-boiled remains were displayed after his execution. He stated that, at that time, the monks believed that the Abbey altar would stand for ever and so Whiting's bones were buried beneath it, subsequently discussing the altar's destruction in Queen Elizabeth's time, when the bones were unearthed by folk with no idea of their identity who promptly reburied them in a different place. Although a high churchman, Carlyle had no problem with the bones' psychical identification and to him they constituted the discovery of a major relic. (Whiting had been beatified, along with John and Roger, by Pope Leo in 1895.) Carlyle himself had been psychic since childhood. He took the bones back to Caldey, where they were placed in a reliquary in the chapel's choir. A kind of "Abbot Whiting Cult" briefly flourished in the community, with the last Abbot being honoured at Vespers, Lauds and High Mass. Caldey, as it happened, converted to Roman Catholicism, precipitated by a visit from Dom Bede Camm.

Although the community's Anglican bosses had not demanded episcopal authentication for the Whiting relics its new Roman Catholic ones DID and in 1913 the bones were put away in the sacristy, perhaps now being a bit of an embarrassment. By 1928 the converted Benedictines had all moved to Prinknash Abbey in Gloucestershire, the Cistercian Order taking over Caldey. Carlyle left the island in 1919 to work in Vancouver, coming eventually to Prinknash as an elderly man. In December 1996 I had an interesting and illuminating discussion with Father Damien of Prinknash, who told me that the bones still lack authentication. They left Caldey with the Benedictines and also found a new home in Gloucestershire. They now reside in a reliquary at Prinknash, each bone being individually wrapped. In some ways it seems like a "Catch 22" situation. In view of the circumstances of Abbot Whiting's death, no pectoral cross or other insignia of office would have survived with the corpse as might have been the case with other abbots.

There seems little chance of the Roman Catholic authorities recognising the bones as being Whiting's as a result of psychic questing material produced in 1908 in the near future. The Glastonbury Three, of course, have not yet been canonised. If this should happen in the future, the status of the bones just MIGHT be reviewed. Who knows?

On 25th August 1917 Bond obtained a message from Whiting himself, in the presence of Basil Blackwell (his publisher) and the novelist Dorothy L. Sayers. In this, Whiting explained how, at Bere's death, Wolsey had appointed him despite his age (he was in his 80's when he was executed). He described the ceremony which took place at Oxford in Wolsey's Chancellorium; having had to be carried to the place on a litter due to his infirmity. He lamented this event which set him on course for his horrific end, wishing that things might have been otherwise. Puzzling comments followed in which Whiting described subsequently sleeping at Westminster where he met the king. The new abbot, apparently, was puzzled as to WHY Henry seemed to want him for a friend.

During the same sitting in which the matter of the skeleton was raised, Bond also asked Johannes about the legendary tunnels and passages under and around the Abbey. Among others discussed (including the drain, found by Bond, in which Johannes stated that things were concealed) the monk mentioned "The Kingsway" which he placed near the abbey gatehouse, obviously the passage under the High Street to Abbot Selwood's pilgrim house, now the *George*. Johannes, in the same context, mentions the cellars "where we worked", but tantalisingly does not say what happened in them. In this comment, we have an economically-worded, throwaway comment about the activities of that daring band of covert alchemists and occultists which so concerns us in this study. As we shall see, a slightly more explicit comment was also received by Bond's psychic in the same year (1908) which provided me with considerable cause for excitement when I discovered it in 1995, for here, at last, was a totally independent statement about the band's activities which had "come through" nearly a century previously! Johannes told Bond that he would find the "Kingsway", which indeed he did.

In one of his archeological reports, Bond wrote up details of his investigation of the tunnel leading from the cellars of the *George*; the "Kingsway" of Johannes. He describes a stone, vaulted cellar reached via a spiral staircase on the Eastern side, noticing traces of a second staircase on the cellar's Western side also. Bond remarks upon a drainage channel in the cellar's floor, intended to deal with water seeping in from under the High Street at the Southern end. (Jo Shrimpton heard continually running water during her 1994 psychic exploration of the area.) After removing some bricks from the wall, Bond found a low crawl tunnel furnished with a segmental, pointed roof fitted on each side with the stone elbow rests noticed by Mrs. Bilborough also. He found the way clear for twenty feet, before it was obstructed by a brick sewer running under the High Street. The tunnel led, Bond stated, in the direction of the Abbey gate.

During sittings on June 16th and 17th, 1908, Bond asked his Tudor informant about the mysterious gargoyle on the tower of St. Benedict's church, erected by Abbot Bere upon the site of an ancient chapel, originally dedicated to St. Benignus and axis-wise aligned with the Abbey, being placed squarely on the "ley" which runs along the Abbey axis, up Dod Lane to the shoulder of Chalice Hill and Jimmy Goddard's "forgotten" sacred site (of which more later) where it is intersected by the Mary energy band, and then on across the country to Stonehenge. The gargoyle resembles a grotesque animal or a churchman's head, depending upon the viewing angle and is located high up on the tower's Western side. Information came through from another monk called Johannes who described himself as a Master Mason of the Guild of St. Andrew, explaining that the gargoyle was ORIGINALLY meant to depict an animal. However, upon viewing it from the bottom of his ladder, Johannes noticed an odd resemblance to the face of the then Abbot (Bere) and accentuated this "visual pun" aspect, the resulting three-dimensional caricature implying no insult. Abbot Bere himself also made a comment, which was followed by the receiving psychic (Bartlett) drawing a barrel, which was Bere's rebus, or pictorial signature device. (It may be seen on the stonework in the Abbey ruins.) Bere remarked *"Wee know not the quips of they who worked for us and did sometimes bee rude to them in powers. "* He went on to say that his only concern was the soundness of the church and that the stonemason's joke did not bother him at all.

Although Bond is perhaps rightly most famous (or infamous) for his discovery of the lost Loretto and Edgar chapels, his psychically-received material positively teems with other snippets of appetite-whetting information which cry out to be followed-up. For instance, he was told of a well which was once to be found close to the Abbot's kitchen. *". . . the well is there, but filled. Certain rude men did go down it to find the treasure, but found it not, though they drew off the water nigh 20 cubits. Then cast they in the walls and filled it up because John Parsons the cowherd fell in and was*

St. Benedict's Church

slain, whereat they said "The spirit of our abbot is abroad and hath taken vengeance." This communication received in 1912 from Johannes Bryant perhaps provides us with a good example of the kind of ill-luck which may result from messing with the energy matrix for greed-motivated purposes. Bond also searched for a secret passage associated with the Lady Chapel's crypt. A cavity was found, but the absence of walling, he said, made identification uncertain. He found Johannes' drain, but not the hidden treasure to which the monk had referred. Local tales told of a passage in the fields South of the Abbey. A subsidence was remembered by an elderly workman interviewed by Bond, who also recalled the passage's reopening by the Abbey's previous owner. Excavation revealed a tunnel just beyond the Abbot's house which was explored by one of Bond's students for some sixty feet.

For me, the real gem is a transmission received on June 16th, 1908. Here we have a brief but clear reference to the activities of a group of mysterious folk referred to collectively as "The Priesthood" whose work seems to have been carried out underground when possible. The "feathery grasses" referred to in the following passage are almost certainly the pampas grass which still grows in the garden on the Western side of Abbey House. "*. . . Dig east beyond the beds of feathered grasses. There was a passage to the East door in the wall to the Street. (The Abbey gateway in Chilkwell Street opposite to Dod Lane.) In the midst it remaineth. There was a lodging where now is the great house and we loved passages. They were safe and the Priesthood loveth secret places. There is somewhat in us that loveth mystical things, so we tell not all, but leave it to the love which seeketh and is not wearied. Use your talents. We guide. It is meet. No work, no wage. All works well. This we tell you. . .*"

The passage referred to above seems to have run roughly along the Dod Lane/Stonehenge ley. Psychometrising a photograph, Carole Young saw a monk offering a chalice to me and telling me that I should return to the Abbey gate to learn about my past life. According to local legend, Abbot Whiting's headless ghost may sometimes be seen at twilight, seated upon the stile at the end of nearby Dod Lane. The transmission corroborated Jo's endless visions of an elite group within the Abbey ranks participating in covert occult activities somewhere below ground. "They were safe. . . " Yes, safe until the last days, when Jo saw the authorities using large dogs and fire to flush the fugitives out of their subterranean hiding places. It is actually admitted that some material is being intentionally omitted from the transmission but may eventually be discovered by one with the

A view down the Abbey axis from the East

The Abbot's kitchen

determination, application and sheer love requisite for the task. (Jenni Stather has long suspected that either Bond or his Otherworldly communicators deliberately left out details of secret group meetings from the material which eventually reached the public.) I had, it seemed, good reason to feel excited by the discovery of this unspectacular, economically-worded script. Two days after finding it, during meditation, I was granted a clear, face to face view of a fresh-faced, flame-haired young monk whom I took to be Roger Wilfred, John's assistant who died beside him on the Tor. On the same day, Carole was shown a candle burning in a still, dark environment and told that this could be regarded as the symbol of the "Priesthood". The group's underground venues, she felt, were more than just a safety factor, they were a core component of the philosophy of a magical order which saw the Underworld as being of particular importance.

Bligh Bond's explorations of sacred geometry were ahead of their time and have been taken up and expanded upon more recently by that arch-geomant John Michell. Their relevance to the Glastonbury Chairs will be discussed in a separate chapter. The science of Gematria merited an entire book from Bond later in his career but as early as 1910 one senses its presence in his work. A plan dated 1770 showed the Edgar Chapel at the Eastern extremity of the Abbey, boasting an apse and bringing the interior length to 581 feet. Bond felt that the apse was needed in order to complete the "ideal" proportions found in many churches in the Middle Ages; esoteric reasons accounting for such a length. A 1913 publication referred to the recurrent module of of 37 feet and a grid of 74 feet squares covering the Abbey groundplan and dictating the layout. 74 feet is equal to 888 inches; 888 being the number which equates with the name Jesus in gematric terms. 74 multiplied by 9 yields the number 666; the Solar number and also the number of The Beast in the *Book of Revelations*; a fact sensibly not underlined by Bond. 666 was a course, a number beloved of Aleister Crowley.

Heady stuff; way too "far out" for the stuffy ecclesiastical authorities of Bond's time. These expressed notions, together with the psychically-received material, his lack of a university background and his sometimes obsessive behaviour in relation to questing work which may have led him to neglect more bread and butter aspects of his occupation such as the clearance of spoil heaps provided his Anglican bosses with all the ammunition which they needed in order to bring him down. To call Bond a "pagan" is ludicrous wishful thinking; he remained a stout Christian to the end of his days. An esoteric Christian, certainly, but a Christian all the same. He blazed the trail

The Abbeys Eastern gateway, now leading to Abbey House, situated on the Stonehenge/Dod Lane "ley"

as a pioneer of an activity field now called psychic questing. He also started a number of balls rolling which are now again gathering momentum. I have the distinct feeling that my own work is leading me to build upon his foundations. We come at things from different angles, he a Christian, myself a pagan, but what are labels in Glastonbury anyway? Largely meaningless, in this Gnostic climate. In September 1995, whilst seated upon a bench in the Abbey grounds, looking down the Abbey axis on a sunny early Autumn afternoon, I suddenly felt his presence beside me on the seat. Being in this great man's presence was a considerable honour as far as I was concerned and, there and then, I pledged to continue his work to the best of my ability. I hope that I may be able to do justice to this task. At least, I'll have a try.

Chapter 13

The Chairmaker

Only one recorded visual image of John Thorne/Arthur survives. The existence of this painting was discovered by me whilst reading Cardinal Gasquet's book *The Last Abbot of Glastonbury*. I was quite excited to find a small, faded photograph of the portrait reproduced in the volume and at once wanted to find out more about it. The Benedictine community at Douai Abbey (who possess the original painting) was once located in France but moved to Berkshire (near Reading) earlier this century. An elderly monk who died not long ago remembered John's portrait hanging in a corridor at the French location, where candles were usually to be found alight beside it. Due to the co-operation and helpfulness of one of the Douai fathers, I was able to borrow the negative of the Abbey's own photograph of the picture and thus obtain a poster-sized copy for my workroom wall.

A question mark hangs over the portrait. National Portrait Gallery experts, when I consulted them, put forward the view that it MAY have been fashioned as an icon due to a) the remembered circumstances of its use in France and b) the fact that the Abbey also possesses a similar portrait of another Reformation martyr. The painted 'oval' which surrounds John is a chronological give-away, being a popular early 17th Century portraiture device. The curators expressed the opinion that the painting was executed maybe a Century after John's death. So, upon which likeness, if any, was it based? The National Portrait Gallery staff suggested that it could be a conjectural image using one of the artist's friends as a model. The Gallery's archives contained no other reference to visual representations of John pre-dating the Douai picture. One of the Abbey's monks wondered if the picture could have been based upon a contemporary drawing which had survived the Reformation plunder. Psychically-received images of John indicate that the portrait DOES resemble him. Several independent psychics have commented upon his "hooked" nose; rather noticeable in the picture. On one occasion, whilst doing some work with a friend in the Chalice Well gardens in the early hours of the morning whilst staying at Little St. Michael, I actually

John Arthur. A portrait at Douai Abbey

underwent an odd transformation, during which my features temporarily changed to John's; my companion remarking upon the nose also. I have seen his image, during meditation, perceiving John as a heavily-built man with a florid complexion who bore something of a resemblance to the Douai picture.

Certainly, the painting is a striking one, judging by the photograph, at least. When I showed it to Carole Young she remarked "This man was definitely into more than orthodox Christianity", also commenting that she felt that he had in some way left some sort of information on the Tor. John's drooping moustache and slightly Jewish appearance are far removed from the popular idea of what a Tudor monk might look like, but then John WAS hardly your everyday monk anyway. As Ian Wicks remarked, watching his back could have been a full-time job and he certainly sailed close to the wind much of the time. Making love in the Abbey Barn, for instance, was rather pushing it. John seems to have lived for his magic, forever driven on by his quest; a true psychonaut, to use a wonderful term which I believe to have been invented by Peter Carrol. After the return of his priestess/lover to France it may well have been the one force that really kept him going as the net tightened around him and the time of his inevitable sacrifice drew closer.

In the portrait, John's hands are crossed over his chest and in the right one he holds two palm leaves, symbols of martyrdom. The hangman's rope is seen around his neck. The expression is one of quiet composure but it has a knowing look and a tiny hint of a smile. Between the corners of the frame and the painted oval decorative scrollwork is painted, forming itself, below the centre of his image, into an elemental-like, non-human head. Such devices are found in many 17th Century portraits, but this head still bears an eerie resemblance to elementals psychically seen by Fay and myself in connection with the Glastonbury quest.

For a few months during late 1994 and early 1995 the image of the lone monk spending long nights working away in the damp seclusion of the George's cellar cropped up whenever I had a telephone conversation with Jo. Always that sense of working against the clock as a tyrannical, murderous authority closed in. At one point Jo was so moved that she drew a picture of a monk hunched over a barrel which he was using as a desk in the shadowy cellar with its Gothic arches, feverishly writing. During one of these visions, she got a closer look at WHAT he was writing: sigils and other occult symbols. The monk suddenly put down his pen, rolled up the parchment upon which he wrote and quickly concealed it inside his habit. He told Jo that he wished to pass the pen on to Jack. The subsequent part of the vision showed him being seized and dragged away, followed by the flushing-out of his colleagues in the secret order to which they belonged. Some were tortured. It was not a pretty experience. Around early 1995 I had repeated psychic impressions of empty monks' habits roaming Glastonbury's deserted, lamplit streets after dark. One inevitably remembers James Turnbull's comments about Glastonbury's unhealed spiritual wound. As we shall see, an event which took place in November 1995 seems to have been a very positive step in the right direction in this respect.

Chapter 14

The Chairs

In 1503 Abbot Richard Bere journeyed to Rome. He led an embassy the purpose of which was to congratulate Pius III on his elevation to the Papacy. Its other aim was to arrange Katherine of Aragon's dispensation to marry Henry, Prince of Wales, later Henry VIII, her brother in law. Due to the death of Pius in the October of that year, Bere returned in 1504. He returned impressed by the flourishing Loretto cult which he had seen in action; an experience resulting in the building of the Loretto Chapel whose footings were later discovered by Bligh Bond. He also had a strong desire to furnish the Abbey with some new chairs, inspired by the comparatively luxurious furniture which he had seen in use by higher-ranking monks in Italy which contrasted strongly with the austere forms used by their English counterparts. Brother John's workmanship eventually gave Bere what he wanted. It seems to be generally believed that the overall design of the chairs, in functional terms, was based upon sketches provided by Bere upon his return, although the decorations carved upon them are a very different matter. Made from stout oak, the Glastonbury chairs could be folded for storage when not in use like a modern director's chair, which they vaguely resembled.

A design student known to me remarked upon the unergonomic quality of the arms, which slope upwards in a curious fashion. A possible reason for this feature may have been that it facilitates the act of resting the elbows on the arms whilst holding a book on the part of the user. I arrived at this idea after carrying out some experiments using a Glastonbury chair in Little St. Michael. Chairs exhibiting this OVERALL design are not uncommon, often to be found in churches and other old buildings up and down the country. These are usually either devoid of decoration entirely or else bear carvings of a noticeably post-Reformation nature. The original chairs and their replicas bear the inscription *"Johanes Arthurus Monacus Glastonie Saluee et Deus Da Pacem Domine Sit Laus Deo"*, or John Arthur Monk of Glastonbury May God Save Him Give Him Peace O Lord, Praise be to God.

A "Glastonbury" chair of John Arthur design, showing the characteristic circle and square motif

It is often said that the Bishop's Palace at Wells houses an original actually made by John, along with Abbot Whiting's mysterious "Trinity" chair made from a multiplicity of triangles, while St. John's church houses another. A closer look at the complex world of antique furniture, however, makes such claims look a little doubtful for, as a *Victoria and Albert Museum* curator told me, the business of positively identifying a chair as an "original" and, for that matter, accurately dating it, is almost impossible. (From the occult angle, perhaps originality is less important than the carved symbology, which, like the runes, definitely exhibits a power uniquely its own.) Writing in 1836 Henry Shaw tells us that a version of the Glastonbury chair once existed at Southwick Priory, Hants; an institution which was plundered by the Reformation agents in April 1539. He does not, unfortunately, tell us whether the chair remained at the priory AFTER 1539. In his book *Specimens of Ancient Furniture*, he reports that this chair displayed a carving of a stag in a square panel below two mitres on the back, which would make it unique as far as I know.

The great 18th Century collector and connoisseur Horace Walpole filled Strawberry Hill, his neo-Gothic villa at Twickenham, with interesting objects; one of which was a Glastonbury chair which stood in the Holbein Chamber. This was said to be "an original" and was also said to be Walpole's oldest and most important collection item. His friend Lord Bathurst also possessed copies. Walpole acquired the chair in 1759, from where we do not know; likewise, we have no idea as to what eventually happened to it. A contemporary engraving shows it to have been original at least in respect of the carving, following John's own designs. Walpole is generally considered to be the first collector to draw attention to this type of chair. The strange triangular chairs of the type favoured by Abbot Whiting were not as rare as one might imagine. In 1761 Walpole discovered a whole "cloisterful" in Herefordshire and has left us with a drawing which clearly identifies the style.

The design of these turned chairs is thought to be of European origin. It was not unknown for them to turn up in West Country farmhouses during the 18th Century. A Reformation commissioners list of 1536 records the existence of two such chairs in the Abbot's Dining Chamber at Tyltey, Essex. In his book *The Romantic Interior* (1989) Clive Wainwright suggests that the supposedly "original" Abbot's triangular chair ("Whiting's Chair") is actually an 18th Century copy. The *Victoria and Albert Museum* also possesses a copy of this chair. I previously referred to this piece of furniture as the

89

"Trinity Chair". History, as far as I know, does not record the name, which was psychically received by Jenni Stather in 1994 who, at the time, was quite unaware that the chair is composed of an assemblage of triangles.

The designs on John's original chairs, with their circle and square motif, merit an in depth study. However, before we embark upon this, some mention should be made of a fascinating alternative version to be found in the Upper Room at Little St. Michael and its relative housed in the *Victoria and Albert Museum*. The chair back on the Little St. Michael version is emblazoned with a beautifully carved double arch motif; two arches sharing a single central pillar against which a sitter may rest her/his spine. To do this is reminiscent of a Qabalistic Tree of Life Central Pillar exercise. Inside the arches may be found two vertically positioned parallelograms, each one containing a central cross. This is a variation on the design to be found on the rear surfaces of the backs on John's "Circle and Square" chairs, in which an equal-armed cross is placed inside a square which has been rotated through 45 degrees and rests upon one corner. (This is a device which I have been repeatedly shown during meditation.) Above the arches, two weird, griffin-like winged creatures support a shield positioned at a curiously oblique angle, bearing a cross.

Meditation upon photographs of this chair has yielded interesting results. On one occasion, I was told that the "diamond" shape was one of the secret order's key symbols and that it can be used as an access portal for gaining entry to the astral plane; the voyager simply stepping through it. This is strongly relevant to the Elder Futhark form of the Ingwaz rune as we shall see, for this rune, too, sports a "diamond" shape and, as we are told in Freya Aswynn's excellent *Leaves of Yggdrasil*, it can be visualised as a gateway through which to pass into the Otherworld. In March 1995, Jo Shrimpton psychometrised a photograph of the chair and made the following comments: "This IS John's chair -his impression is still in it. In front of a desk, writing on parchment. He uses a quill pen. Dim lighting like I saw in the cellar. Torch lighting. A mystery surrounds the chair. A name: Peter. " In the same month Carole repeated the exercise with another photograph: "Seat of honour. Holding the Sacred Land for the people. Voices of a spiritual choir. Written knowledge of nature -science -the Land and Sacred building. Geomancy. The Laws. Laws of High Magic. A powerful image. Through religion and beyond to magical knowledge."

The Little St. Michael chair's relative in the *Victoria and Albert* is impossible to date with accuracy, so a curator told me. It is less spectacular than its cousin, the griffins and shield being replaced by simple abstract decoration. The double arches house diamonds, and within the semi-circle of each arch is located half a sunflower in bloom.

Gordon Browning is a long-standing Glastonbury resident who, over the years, has lovingly and skillfully crafted a number of replica chairs exhibiting the original circle and square pattern. He at one time issued a statement, available to buyers, which gave his view of the symbolism which he had reproduced. He does not, as far as I know, claim this statement to be definitive and remains open to the interpretations of others. He describes the geometrical patterns as being thought to be related to "astro-masonry".

Gordon Browning interprets the interlacing circles on the top rail as symbolising brotherhood and pointing heavenwards and he sees the leaf motif on the back and side rails as referring to life. These leaves actually survived on some of the post-Reformation versions. The square on the front panel of the chairback he takes to symbolise Earth (very reasonably) whilst seeing the circle as eternity. The meeting of the circle and the square can be interpreted in a number of ways and is in fact a highly profound concept to which we shall return presently. With regard to the conspicuous back panel of the chairback with its square containing an equal-armed cross and part-circles at the square's corners, Gordon sees the latter as being representative of planets. On 12th January 1994 Jo Shrimpton psychically received information to the effect that the carving "includes a secret, possibly on the back". A square thus positioned echoes the Elder Futhark Ingwaz rune already discussed; an ideal symbol for use an an astral travelling portal and certainly the covert order's chosen insignia. On 18th December 1994 I had a vivid hypnogogic vision of the back of a chair, broken circles suddenly folding back to reveal a staring "all-seeing eye" (an ancient symbol of the Western esoteric tradition).

The squared circle is a very dominant feature of the design and the time has come to look at its implications in a little more detail. The Earth is finite and measurable; the rigid square thus being an ideal symbol. The circle is a different matter; its proportions governed by the irrational quantity pi. Any calculations governed by pi are endless; the mathematician ever going on to the next decimal place until he has to stop somewhere. The circle is thus a good symbol for the heavens or, for that matter, eternity; that which cannot be measured finitely. The squared circle symbolising the temple as a place of union between Earth and Heavens is a universal concept as John Michell demonstrates in his book *City of Revelation.*

Male devotees of the Sikh faith wear a bangle which represents the boundless, endless nature of the divine. The square is hard and angular; the number four relating to the four elements of worldly existence which, when spirit is added, can be redrawn as the pentagram. The merger of square and circle is to some extent a reconciliation of opposites. To the alchemists, the squared circle represented male and female merging to form the ultimate, sought-after androgynous product. The Continental alchemical textbooks of the 17th Century contain a number of engraved illustrations which interpret this notion in pictorial form, some showing the mystic marriage of King Sol and Queen Luna. This has the directest bearing upon our study as John and his French priestess Madeleine used exactly such a format when jointly creating the androgynous product which was stored under Glastonbury High Street for 450 years until its intended release into the terrestrial energy matrix on the 1996 Summer Solstice, but of that much more later.

Keith Critchlow's book *Time Stands Still* describes an ancient Hindu manuscript, the *Manasara Shilpa Shastra*, which provides instructions for precise temple layout aligned to the cardinal points using a simple stake and rope compass. Correct alignment and the knowledge of divine proportion seems to have been of paramount importance across the globe where sacred places were concerned. John Michell refers to the dream of the early Christian Gnostics (not without covert influence at Glastonbury), hermeticists, Knights Templars, Caballists, magicians and Masons; a dream of restoring the temple as a symbol of revealed world order. The squared circle temple, in this context, represents a New Jerusalem, using Solomon's Temple as a point of reference. Over the centuries, prophecies have heralded the future realisation of Glastonbury's spiritual potential. Such a prophet was Austin Ringwode; a contemporary of the Glastonbury Three who survived the Dissolution. On his deathbed he announced: *"The Abbey will one day be repaired and rebuilt for the like worship which has ceased; and then peace and plenty will for a long time abound. "*

Building on research and speculative foundations provided by Bligh Bond, John Michell's *City of Revelation* portrays Glastonbury as a temple of the Holy City; a reflection of the temple described in the Revelation of St. John. To Michell, numerical values are more important than comparative size and

92

he juggles with several ancient measurement systems in order to correlate St. John's New Jerusalem with Glastonbury's Abbey groundplan. A student of gematria, Bond had similar views regarding sacred numbers. At the heart of Michell's New Jerusalem lies the squared circle, uniting matter and spirit. The square is simple, its perimeter four times the length of its side. Precise determination of the circle's perimeter is impossible as irrational pi is involved (circumference being equal to the diameter multiplied by pi) so, in simplest terms, we are here merging the finite (square) with the infinite (circle).

Anyone seriously interested in the mathematics of the squared circle/ New Jerusalem diagram is urged to read *City of Revelation* and other earlier works by John Michell. To do so is to see the *Book of Revelation* in a new light. We have space here for little more than a superficial glance. Verses 15-17 of St. John provide a suitable appetite whetter: *"And he that talked with me had a golden reed to measure the city, and the gates thereof and the wall thereof. And the city lies foursquare, and the length is as large as the breadth: and he measured the city with the reed, twelve thousand furlongs. The length and the breadth and the height of it are equal. And he measured the wall thereof, one hundred and forty and four cubits, according to the measure of a man, that is, of the angel. "*

In comparing ancient measurement systems Michell stresses the importance of the number 6; a unique number which is both the sum and product of its factors. In other words 1+2+3=6, and 1x2x3=6. He demonstrates a groundplan in which the side of a square measures 7920 feet with a perimeter of 6 miles, the square enclosed in a circle of circumference 6. 660 miles with an area of 33, 300, 000 square cubits. As on the chairs, the square encloses a circle, this one having an area of 6, 660, 000 square megalithic yards (my). (The megalithic yard is a prehistoric unit of measurement found via the surveying of stone circles. etc, and discovered by Prof. Alexander Thom.) Michell uses four systems of measurement. Michell's Masonic architect could combine a range of sacred numbers in one scheme by following canonical geometrical principles. Numbers prominent in his New Jerusalem scheme are 864, 666, 144, 7920 and 1728; all multiples of both 6 and 9; the latter being a number of judgment, finality and prophecy fulfilment; the trinity of trinities.

Michell attaches significance to St. Philip's sending of 12 missionaries from Gaul (including Joseph of Arimathea) to Britain. King Aviragus granted each of the 12 a hide of land. At the present Abbey site a timber and wattle structure was erected, surrounded by a circle of 12 huts. Until dissolved the Abbey ruled the 12 hides with an absolutist authority; its rights respected by both Normans and Saxons. A hide was defined as the amount of land which could be cultivated by one man and support a family; an area accepted in Glastonbury as 120 acres. 12 hides would equal 1440 acres, the area of St. John's New Jerusalem plan, as demonstrated by Michell.

A square with an area of 1440 acres boasts a side of 7920 feet or 12 furlongs. Twelve hides thus becomes a model of St. John's Holy City; a square of 12, 000 furlongs. (Numerology rather than units is the important factor here.) A circle inserted in the square would be 14,400 cubits round.

At the end of all this, we are left with some highly tantalising possibilities. Were John Thorne's squared circles on the chairs motifs relating to alchemical activity and the fusion of polar male and female to create the ultimate androgynous product? Were they visual representations of the potential New Jerusalem which is Glastonbury, masquerading as pretty decorations? There are many questions to be pondered here; much food for thought.

Chapter 15

The Magus from Mortlake

Perhaps it seems almost inevitable that John Dee, that unique Elizabethan cartographer, astrologer, secret agent, mathematician, alchemist, occultist and man of many parts should enter our tale sooner or later. Recorded references to his presence in my native Greenwich are many; those to his presence at Glastonbury sparse. Katherine Maltwood (re)discovered the existence of the vast terrestrial landscape zodiac at Glastonbury in the inter-war years and her researches have been more recently built upon and extended by Mary Caine.

More recently still, (1985, 1990) intrepid psychic questers including Paul Weston and Andrew Collins have tackled the zodiac using a very physical shamanic vision quest approach, with amazing results. As we shall see, the great zodiac is also of very particular relevance to our study also. Did John Dee know of its existence? Did he actually provide us with a brief but telling description of a vast planisphere moulded by the Avalonian soil? Richard Deacon's biography mentions a map housed in the Warburg Institute in London (not available for scrutiny by the general public) which bears marginal notes regarding the zodiac scribbled by Dee. The notes refer to constellations projected down onto the Earth.

In the last article written before he died as a result of a heart attack suffered whilst climbing the Tor (what a way to go!) the late Anthony Roberts, in the first issue of *The Glastonbury Zodiac Companion* (an occasional newsletter) states that on one visit to Glastonbury, Dee stayed at Sharpham Manor; the one-time Abbot's private residence where Whiting was arrested, where he found books which had been rescued from the Abbey library before its destruction. Unfortunately, the source of this information is not given. In Robert Coon's 1993 booklet *The Glastonbury Zodiac*, the author tells us that Dee did spend much time at Sharpham (about a mile from Glastonbury) because it was the residence of Elizabeth's Chancellor of the Knights of the Order of the Garter, Sir Edward Dyer. This gentleman was the godfather of Dee's son Arthur. Coon suggests that Dee searched for the legendary cruits of Joseph of Arimathea once rehidden by St. Dunstan, but considers the question of his knowledge of the Zodiac to be a matter for debate. As my friend Ian Freer has observed, Dee's doings in Glastonbury are shrouded in mystery. What he MAY have done is preserved in a kind of whispered hearsay passed-on down the ages. Writing in the seventeenth century, Elias Ashmole stated that Dee and his sidekick Edward Kelly found the Philosophers' Stone in the Abbey ruins, wasting much of it before fully comprehending its true worth and best usage. Other writers hint that Dee and Kelly found Joseph's cruets containing Christ's sweat and blood -the red and white of the alchemists. Still other writers state that Kelly found the red and white substances in a tomb in Wales. The term "The diggings in England" is often used historically to describe Dee's shadowy unearthing of these fabled commodities.

From time to time, the man from Mortlake has, in a modest way in keeping with his personality, made his presence felt in my researches. All this began in 1992, with a brief glimpse received by Jo. No name was given but the description provided at once brought Dee to mind, although at THAT time there was no obvious reason for his making contact. On 24th October 1994 something happened during a telephone chat with Tony Lee, another psychic. He was told: "*A book open in a book-filled room in Jack's house should be found.* . . ." this coming after Tony had felt a sudden and unaccountable need to speak the name of the magus. After a quick look round I did indeed find the open book: James Carley's fine volume on Glastonbury Abbey. Sure enough, it was open at a reference to Dee; the latter coming under focus in relation to the whispered tradition of secret alchemical activities at Glastonbury. Carley links this alchemy with Melkin the Bard's 14th Century prophecy, believed to have actually been spoken in the 5th Century but committed to paper much later. Melkin announces that when Joseph of Arimathea's body is found the Glastonbury folk will not be lacking in water or heavenly dew (ros caeli). As Carley tells us, these people lived under constant threat of flooding even after the construction of moor drains, and they certainly had enough water! Alchemically, however, ros caeli has a different significance. Such an interpretation of dew was not lost on Dee, who focussed upon it in his mid-16th Century work *Monas Hieroglyphica*.

On 27th October 1994 Tony Lee was once more aware of John Dee in a Glastonbury context. He was shown a vision of a monk talking to a boy aged about 11 and giving him a piece of highly confidential information. The monk was then arrested and hung. Dee was then seen returning to Avalon as an adult and communicating with John Thorne's ghost in the Abbey ruins. At first sight the notion of Dee and John meeting may seem ludicrous given that Dee would only have been 11 years of age at the time of John's death. Dee, however, was a prodigy; certainly no ordinary boy. (He went to university at 16 and thought nothing of working an 18-hour day, such was his application.) While it seems unlikely that Dee journeyed from London to Glastonbury alone at such a tender age, he could well have been taken by his parents.

Interestingly, a Druid friend of mine recalls once reading, in an unfortunately now lost (through theft) biography of Dee, information to the effect that Dee WAS taken to Glastonbury as a child. This precocious boy, intellectually and academically far ahead of his chronological age, would have been an ideal "carrier" of secret information. Who, after all, would have suspected a boy of 11? He would hardly have constituted a threat to the Reformation agents.

On January 19th, 1996, I found myself in the *British Museum*. Ian Freer had recently been talking to me about the Dee relics on view in that institution and I was keen to find them. I had only said a few words when the enquiry desk assistant said *"Oh, you mean that crystal ball."* She then told me the location: Room 46, also telling me that the Dee relics are much sought by visitors; particularly, I assume, odd folk like myself! As I approached the tall showcase I felt a strong "left-hand tingle". The actual crystal ball said little to me; my attention was at once grabbed by the black obsidian scrying mirror. THIS exhibit positively seethed with psychic energy. Standing before the glass-fronted case I did my best to look unobtrusive as I endeavoured to contact the Tudor magus. I was immediately answered by a flash of light on the obsidian mirror. Communication had been established!

A meaningful dialogue followed. Dee was now no longer a precocious 11 year-old but a one-time magus with a considerable reputation; like many, perhaps, more highly thought-of now than when he was on the physical plane, which he left nearly 389 years ago. As we "talked" I explained that "the work" in Glastonbury was being continued and that I was continuing where I had, through unavoidable circumstances, left off. Waves of energy surged about inside the showcase and an amethyst-coloured sphere began to build above the scrying mirror. It occurred to me that although the relic was attributed to Dee, the mirror and ball would, in reality, have been used by Edward Kelly; Dee's psychic. The Magus complained to me that Kelly received no mention on the showcase labels, which he felt to be rather an oversight on the part of the museum. Dee struck me as a likable man; friendly and polite. When I finally said "farewell" he answered me with another flash of light above the mirror. It had been a good meeting.

Chapter 16

Out and About in the Ritual Landscape

On 27th March 1995, I returned to Glastonbury after a year's absence. After several days' uncharacteristically warm weather, snow was falling as my suburban train pulled out of London Bridge. It was to briefly fall again the following day as I climbed the Tor, but generally the weather during my stay was ideally suited to open air questing activities; cool but bright with crystal-clear visibility. By 2p.m. I was drinking tea in the kitchen of Little St. Michael; glad to be back at Chalice Well. I soon got to know my fellow-residents; pleased to find that I was not staying at the retreat house alone this time. Questing can get very intense without company, particularly in the quiet of Little St. Michael and I welcomed the balancing effect of being able to "knock off" for a chat or a shared cup of tea at the kitchen table. Unpacked, I made for the town. Following the usual wander round, I visited my favoured vegetarian restaurant for a delicious lasagne.

Having consumed the meal, I made for St. Benedict's Church, eager to find the mysterious gargoyle, or corbel, to use the precise term, of which Bond had written. It was far higher than I imagined it to be, on the tower's West wall above the main entrance. "Rather him than me" I thought, picturing Johannes' long ladder (referred to in Bond's script) shaking ominously in the chilly October wind. I realised, to my annoyance, that I had left my binoculars back at base but, of course, the stonemason had not fashioned it with optical aids in mind, and I should be able to see it as well as anyone else, despite the height. Walking towards and then away from the church repeatedly I was able to see precisely the effect described in Bond's received script. Walking away from the town on that chilly but bright March evening I soon reached Dod Lane.

Heading up the little turning I came to the point where the road ended; the Lane continued by a footpath leading up to the shoulder of Chalice Hill

The Dod Lane stile; a psychically active site said, according to local lore, to be haunted by Abbot Whiting's headless ghost

beyond a stile. I saw much psychic activity ahead of me on the footpath. I had previously heard tales of people suffering terrifying experiences on the Dod Lane -Stonehenge alignment in Glastonbury although I subsequently slept upon it peacefully on several occasions; one of them being in a house where the "ley" actually ran through my bed head! In local legend the stile is haunted by Abbot Whiting's headless ghost. Among moving pinpoints of light (my usual way of seeing psychic activity) I discerned a dark, ill-defined shape flitting across the footpath. No, the place was NOT letting me down! T. Scott-Holmes' 1908 book *Wells and Glastonbury* contains an evocative passage regarding the stile: "*. . . Dods Lane, so called because it was noted for its wet dirty condition. It leads us on to Bushey Combe and Chalice Hill, and here at times in the twilight might be seen sitting on the stile an old headless man said to be the ghost of poor Abbot Whyting. This vision, however, is not guaranteed to every visitor, since there are certain qualifications necessary for this power of sight, and these are by by no means universal.* "

John Michell translates Dods Lane as "Dead Man's Lane", seeing it, like Ross Nichols, as the processional route to the Tor; a view supported by the many sandalled feet psychometrically seen passing up and down the path by Carole and Jo. In *The New View over Atlantis* (1983) Michell referred to the German word *Tod* (meaning death), stating that Alfred Watkins often found this name and linking the notion of "spirit paths" which correspond to Chinese lung-mei, or dragon current paths relating to royal burials. "Arthur's Tomb" lies, as Michell points out, on the Stonehenge/Dod Lane ley, which corresponds with the Abbey's axis.

After climbing some way up the muddy footpath I paused and looked back at the town and the Abbey spread out below me. The view reinforced the fact that Abbot Bere had built St. Benedict's Church on a spot where it aligned perfectly with the Abbey axis and the Dod Lane/Stonehenge ley. It suddenly struck me that this was the route taken by the Glastonbury Three on the occasion of their last, painful journey up to the Tor. (Jo Shrimpton was later to sense an association with hanging when psychometrising a site photograph.) Standing there, one remembers Ross Nichols' comment about the Dod Lane footpath being a "causewayed spirit path".

The evening continued with a walk which, inevitably, took me up to the Tor and then back the long way via Edgarley. Back at Little St. Michael, I made some tea and then relaxed in the lounge, chatting to a young Dutch couple

Bushey Combe and the Dod Lane pathway on a Summer morning

who were staying with me at the retreat house and who seemed to have become captivated by the spirit of Glastonbury. The following morning dawned overcast and a little chilly. Over breakfast, it transpired that no-one had slept well; nothing to do with "bad vibes" -just an inability to sleep. We later found that this was hardly surprising. A dowsing check on the serpentine Michael band revealed that it came very close to the house as it swept across the "private" part of the garden only accessible to Little St. Michael's residents, bound for its crossing of the Mary band at Arthur's Court. Yes, the Michael male energy was certainly throbbing away, causing it to measure a width of 17 of my paces! With the geomantic "sap" rising in this fashion it was, perhaps, inevitable that sleep would be difficult as we were surely riding on the band's radiations even if not exactly on it in the house. A female friend to whom I later related this experience remarked "Now you know what it's like for us when a randy male keeps US awake all night!"

Another pleasant day was spent walking old sites and trackways, with a stop-off at the *George*, where the atmosphere was as strong as ever.

By 9.15 p.m. night was well established. The days still seemed quite short and the evenings were chilly. I was alone in the peace and calm of WTP's Upper Room at Little St. Michael; the spiritual space gently illuminated by the low-powered lighting panels in the ceiling and a single flickering candle. The bubbly amber windows afford a hazy view of the Somerset Levels by day, but now one could see only streetlights burning out in Chilkwell Street. I had tried a simple open meditation while seated in one of the room's Glastonbury chairs the previous day and had been rewarded with glimpses of the Abbey in its glorious heyday. It was now, I felt, time for something a bit more prolonged.

Seated in the chair decorated with John's squared circle motif, I centred myself via some rhythmic breathing. The Upper Room's atmosphere was perfect for meditation, the only sound being that made by the occasional passing car in the street outside. After a while, I saw, behind closed lids, the diamond shape located within the double arches of the room's other chair. I was then suddenly aware of a dignified-sounding, male voice saying "I am Abbot Richard Whiting and I would speak with you." I was surprised, as I had been half-hoping for John-related material. The Abbot sounded calm and purposeful. A dialogue followed during which I addressed him respectfully as "reverend father". He expressed a preference for being buried in

Glastonbury, and I had the impression that the bones once found by Bligh Bond, now at Prinknash, were indeed Whiting's and that he had not been fully in favour of Dom Aelred Carlyle's removal of them to Caldey in the century's early years. Regarding the Glastonbury Three, Abbot Whiting said "We were left. . . "; somehow indicating an unfinished business scenario. When I asked him what I could do to help the situation, he replied "The Abbey. . . " At this point I lost him as a new vision took over and I briefly became John Thorne, sitting in the chair which he designed and looking out through his eyes as I witnessed some events of his time, including secret writing sessions in the George's cellar. I then returned to normal consciousness, grounded myself and opened my eyes. Going downstairs, I found the kitchen deserted and made some tea, always a good move (a hot drink) if one wishes to reinforce one's groundedness after a session. As I drank tea and munched biscuits, I mentally chewed-over Abbot Whiting's words.

I had to do something, it seemed. The Abbot MUST have "come through" for a good reason, otherwise why should he bother? However, another matter kept creeping into my head -that of the Upper Room's other chair, with its mysterious shield guarded by two equally strange creatures and featuring the double arch motif also to be found on the seal of St. Dunstan; an influential Abbot from Saxon days who also had a shadowy, half-remembered reputation as an alchemist. Although the creatures were not strictly griffins they nevertheless brought these mythical beasts to mind, as they seem to be very much at home on Glastonbury (particularly on the inner planes), having an intimate association with St. Dunstan. It has been my impression that magician-created site guardians were fashioned with the outer form of griffins by Glastonbury occultists long ago; John Thorne being one of them. For a good, concise, modern overview of the creation and function of such artificially-created thought-forms, elementals or servitors (whatever one wishes to call them) interested readers are referred to Phil Hine's excellent book *Condensed Chaos* and Dave Lee's illuminating article *The Cyber Zoo* in issue 17 of the magazine *Chaos International*. Carole Young became aware of a griffin flying round the tower of St. Benedict's Church when she psychometrised a photograph which I had taken during my March 1995 visit. A young man who wishes to remain anonymous once told me how he "startled" a griffin outside St. Patrick's Chapel in the Abbey grounds. Its long tail certainly sounded very similar to those sported by the creatures on the "other" chair in the Upper Room; its gaping mouth and razor-sharp teeth reinforcing speculations regarding its guardian function.

The next morning found me revelling in the airy vitality of Wearyall Hill. It was hard to say why but the "vibes" felt wonderful up here. John of Glastonbury placed it as the site of the convent of St. Peter. Professor Rahtz tells us that vineyards were once to be found on the Hill's Southern slopes. Local lore, of course, also identifies it as the site where Joseph of Arimathea once plunged his flowering staff into the Avalonian earth (a very male piece of symbolism) and the good old Michael line runs along the spine of the hill, being deflected away towards the town as it reaches the Holy Thorn; a distant descendant (via cuttings) of the original which was cut down by the puritans.

During a meditation on the hill's sunwashed summit on that glorious Spring day, I was shown Gebo runes (the rune of energy exchange), pentagrams and, interestingly, a Thelemic Unicursal Hexagram (Crowley's "Hexagram of the Beast"); the latter presented in dazzling clarity. I later learned that the Hexagram vision was intended to focus my attention upon Tiphareth; the heart/Solar station of the Qabalistic Tree of Life. Follow-up research led me to ponder upon the profound alchemical implications of Tiphareth and as intermediary between higher and lower energy states as revealed in the works of Dion Fortune and also the status of Glastonbury as a planetary heart chakra. This might sound a wee bit twee and 'New Agey', but it is vital to stress that the Thelemic author Kenneth Grant (not noted for his "fluffy bunny" attitudes) expresses a view of Glaston occupying such a role in the section of his book *The Magical Revival* which deals with power centres, as Paul Weston has pointed out. The Michael band's throbbing energy on the hill was later felt by Jo when she psychometrised a photograph taken that morning. She was aware of a link with underground passages and secret meetings at the *George*. Oddly enough, after being deflected under the Holy Thorn, the band goes straight to the town, running across the cobbles at the rear of the Pilgrim House. According to my own dowsing work, it is sometimes so wide that it passes through the George's restaurant.

After Wearyall Hill I went to the Abbey. The wind seemed to be blowing more keenly as I entered the grounds and I suddenly felt myself becoming attuned to the frequency of unease left by the events of 1539. As I wandered round, an inner voice told me: "There's no sense in you reliving the bad events from the past. It's NOW that matters". Short and to the point, this message clarified something for me. I had previously considered undergoing a past-life regression session which some mates from The Association for the Scientific Study of Anomalous Phenomena had offered to conduct. "You will learn what you need to know about the past as it becomes necessary", the

The Holy Thorn on Wearyall Hill

voice went on. Fair enough. This is not to criticise regression sessions, but such an approach was obviously not at all appropriate in my case; particularly in view of the immense volume of material which would gradually trickle through. As for reliving the horrors of torture and execution, this would have been a pointless act of self-indulgence; quite negative when contrasted with the essentially positive activity of going forward through the mid-'90's, carrying on where I had left off four centuries ago. This whole thing was NOT about living in the past anyway, it was about progression and continuity.

St. Patrick's Chapel presented a rather different "feel" to that experienced by Jenni and myself a year previously. There was no overpowering smell. Finding myself alone, I felt very welcome in this little sacred space. Remembering Abbot Whiting's words the night before, I impulsively conducted a simple solo ceremony. Concentrating upon The Three, I wished them honour, blessings, peace and the fruition of their work. When I had finished, the chapel's atmosphere felt warm, friendly and positive; sparks of psychic energy around the altar demonstrating a response to my endeavours. If a solo effort could produce such a response, what might be achieved by a corporate event held in the Abbey? Such a ceremony, apart from its central purpose of healing the etheric wound left by the 1539 hangings could also have some other beneficial "spin-off" if it were of an ecumenical nature, for participation could be quite a unifying experience. By ecumenical, I meant not simply a mixture of Christian denominations but also the participation of folk of various pagan paths. Too much to hope for? Maybe, but at that time a number of multi-faith events WERE taking place and have done so since.

When I returned to London I contacted various folk with a proposition structured along the lines described above. Various well-known figures on the pagan scene were approached; Wiccans, Druids, etc, and all responded enthusiastically, keen to participate. But could we get such an event off the ground in the Abbey? During the weeks that followed I wrote a series of letters to people who would need to be approached in this respect, including the retired clergyman whom I had met a year previously. I was told that the Abbey normally only hosts events of a specifically Christian nature. A letter applying for the Abbey as a venue and outlining my proposal was finally left with the relevant authorities in Glastonbury. As the months went by I heard nothing. I was becoming increasingly involved in other questing aspects and assumed that the idea had turned out to be a "no go". It was not until December 1996 that I learned, by chance, that a ceremony honouring The

The Author standing at the dowsed site of the 1539 executions

Three HAD taken place in 1995; on the Tor, on the 15th December; the day of the executions! Although initially a little "put out" that I had not been informed, I realised, talking things over with Paul Weston, that the important thing was that the event TOOK PLACE. Paul had been present on the day and assured me that it had been a very positive, "happening event". The ceremony had been organised under a basically Christian "umbrella". My continued involvement might have meant that the ecumenical side never really got off the ground due to involved folk finding it impossible to agree on what they would do or who would or could not be included. Pope Leo's 19th Century beatification of The Three along with many other Reformation martyrs did seem just a trifle tokenistic, whereas this ceremony, held at the site of the executions, seemed to have made a real attempt at healing the past and honouring the memories of three brave men.

I rounded off the day dowsing the nodal (intersection) point of the Michael and Mary bands at Arthur's Court, finding a huge square of mixed male/female energy at the cascade. This accomplished, I climbed the base of Chalice Hill, passing several badger setts and observing the tail-end of a glorious Avalonian sunset. It was a good end to a very positive three days. My stay at Little St. Michael had been fairly unspectacular but valuable. The Abbot Whiting communication eventually seemed to lead, in a roundabout way, to the ceremony on the Tor eight months later which, hopefully, contributed something towards laying some ghosts to rest (speaking loosely), recognising the memory of three brave men and attempting to heal wounds left by the past. The Abbot implied a wish for his bones to lie in his beloved Glastonbury. At present, bones identified as his by Bond's psychic but unauthenticated as official relics by the Catholic Church are respectfully kept at Prinknash Abbey in a reliquary. Perhaps if, or more positively, when the remains of this skeleton are buried in the Avalonian earth from which they were taken in 1907 this aspect of the affair may be considered to have reached a satisfactory conclusion; to be "sorted", as they say.

Chapter 17

The Alchemists of Avalon

Following my March 1995 trip to Glastonbury, I continued intensive research in the *British Library*, which I had found to be an absolute storehouse of precious information. Around this time, I discovered that the executions of the Three were not the only ones to have taken place on that fateful day in 1539, according to correspondence between Vicar General Thomas Cromwell and the Commissioners stationed in Avalon. Lord Russel's letter to Cromwell, dated 16th November, 1539 (the day after the hangings) detailed the fate of The Three, then went on: "... *Rape and burglary committed, these parties are all condemned, all four of them put to execution at the place of the act, which is called the Were (Wearyall?) and these adjudged to hang in chains to the example of others. As for Capon, one of the said offenders, I have reprieved according to your Lordship's letters. . .* " Cromwell's previous letters to Russel, to which the letters refers in this report, have not, unfortunately, survived. It is more than a little interesting that four other folk were executed on the same day and one wonders what was really behind it all, just as one also wonders why Cromwell decided to spare Capon from the fate of his fellows.

Another interesting piece of documentation discovered was a description of the tunnel connecting the *George*'s cellar with the Abbey found in Collinson's 1791 history of Somerset, written before the construction of the sewer below the High Street found by Bligh Bond. Collinson writes: "*Underneath this house is a vault which comes out quite under the town, and leads to the Abbey, so low that a man must crawl on his knees to pass it, but there are benches at little or narrow places to rest the elbows on, in order to ease the knees. It comes out into a large vaulted place, used for a cellar, and after about 5 or 6 paces turns aside to the right into another passage large enough for a man to walk upright, this passage is about 5 or 6 paces long, and leads to a flight of steps which conducted privately to the Abbot's chamber, wherein was a large, handsome bedstead, on which King Henry VIII once lay.* "

To the serious historian, the above account contains some curious inconsistencies. The building which served as the Abbot's private residence at the Abbey had been demolished over fifty years before the publication of Collinson's book. Charles Eyston wrote an account of its state on the occasion of his 1712 visit, not long before its demolition. He describes "stately" rooms wainscotted with oak. I was once psychically afforded a glimpse of the rooms as they were in John's time, and was impressed by the dark oak panelling which was decorated by what appeared to be gold leaf lining. Eyston locates the Abbot's bedchamber at the building's Southeastern end, He describes the remains of a bedstead locally believed to have been used by Abbot Whiting, also the poor condition of the room, with its broken windows and holes in the roof through which rainwater had dripped. Collinson, then, could not have seen the building for himself in 1791, and his account obviously refers to the same bedstead and building as that described by Eyston. It seems likely, therefore, that his account of the tunnel must be based on a historical one provided by one who had explored the passage some years previously.

Reading the works of Elias Ashmole, I came across the curious reference to Edward Kelly's discovery of the Elixir, or Philosophers' Stone, in the Abbey ruins. Pondering upon this, and reading Frances Yates' book *The Rosicrucian Enlightenment*, it suddenly dawned upon me that John and his brothers in the "underground" (in more than one sense) order were, among other things, alchemists. This notion was at once psychically confirmed for me. As we have seen, James Carley's book briefly mentions a shadowy but continued link with alchemical tradition at the Abbey. There is a medieval tradition which associates St. Dunstan (patron saint of goldsmiths) with alchemical texts, particularly *De Lapide Philosophorum*, a manuscript preserved at Corpus Christi College, Oxford. The 17th Century esotericist Ashmole also mentioned a manuscript in his own collection, now held by the *Bodleian Library*, which is a Latin translation from an English original found in the Abbey treasury (John's domain!) in 1539! (*The British Library* had a later English translation which was apparently stolen in 1957.) Dunstan's authorship of texts attributed to him after his death has been questioned by several writers, among them A. E. Waite. Dee's diary refers to "*The Book of St. Dunstan*" when referring to "*powder found at the diggings in England*". Ashmole's *Theatricum Chemicum Britannicum* contained two metrical treatises also attributed to the saint. They are packed with practical, "bread and butter" alchemical information.

The *Bodleian Library* informed me that the Latin copy of the manuscript which Ashmole claimed to have been found in the Abbey's treasury in 1539 likewise contains a series of recipes. Ashmole reports that the original was written on parchment (Jo repeatedly saw John writing on this material) and for some reason escaped destruction; the fate of the greater part of the Abbey library. The Latin translation is bound in a volume with other texts from Ashmole's collection. The *Bodleian Museum's* 1845 catalogue of the Ashmole manuscripts contains the following entry: "*Tractatus Alchemiae ex antiquo libro. Manuscripto, Anglice ab Authore Scripto, et postea in Latinumm verso 125 -137. This book I hear was found in the treasury of Glastonbury Abbey at the time of the suppression of the Abbey, the original copy whereof, I hear, remaineth yet written in parchment in a friend's hand whom I know.* "

Ashmole dwells upon the wanton destruction of priceless volumes during the Dissolution and laments a fanaticism which could lead to a book's being torn apart because it contained "*a red letter or a mathematical diagram*". The Theatricum edition which I consulted contained another work attributed to Dunstan: *De Occulta Philosophia*; a real alchemist's working manual. The Benedictine link was also echoed by three alchemical tracts by one Pearce, the Black Monk. Among the tracts which make up *Theatricum Chemicum Britannicum* is an "emblematic scroll" attributed to George Ripley, Canon of Bridlington; a mysterious and highly-influential alchemist who was active during the Wars of the Roses in the second half of the 15th Century. Here is the classic example of an alchemist concealing arcane formulae within a verse structure, to be found by those with eyes to see. As C. G. Jung had apparently been, I too was fascinated by this man's work, which at once struck me as highly significant and VERY relevant to my quest.

Ripley, at his own admission, wrote to confuse the many and enlighten the few, intending to puzzle and confound the "owls and bats" as he called them. To read a Ripley text for the first time is like being dropped into a labyrinthine hall of mirrors; it seems quite "mad"; it is meant to. Getting anywhere at all with it is, in itself, like a sort of initiation; completing (or at last going some way round) an intellectual assault course. As soon as she became aware of this man's work, Carole was psychically told that he was a KEY. The key turned and the yellowing pages of obscure alchemical tracts suddenly erupted into crackling, firey life, as we shall see. I saw old George - a figure of endless mystery -an archetypal magician figure with echoes of Merlin, Odin and Aleister Crowley, returning after his death as the puppeteer; the choreographer of the dance performed by John and his priestess Madeleine. I saw him watching as they lived out the ritual drama concealed within his wheel mandala. I saw him calling the tune as, behind a locked door upstairs at the *George*, they enacted their alchemical wedding, reaching orgasmic ecstasy within a circle of flickering candles. I saw him watching as Madeleine became Queen Luna and John became King Sol, fusing their energies to create the ultimate androgynous product. I saw him watch as John took on the mantle of the sacrificed Solar God, living that role to the end. I saw the wheel turn; the heavens conspire and a vice tightening about the Sun King. I saw John identifying with the Sagittarius figure in the great Zodiac of Glastonbury, a stricken Sun King rising in the saddle and falling over his horse's head, outstretched arms echoing the form of the crucified Christ. I saw the year turn, leaves falling and skies darkening as the Sun God sank below the horizon, paying, in Mary Caine's words, the price for "quickening inert matter". I saw the King die, hanging upon a wooden scaffold and being dismembered, sharing the fate of many Solar Gods. . . Odin, Christ, Osiris. . . . The King is dead -long live the King!

Chapter 18

The Canon of Bridlington

George Ripley died as he had lived, with style. He was laid to rest in an ornate tomb decorated with alchemical symbols which were to be hacked off three centuries later by an outraged new vicar who was horrified at finding such pagan symbolism in Bridlington Church. If there was ever a man who knew how to work the system, as we would say today, it was old George, actually going so far as to obtain a papal dispensation which freed him from all monastic observations and meant, in effect, that he could take full advantage of the free board and lodging offered by living in a monastery whilst following alchemical pursuits twenty-four hours a day if he so desired. It is believed that he died during or close to 1490; probably around the time of John Thorne's birth, given that the latter was described as middle-aged when he was executed in 1539. At different times he was Canon of Bridlington, curate of Fox Bulbergh, a monk and an Anchorite hermit at Boston. He found time, along the way, to collect a knighthood.

Sir George was actually born at Ripley in Yorkshire. In the 1470's he was (in name, at least) canon of an Augustinian priory at Bridlington. During his long career he studied esoteric science on Rhodes with the Knights of St. John. He is said to have written twenty-five books during his last years at Boston. His great book *The Compound of Alchemy*, first released in 1471, was dedicated to Edward IV, indicating either Yorkist sympathies or a shrewd ability to curry favour with those currently in power. Showing characteristic nerve, Ripley saw fit to address lengthy words of caution to the hell-raising monarch in the course of the book's dedication, advising Edward to limit his alcoholic intake if he wished to live for a few more years! Ripley's *Medulla Alchimiae* (Marrow of Alchemy) was dedicated to George Neville, Archbishop of York. Not always popular with other monks with whom he lived, complaints were occasionally made about the odd and offensive chemical aromas issuing from his quarters.

Ripley's metrical treatises have an oddly disturbing quality even if one knows that the imagery is symbolical and metaphorical, relating to alchemical process. Like Crowley, he seems to have enjoyed confusing "the owls and bats". Although he could write in a bread and butter instruction manual style he more often wrote in a verse format which heavily disguised the marrow of his subject matter. Psychologists could really go to town on Ripley's imagery, as C. G. Jung certainly did. The weird *Cantilena* has been claimed by some (naively, I believe) to be a projection of old George's incest fantasies; a piece in which a king returns to the womb and is reborn as the "Son of the Philosophers". Jung felt *Cantilena* to merit analysis, discovering it as a result of his interest in the psychological aspects of alchemical science.

The Compound of Alchemy describes a bizarre vision of a suicidal toad which, is, in fact, a series of metaphors for alchemical processes. The edition printed in 1591 (a century after Ripley's death) follows the poem with a plate showing Ripley's "Wheel" or mandala diagram, which relates more than a little to our study. The wheel is an illuminating demonstration of the various esoteric schools of thought which influenced this amazing and eclectic man. Under the title, the plate bears the words: "*In the Sun he puts his tabernacle. Sun and Moon blessed be ye.*" The diagram teems with astronomical/ astrological/ alchemical/ religious/ occult correspondences, seeming to simultaneously represent a ritual working space, wheel of the year, diagram of alchemical processes and symbolic representation of the life and death of Jesus Christ as the sacrificed Solar God, equating him with the King Sol of the alchemists. At the end of one's passage around the wheel one finds the words: "*When thou hast made the quadrangle round, then is all the secret found.*" In addition to the Wheel, Ripley produced a profile of the twelve "gates" through which a voyager passes in the course of the alchemical process journey. Towards the end of 1995, I received a forceful psychic message informing me that I should superimpose a plan of the great Terrestrial zodiac at Glastonbury upon a similarly-sized copy of the wheel; also taking into account the twelve gates. This, apparently, would go a considerable way towards clarifying what John was up to and how it eventually affected the role which he opted to live out magically. Faced with the wheel's bewildering complexities, I decided that the best way to get to grips with it was to strip it down to its component parts as one might dismantle a machine and then reassemble it, at the same time checking the various rings so derived against a zodiac template. This process may sound both idiosyncratic and cumbersome, but, strangely enough, it proved to be quite illuminating.

Ripley's wheel shows the four cardinal points and the related seasons. His elemental attributions to the four quarters has left many puzzled, differing considerably from standard magical practise. Fire he places in the South, Water in the North, Earth in the East and Air in the West. My friend Ian Freer has suggested that this scheme of attributions may have been a result of factors imposed by the geographical location at which old George was working when the diagram was constructed.

For the benefit of those unfamiliar with it, the great Glastonbury landscape zodiac was discovered by the artist Katherine Maltwood in 1929 when she was working on the illustrations for a new edition of *The High History of the Holy Grail*. In a revelatory vision she saw a vast planispheric round table representing versions of the twelve zodiacal constellations imprinted on the Somerset landscape; natural and human-created features combining to mould gigantic figures; the whole stretching over a diameter of about 10 miles. Whether the zodiac's existence can be "proved" or whether it really was the work of Sumerian visitors 5000 years ago need not concern us here. We shall look at it in greater detail a little later in this volume, but it suffices here to state that the zodiac has an intensely powerful etheric reality, invested belief having built up an immensely powerful thought form which can be, has been and still is worked with on a magical level. The comparative super-imposition process which had been psychically dictated to me required a degree of "thinking round corners"; an approach often resorted to by questers and magicians.

The Glastonbury Zodiac is essentially the result of the projection of relevant constellation images from a planisphere down onto the Earth's surface. This explains how they may appear in reverse order as a planisphere gives the view of the heavens seen when one looks up from below them, whereas in Mrs. Maltwood's plan we are looking DOWN onto a planisphere from above. This involves lateral inversion; left becomes right, etc. At Avalon, local place names and customs correspond disarmingly with the zodiacal figure covering their area of location. Placing the zodiac on Ripley's Wheel means that we must return it to conventionally represented order via rotating it through one hundred and eighty degrees about a polar axis; this axis being aligned with that of The Wheel. At Autumn, the Wheel's Western quarter corresponds with the zodiac's Scorpio. Ripley sees this point as representing Christ's decision to descend from heaven to Earth as the Sun, too, falls in the West. This links directly to the "position of the stone" band of the Wheel, here entering "into practice -Earthing in quality". (Ripley's words.) On Earth

116

another conception takes place as "The Red Man and his Wife are espoused with the spirit of life". Ripley assigns red as this sector's principal colour. To the North-West the Solar God figure of the zodiac's Sagittarius falls below the skyline, his energies all spent.

In the North, Christ assumes human form, his "divinity hidden" as the Sun's beams are hidden. Eclipsed by the moon the Solar disc "dies in order to multiply". Sagittarius/Arthur has now vanished below the horizon and the "stone" is described as being "in the sphere of purgatory". The red man and his lady also go to purgation, purged by pain and woe. As we go into the North-East the colour pales and we find Pisces (taking in Bride's Mound and Wearyall Hill) followed by Aries and the Holy Child of Gemini, rising and long-awaited. In the East Christ is in his tomb but "uprose indewed with clarity". The Sun is eclipsed by various colours and then rises in "incomparable whiteness". The stone enters the "light sphere of paradise" and the Moon is full. "Pains passed" the red and white lovers become "resplendent in crystal". In the South, at Summer, Christ ascends and the Sun, "now made our stone" has its first glory "renewed with youth". The stone, fiery in quality, shines "more than quintessence". It is "the end of practice". As for the lovers, "Here to paradise they go to one, Brighter than is made the Sun". In the South-West we have Virgo, the Glastonbury zodiac's mother of the messiah/holy child whose birth results from her union with the sacrificed equestrian Solar God who then sank in the North-West.

From the above very brief summary it will be seen that The Wheel is a highly complex diagram. The concentric discs (called "spheres" by Ripley) closer to the hub contain the "heavenly bodies" Sun, Moon, Venus, and Mercury and we have the "principal colours" sphere/disc containing pale (North-East), black (South-East), white (South-West) and red (West). Use of verse as a vehicle of camouflage was common among Ripley's alchemical contemporaries. He makes much use of sexual metaphor. Gate 4, for example, he calls "copulation". In a short piece called *The Mystery of Alchemy* he exhibited a feeling for the seasons and the Wheel of the year which his own Wheel represented, among other things.

> *"When the Sun is in Aries and Phoebus shines bright*
> *The elements reviving the new year springing*
> *The Sun by his virtue gives nature and light*
> *And by moisture refresheth all things growing:*
> *In the season of the year then the Sun waxeth warm*

Freshly and fragrant the flowers do grow
Of nature's subtle workings we cannot discern
Nor yet by our reason we cannot it know
In four elements is comprehended things three
Animals, vegetables and minerals must be
Of this is our principle that we make our stone
Quality and quantity is unknown to many one.
.. ..With our fixed body we must thus begin
Of him made mercury and water clear,
Man and woman is them within
Married together by virtue of our fire,
The woman in her working is full wild
Be well aware she goes not out
T'ill she hath conceived and born a child. "

At the end of the *Compound of Alchemy* Ripley provides a "Recapitulation". This section indicates that a copy of the Wheel would have been provided with each copy of the book. The most complete version of the Wheel which I have seen was bound with the text of the Compound of Alchemy in a 1652 edition of Ashmole's compendium work *Theatricum Chemicum Britannicum*. The recapitulation refers to the Wheel. It shows Ripley again using verse as a vehicle with which to juxtapose alchemical laboratory procedures, wheel of the year imagery and the fates of sacrificed Solar God and Lunar Goddess. It closes: "*Then to win to our desire thou needest not be in doubt For the wheel of our philosophy thou hast turned about. "* Anyone whose appetite is whetted by this chapter is urged to visit the *British Library* and attempt to plumb the strange Riplean depths for themselves. As the Canon himself made clear, he wrote ". *. . to discourage the fools, for although we write primarily for the edification of the disciples of the art, we also write for the mystification of those owls and bats which can neither bear the splendour of the Sun nor the light of the Moon. . . "*

There seems little doubt that John and his brothers in their covert order would have known of Ripley's then-influential works. (His *Compound* was written around the time that Abbot Selwood's pilgrims' house was nearing completion.) Psychically-received input indicates Ripley to have been a major influence on John. Further input made clear the notion that old George's Wheel and the great Glastonbury Zodiac, when studied together, provide a key to the mysteries that lie hidden at the George. In the Summer of 1995 Carole Young carried out a long psychometric session using rubbings taken from furniture in the pilgrims' house (a chest from the Monk's Cell and chairs from the bar) and also using photographs and a scale plan taken from a book by Prof. Rahtz. Something profound had not only taken place at the *George* four hundred years ago but had resulted in the creation of a product which was STILL there; hidden away and incubating over the centuries, patiently awaiting the time of its realisation; its release. "*The great zodiac with its twelve mansions*", Carole was told, also played a key part. Perhaps it is now time to look a little more closely at Mrs. Maltwood's discovery.

Chapter 19

The Great Zodiac

As stated earlier, the landscape zodiac at Glastonbury was (re)discovered by the artist Katherine Maltwood in 1929, whilst producing illustrations for *The High History of the Holy Grail*. Initially, it was the Leo figure which struck her. Her perceptive research on the subject has been continued by the brilliant geomantic researcher Mary Caine, who has produced two illuminating books and a video tape. As also stated earlier, I do not feel that it really matters whether or not we go along with the notion of the initial moulding of the landscape having taken place 5000 years ago at the hands of visiting Sumerians. The figures found by Maltwood are created by a mixture of manmade features and natural forms. The academic will inevitably shoot the whole thing down in flames, yet her/his arguments never quite explain away how it is that so much placename lore and so many local legends seem to crop up time and time again in the right place within the context of a given figure; for example, Wagg on the tail of the Girt Dog of Langport and Wimble Toot on the nipple of the great Virgo figure. The standard objection is that one can find ANY image in the abstract forms presented by a map or aerial view if one so desires, which may well be true but it does seem to be rather "pushing it" a bit when one considers that Katherine Maltwood found not one but TWELVE figures, in the right order and fashioned to a compatible scale. At the end of the day, the zodiac, in any case, emerges, from the occultist's viewpoint, as an immensely powerful thought-form which can be effectively worked-with on a magical level, as we shall see. Readers interested in finding out more about the zodiac, its figures and its lore, are advised to read the works of Maltwood and Caine for themselves.

Mary Caine's writings on the zodiac discuss the significance of the "Law of Three", which she finds to be common to a number of religions. In terms of the Glastonbury configuration, she highlights an equilateral triangle which is produced by connecting the three signs which are represented by images of human figures: Virgo, Sagittarius and Gemini. On several occasions I had been psychically shown such a triangle, during "on site" meditations at

Glastonbury, and had assumed it to be the pattern created by three sites. Mary Caine has developed Mrs. Maltwood's original interpretation to show the Gemini twin as a divine male child riding in a Moon boat, ark or cradle. Sagittarius and Virgo, its parents to whom it is connected by the triangle, are the zodiac's two largest signs, each 5 miles across. If John had played the part of the doomed Solar king and his priestess (as I later learned) had played the part of the Lunar Goddess, the Gemini child echoed whatever it was that their union produced. Caine's linking of the equestrian Sagittarius figure with Arthur brought to mind the fact that John opted for adopting this name when he entered the Benedictine brotherhood. Caine's Gemini child seems to stir from a foetal position; filled with promise and awakening from incubation. The finding of a church dedicated to Mary Magdalene in the area occupied by the Virgo figure seems like an added bonus, for, as we shall see, the Bride of Christ is highly relevant to our quest.

Much of the Virgo figure's outline is defined by the River Carey. Caine links the figure to the grain deities Ceres and Ceridwen, for in the landscape image she seems to hold a sheaf of corn. At Babcary, Mary Caine sees the swelling shape of the divine child in the pregnant folds of the clothing of the Goddess. Placed appropriately in the calendar after Scorpio, Sagittarius is seen by Caine as a doomed Solar God, occupying the classic pagan role of the Sun deity who mates and then is sacrificed and dies, just as every man "dies" after the physical climax of orgasm, subsequently to rise again. Following the Sun king's death, a child is born. Caine refers us to E. M. Plunkett's *Ancient Calendars and Constellations* and W. T. Olcott's *Star Lore of All Ages* in relation to Sagittarian correspondences, identifying the figure with the Assyrian Sun God Ahura -a name obviously similar to Arthur. As Arthur, Caine sees his glories lying in the past, cuckolded by Lancelot. The zodiac's Sagittarius figure does not appear as the more familiar centaur but as a warrior dragged over his horse; arms upraised to form a cross. Caine feels that he could also be identified with St. George, or a mounted St. Michael. And, of course, an echo of the figure of the crucified Christ, whilst on the subject of Solar Gods, inevitably comes to mind.

In an article entitled *The Great Zodiac of Glastonbury*, published in the original series of the magazine *The Occult Observer*, Ross Nichols waxed lyrical on the subject. He, too, described the "dwarf-giant of Dundon" (in Gemini) as the "child of the Sun hero". Sagittarius he calls "the year hero of the Zodiac" and "the Celtic Sagittarius who is Arthur". Nichols, like Maltwood and Caine, also dwells upon the strong relevance of placenames to given figures, drawing our attention to the fact that the fork of the Sagittarius figure's buttocks is marked as Breech Lane on the map, while Canter's Green runs up his thigh. His arms forming a cross, Nichols suggests, mark, in a sense, a crucifixion on the Winter Solstice. He sees this crucifixion as being of pre-Christian origin and more related to mystery initiation, quoting Blavatsky on the subject. He, too, equates the Virgo figure with Ceridwen. Summing up, Nichols expresses the view that local names and traditions support the validity of the concept of the Glastonbury zodiac. Mary Caine's video makes the same point, showing us the places involved. There is something oddly magical about this film, which repays endlessly repeated viewing. I frequently watch it very late at night, often whilst in a near-hypnogogic state. Sometimes, I use the pause button on my machine to freeze a particular shot on the screen, perhaps psychically attuning to the place shown or picking out landscape details in the case of aerial views. The film is subtle; its true magic not being immediately apparent. In an inspiring climactic sequence it demonstrates the significance of the triangular Virgo/Gemini/Sagittarius configuration.

It is important to bear in mind that the great Zodiac exists to be USED magically as well as to be studied. Far from being a fossilised example of a world-view illustration of some archaic culture it is, on the contrary, a living magical reality with an immensely powerful etheric existence. Magically, if the occultist CHOOSES to invest energy in a concept/proposition, whatever, and act AS IF it is totally "real" then she/he is more than likely to get results, as Aleister Crowley once pointed out. Chaos magicians, as an example, sometimes work magically with a fictional mythos. In his book *Prime Chaos* Phil Hine describes approaches to working with H. P. Lovecraft's Cthulhu mythos. Using the zodiac is little different. For an example of such working, the reader is urged to buy a copy of Paul Weston's recorded lecture *Avalonian Aeon* from the Avalon Foundation.

Veteran psychic quester Andrew Collins once intriguingly described the Glastonbury Zodiac as a psychic assault course. During some solo workings of a shamanic nature in 1985 he treated it as just that, hurling himself into the Baltonsborough Flights weir one night. Working with his psychic colleague Bernard, immortalised in the books *The Black Alchemist* and *The Second Coming*, he was led to uncover concealed artifacts from areas of the landscape, such as the finding of a hidden 17th Century crucifix at Wimble Toot on the Virgo figure's breast. The weir episode at Baltonsborough (Dunstan's birthplace) took place on the tail of the bird which, in the Zodiac,

122

represents Libra. With the weir in full flood, this re-birth experience COULD have proved fatal. He later saw Solomon's ship sailing across the Somerset Levels whilst in a shamanic, sleep-deprived state. In 1990, Andrew returned to the Zodiac with a group of questing colleagues. The plan was to access the zodiac using an intensive shamanic three-day "vision quest" format, covering a lot of ground with little (if any) sleep. The aim was to culminate this spiritual and very physical journey with a powerful meditation at Butleigh, the circle's centre. In preparation, Paul read all that he could find on the Glastonbury Zodiac, discovering that the notion of its existence went heavily against the grain of common-sense from the viewpoints of academic, archaeologist or "normal" thinking person. He went ahead, CHOOSING to believe in it and work with it magically. The results, at any rate, were certainly magical, with several aspects of Paul's life experiencing profound changes which strongly affected his future.

With the Tor configuration of the Michael and Mary bands, as Miller and Broadhurst have shown, we have another instance of a cosmic coupling at Glastonbury. The amazing pattern which they dowsed showed the serpentine Mary band forming the shape of a double-lipped cup or chalice (Grail?), with a phallus shape outlined by the sinuous Michael band plunging into it at what was probably the location of the altar of St. Michael's church. A Goddess and God copulating on the Tor! As Miller and Broadhurst stated, the implications of this discovery are indeed profound.

A dying God. . . John, as we are seeing, seems to have stepped into such an archetype; his identification with it somehow invoking the hideous sacrifice which was to follow. Much of what John loved and cherished may appear, at first sight to have died with him. The "Priesthood", according to psychic sources, was ruthlessly wiped-out in a manner characteristic of Stalin's Russia or Hitler's Germany. The great Abbey was desecrated and vandalised; its priceless library scattered and its fabric ripped apart by builders hungry for cheap materials.

An era ended. . . or did it? Psychically-received material indicates John's secret order never ceased functioning on the inner planes while, similarly, those parts of the Abbey's structure which were rendered physically invisible following 1539 still have a strong etheric existence, glimpsed by various friends and myself whilst hovering on the borders of sleeping and waking. Glastonbury lore, too, abounds with prophecies of a fabled return -a promised time of glory when the place will again come into its own. The zodiac figure which occupies the Aquarius position perhaps says it all. Stretched across both the Tor and Chalice Hill Mrs. Maltwood saw a phoenix. . .

Mary Caine has written about Solar energy absorption giving life, but in so doing slowing down its own vibrations to the point of death. This results in the end of the Sun King's life, for he already has "one foot in the grave" of Ponter's Ball; that mysterious ancient earthwork beyond Edgarley once known locally as The Golden Coffin. On the zodiac, this earthwork forms the horn of Capricorn; the "frosty grave of the year". Caine equates the Sagittarius figure with the Tarot's Hanged Man, crucified upside-down, engaging in the "divine foolishness of self-sacrifice. In addition to its archetypal symbolism, the great Zodiac seems to constitute an immense visual metaphor of Glastonbury's past, present and future; also a metaphor of John's life and spectacular death, as we shall see. The mating Michael and Mary bands on the Tor reinforce such a notion. But HOW did the actual execution, which had undertones of a ritual sacrifice, fit into all this?

Dowsing the precise site of one's OWN execution in a past-life might seem to be a slightly dodgy thing to do on a map, let alone on site. However, I did both. I had repeatedly been told that to relive those last moments on the Tor would be a pointless, negative exercise and I had no wish to anyway. Pinpointing where it happened in the spirit of geomantic enquiry, hoping to develop a fuller overall picture, however, was a different matter. Having found the spot at home using a map, I repeated the exercise alone on the Tor on a cold, misty morning in January 1996. Both exercises came up with the same location. My pendulum indicated that the gallows had been situated on the South-Western side of the tower just below it, before the angle of the gradient increases, and actually ON the straight St. Michael alignment of sites. In terms of Miller and Broadhurst's findings, the gallows siting was VERY interesting. There, within the Michael band's gigantic phallus form, in line with the inner lips of Mary's gigantic chalice/vagina receptacle, John Thorne was hung and dismembered, living out the ultimate fate of the Solar God. The Tor suddenly emerged as a place of sex and death -creation and destruction -echoing the functions of the great cauldrons of the Celts.

Kathy Jones' book *The Goddess in Glastonbury* contains a sketch of a French statue of Mary Magdalene in her barely-concealed role of Death Goddess, holding a vase of anointing substance with a skull at her feet. In ancient tradition, a priest/king chosen to die was first anointed. The now much-maligned writer Margaret Murray makes some comments in her books *The God of the Witches* and *The Divine King in England* which are strongly relevant to John's death. She studied the lore surrounding sacrificial deaths; the death of William Rufus in the New Forest seeming to her to be a good example. As well as mentioning the inevitable dismemberment and transportation of various bodily parts to separate locations, Murray also states that the months seen as those in which the Celtic fire festivals fell were also the months of sacrifice: February, May, August and November. In his book *Earth God Rising*, Alan Richardson looks at the assassination of John F. Kennedy in such a light. It took place on 22nd November, 1963. Richardson does NOT hint that Kennedy's death was really a previously-planned ritual murder by a secret occult society. Instead, he suggests the subtle existence of a consciousness matrix like that found in copper sulphate solutions, which ensures that crystals are always formed in the same shape -an ancient matrix and its energy at work.

Looking at the circumstances of John's death, one is reminded of the fates of Odin's chosen heroes in Norse mythology; seemingly "betrayed" by him but subsequently being taken to Valhalla in triumph. Odin's own sacrifice was voluntary, hanging on the windswept tree for nine days and nights, pierced by his own spear but eventually rising again with the knowledge of the runes. Like Odin, Christ too was sacrificed on a tree (cross), pierced by a spear and then rising again to be met by Magdalene. Osiris, in Egyptian tradition, suffered bodily dismemberment. And then there is our own John Barleycorn. Ostensibly this is a lusty traditional English drinking song. However, the pagan theme of the sacrificed God lies just below the surface. Barleycorn's fate, plotted by three mysterious men from the West, is grim indeed; formulated by them even before the seeds are sown. Once grown, he is cut with scythes, pricked with pitchforks, split skin from bone with sticks and finally ground between stones. Yet John B, finally triumphant, lives again in "good strong ale". John Barleycorn is dead -long live John Barleycorn!

Chapter 20

Signs in the Heavens

As 1995 wore on, a bizarre picture began to form. It seemed that John Thorne/Arthur had in some way invoked an archetype whose role he had then lived out to the bitter end. The reason WHY at that time was far from clear. Alan Richardson's comments about Kennedy's assassination which, like John's execution, took place in November, fascinated me. I vividly remember hearing about this event which sent shock waves around the world for the first time. On the evening of that fateful day I was employed on counter duty at the public library where I earned my living as an assistant. During the quiet "tea time" slot a stunned member of the public burst in through the swing doors and made the terse announcement *"They've killed Kennedy."* As Richardson points out, Kennedy was in many ways a modern embodiment of a Solar God myth figure. Even the Arthurian connection was there; his "court" sometimes being referred to as Camelot. John Thorne's assumption of the sacrificed God role appeared to be supported by alchemical factors (the powerful influence of Ripley), geomantic factors (relevant imagery in the Glastonbury zodiac and Michael and Mary configuration) and, of course, psychically-received material. Richardson's remarks about "sacrificial months" prompted me to ponder upon possible astrological implications. My astrological knowledge was pathetically limited, but two highly-experienced and skilled astrologer friends at once came to mind -Ian and Jackie Freer.

Ian and Jackie ran their own Druidic order and Druidic college in West London. Their particular area of interest was star lore. I at once rang them and asked them for any observations which they would care to make regarding the astrological configuration on 15th November, 1539. Ian set about investigating the matter with the aid of a computer programme. With no knowledge of my recent discovery of Richardson's comments, he subsequently remarked that if one took calendric changes into account, the Sun's astrological position at John's death was the same as it would have been when Kennedy was assassinated! (I had not told Ian WHAT happened on 15th November.) Ian's impression was that a vice-like grip had been slowly tightening upon the victim concerned. He sensed a turbulent conflict situation with long-term consequences, leaving a lot to be resolved.

The entire chart, in fact, spelled out conflict. The Sun was found to be in the same degree of Sagittarius which it was to occupy four centuries later on the day of the Dallas tragedy. The slow-moving planets at the Solar System's extremity exerted an influence over long-term aspects, illustrated by the opposition of Saturn and Neptune, Uranus and Pluto. The Saturn/Neptune configuration heralded a dissolution of social structures (how pertinent to the monastic situation) while Neptune in Britain's Sun sign Aries indicated a national identity crisis. (Neptune also relates to mystical and religious matters.) Saturn in Libra indicated a weighing in the balance and passing of judgment. A nodal axis was produced by the Moon's passage over the ecliptic (the Sun's yearly path). Jupiter created a "T-square" to this axis highlighting legal and religious affairs. The Lunar opposition with Jupiter made a "grand cross" which produced a "no way out" scenario. If the Moon symbolised the body of a person under interrogation (John) then the Jupiterian opposition signified defeat. The Uranus/Pluto opposition resulted in a "shocking manifestation" of a "murky" yet at the same time transformative nature. Mars, a traditionally malefic sign, aspected Mercury, Jupiter and Uranus. If Capricorn was rising (which it did for two hours) then the whole chart came under the "malefic" rule of Saturn. The conditions, then, were hardly tranquil!

Jackie, knowledgeable on the Tudor period, also supplied some notes. Curiously, 15th November 1539 marked the beginning of the end for Thomas Cromwell, whose policies directly resulted in the holocaust which had descended on Glastonbury. As the Three died, Ann of Cleaves arrived at Rochester. Cromwell, who had urged the king to marry her, was present. It was found that the latter had been altering accounts of the lady which had been sent to the Henry in order to give a favourable impression. In May 1540 Cromwell was dismissed from office. The block followed. With Cromwell's death, the monastic Dissolution ran out of steam, with only Waltham following Glastonbury. The Saturn/Capricorn situation in the chart seemingly spelled the end of more than one thing.

After receiving Ian's astrological analysis I had a dream in which I saw John Thorne crucified at the Tor's summit; the familiar (from the portrait)head topped by a crown of thorns. (This was seen from the observer's viewpoint, not that of the participant.) This dream, as it happened, coincided with Jenni Stather being psychically told that I should research the origins of the surname Thorne, which John swopped for that of Arthur when taking his vows.

In Christian symbolism the thorn represents grief, tribulation and sin. When worn by a saint it signifies martyrdom. Christ's crown, placed on his head by Romans, has been taken to be a parody of the festal rose crown of a Roman emperor. In English surname lore, Thorne, or Thorn, means exactly that - thorns; a reference to one who lived near a hawthorn bush or hedge. It may also refer to a person who originated from one of the places which carry the name, examples being found in Devon, Dorset, Wiltshire, Berkshire, Buckinghamshire, Kent and Somerset. It is not impossible that John, a Glastonbury monk, might have been born at the latter location. Given the Christian significance of the crown of thorns, even John's surname, carried from birth, seems like a reference to his eventual fate.

"Thorn" is the old English name for the phonetic sound of the letter combination th and it also refers to a rune, whose corresponding sacred tree is the hawthorn. In *The New Celtic Oracle,* Nigel Pennick links hawthorn to the Welsh Goddess Olwen; she of the "white track", a Spring renewal deity. Hawthorn bushes, in Celtic lore, Pennick states, are Otherworldly gateways. In the Northern Tradition hawthorn links with the God Thor and the Thurisaz rune; known by the name Thorn in the Anglo-Saxon rune Futhark. The rune's shape continues to be used in the Icelandic alphabet.

In his book *Rune Magic* the versatile Pennick assigns a male polarity to this rune, corresponding with the element Fire and representing the willed direction of male creative force. Pennick draws our attention to places with names derived from Thor's, such as Thorney and Thornbury. In magical terms Thurisaz/Thorn can represent passive defence/protection. However, it has a rather "dodgy" side. Freya Aswynn, a rune expert NOT noted for a cautious attitude, urges care if using this rune in a magical working. In her book *Leaves of Yggdrasil* she reminds us that Thurisaz also refers to the "thurs", or giants of Northern mythology; often the enemies of the Gods. She informs us of the rune's disconcerting ability to suddenly backfire during a working, despite its potential for protective use. She also comments upon the rune's phallic shape. Thor, after all, is a deity concerned with fertility. Rain falling as a result of his storms was needed for a successful harvest. Thor was a God of the farming folk, dependable and straightforward; lacking the

128

deviousness of Odin; a God of rulers, aristocracy and workers of sorcery. Looking at the evolution of Odin/Woden, one can see the gradual development of a composite figure who ended up as a very complex deity indeed, progressing from the simple mountain-dwelling storm God Wode, honoured in central Germany, to the multi-layered "Allfather"; warrior, shaman and wanderer, forever questing for yet more knowledge.

Thorne, thus, seems to have been an appropriate name for a man who stepped into the Solar God role, whose function, via mating and sacrifice, was to ensure generation, incubation and growth. Thor's association with fire and the colour red, which also represents the final alchemical process, is also interesting in this context. Runes and Celtic/Northern lore apart, the links with the crucified Christ's crown of thorns make the treasurer's surname a particularly apt one.

Some very weird patterns were beginning to outline themselves. If John HAD identified with the Solar God figure from many traditions, WHY had he done this? The king, too, inevitably had a queen somewhere around. Did anyone fulfil this role in John's "secret" life? I decided that it was high time to lift my head from the mountain of research material which I had assembled through the Summer of 1995. A return trip to Glastonbury was definitely in order. There was a need to physically get back to where it all happened again. Perhaps I might even get some answers.

St. Joseph's Well

Chapter 21

St. Joseph's Well

27th September, 1995. The Somerset countryside looked glorious as Autumn crept over it. I felt a growing sense of excited anticipation at the prospect of seeing the Avalonian skyline once more, with that first glimpse of the distant Tor reigning in majesty above the Vale. It was a day of azure skies, dazzling sunshine and fresh breezes. Ideal questing weather!

Quest momentum had definitely speeded-up. Things "kicked in" as soon as I had booked in at a bed and breakfast conveniently situated in the High Street. After a short while I found myself standing in a little "New Age" shop into which I had wandered in search of the inevitable gifts for the folks back home. The proprietor was a friendly and very knowledgeable woman, who, by her conversation, exhibited a good grasp of handling problems presented by living in Glastonbury experienced by those who have moved to the area from elsewhere. She told me, unprompted, that the presence of the great Celtic Underworld Goddess Ceridwen was currently being experienced in Glastonbury by a number of independent folk, mainly women. The woman herself felt particularly aware of this deity when close to water; the Holy Well in St. Joseph's Chapel (the crypt of Abbot Bere) being a good example of such a place. The crypt was excavated with some difficulty centuries after the structure above it had been erected, on the order of the charismatic Bere. Synchronicity was wasting no time in getting going on this visit and I had little doubt that this apparently "chance" meeting and conversation were somehow significant. Ten minutes later I was standing at the well, having first parted with the requisite Abbey entrance fee.

The general atmosphere of the Abbey on that fresh, bright afternoon was one of peaceful tranquility. My footsteps echoed in the empty crypt, open to an intensely blue sky flecked with high, feathery cirrus clouds. Passing through the dark opening in the crypt's wall, I greeted the guardian of the well. Meditation seemed a good idea. After petitioning my usual inner plane contacts for inspiration, I settled myself on the worn old stone steps which so

A piece of Abbey masonry decorated with thw 'World Tree' form of the Elhaz/Algiz rune many sandalled feet must have trodden so long ago and closed my eyes, opening with some slow, rhythmic breathing.

Almost at once I was shown a familiar sigil which identifies with the Anglo-Saxon form of the Ing rune; a symbol which the inner priesthood of Glastonbury had repeatedly shown to me at that time. It seemed that my Otherworldly contacts were bent on using the rune as a kind of psychic microchip; a carrier of information which needed to be relayed. In the Elder Germanic rune futhark Inguz/Ing has a different shape, but one which had also been repeatedly shown to me psychically and which appears on several variants of the Glastonbury chair; also appearing in the Sacred landscape South of the Tor as an immense geomantic figure linking Cadbury Castle, Hamdon Hill, Burrowbridge Mump and the Tor; the side of this huge diamond/rhombus shape connecting the two last-mentioned sites coinciding with the Beltane sunrise St. Michael alignment around which the Michael and Mary bands weave their course. Nicholas Mann's excellent book *The Isle of Avalon* focuses at length upon this figure; interested readers being referred to that work. The Arthurian associations of this landscape rhombus are strong, given that some believe Cadbury to have been the historical Camelot. Mann tells us about the old local legend of Arthur galloping down his hunting path from Cadbury to Glastonbury on stormy nights. All four sites have Michael and Grail associations. Each side of this precise figure measures 11 miles, with a 2 percent accuracy, according to Nicholas Mann.

The Elder Futhark Inguz rune is a vertically positioned rhombus/diamond stood on one corner. During meditation I had seen it opening as if acting as a gateway or portal, and on one such occasion I had actually been told that it IS a gateway through which I may pass in order to access other realms of being. A look through Freya Aswynn's Leaves of Yggdrasil, Nigel Pennick's *Rune Magic* and Kveldulf Gundarsson's *Teutonic Magic* bring some interesting aspects of Ing/Inguz to light. It seems generally agreed that the Elder, "diamond" form, if projected onto a wall or curtain, is an ideal vehicle for accessing astral realms. A portal indeed! The secret order, then, obviously possessed and used runic knowledge. Concrete proof of an interest in things runic in Glastonbury Abbey may be easily found just inside the Abbey gateway in Magdalene Street. It will be seen that a long chunk of masonry resting against the wall is decorated with the "World Tree" form of the Elhaz/Algiz rune. At St. Joseph's Well, it was the Anglo-Saxon form of the Ing rune which I was again shown. My astral contacts had been relentlessly showing me this rune since the previous July, when it had suddenly turned up in amazing clarity whilst I was sitting on the toilet in Maria Assumpta Centre, Kensington, prior to a London Earth Mysteries Circle meeting! In this form the rune's shape, as Jan Fries points out in his book *Helrunar*, resembles the entwined legs of a copulating couple; very apt for a rune with a fertility connection.

Freya Aswynn refers to the rune's connection with worship at Holy wells and its corresponding tree, which, pertinently for Glastonbury, is the apple. Gestation and incubation are terms which often occur in writings which deal with the Ing rune and I soon saw its relevance to material left "in suspension" since 1539. Aswynn further points out that if the rune's Anglo-Saxon form be depicted vertically and then extended in an unbroken chain, a shape reminiscent of the DNA double helix emerges. She sees Ing as a genetic material carrier which confers inherited characteristics and takes this context still further by discussing the rune's relevance to reincarnation. All in all it would be hard to find a rune more appropriate to our quest!

Given the ancient sanctity of this well in the depths of the mysterious crypt which became Joseph of Arimathea's cult pilgrimage centre and a handy revenue source for Bere's regime and in view of comments about Cerridwen's presence I decided to make a simple offering to the Goddess at this hallowed site. This act prompted a powerful surge of psychic energy and my inner ears heard the words "Place of initiation -cauldron". I experienced an intuitive feeling that the place may have had an initiatory function which survived, if in covert form, until the Reformation. Looking down at the modern perspex well covering I noticed that someone had traced the diamond form of the inguz rune in the layer of dust which covered it. Taking a torch from my coat pocket I shone its beam down into the well shaft, seeing crystal-clear water just below the transparent cover.

During my initial meditation I had been told: "research the well's history and then put two and two together". This was typical of the kind of terse Otherworldly information which I receive. Few words are wasted. It sounded like a good piece of advice. In his book *The Subterranean Kingdom*, Nigel Pennick describes the crypt as being rather unusual. To begin with, it was excavated in 1500 below a large existing building, the floor of which had to be raised as the crypt not fully below ground level. It was constructed in two stages, initially below the Galilee Porch but then extended to run under St. Mary's Chapel. Some Norman vaulting ribs were recycled in the process. Following the dissolution it was filled with earth, but reopened during the

1825 Abbey excavations when 18 coffins and the well were discovered. The crypt's construction was an astute move on Bere's part, difficult though it must have been, for it became a magnet for thousands of pilgrims. Pennick hints at a surmise that the crypt may have had some other, now unknown use. For an accessible, "hard facts" account of the well, Prof. Philip Rahtz's book *Glastonbury* is hard to beat. He describes the shaft as being spring-fed via a hole in the rock. Historically, it has been suggested that the well could have been an ancient site feature pre-dating the surrounding structures by centuries, possibly of Roman origin. This raises questions of original depth and some possible means of truncation being used when the crypt was built as the present shaft top's level is around 10 feet below the original level of the Lady Chapel's floor. This means that either the head was much higher than at present or that the well, pre-1500's, was reached by steps and has always sported its own little subterranean compartment.

Detailed examination took place in 1991 and 1992. Two-feet deep water was bailed out to reveal little of interest; mud and rubbish being found together with a quantity of post-1960 coins. Removal of this layer exposed a further three feet of shaft, built from limestone and, to the archaeologist, reminiscent of other shafts of known Roman origin. Rahtz comments that IF the well is pre-Norman then it could well be the Abbey site's primary feature.

So much for archaeology, but what of local myth and folklore? In Bligh Bond's time some intriguing old tales crept out of the woodwork. One of these focuses upon a secret passage running in a Southerly direction from the well chamber. A local legend came to light, relayed by a veteran Glastonbury curator, regarding a tunnel leading to subterranean rooms used as a "treasury", the fact of the existence of which was never entrusted to more than three monks; an interesting correspondence with the number executed on the Tor in 1539: Abbot, Treasurer and Under-Treasurer! Following the Dissolution a vague local rumour stubbornly survived. An elderly woman backed-up this rumour in conversation with Bond, reminiscing about her discovery of what had once been a torch-lit stone corridor during her sheep-minding employment at the Abbey ruins in the late 19th Century. The Abbey's owner at the time apparently walled-up the tunnel entrance due to frequent disappearances of flock members! Intrigued, Bond sank a trench to a depth of ten feet to the South of the Chapel wall. No corridor was found, but a not-easily explained soil change hinted mysteriously at earlier filling-in.

"Put two and two together. . . " I began to see what my Otherworldly communicator was getting at. If there was any factual foundation in the old curator's tale of a subterranean treasury, then the questing implications were considerable. If Bere excavated the crypt then it follows that he would have constructed the treasury, assuming, for a moment, that it DID exist; likewise its access passage from the well chamber. Psychic work has indicated that the dynamic Bere, astute, charismatic and intellectual, to have been a significant (if secret) "Priesthood" driving force during his Abbacy; a role which seems to have been assumed by John at Bere's death. (We know Thorne to have been on the Abbey staff at the time as his name appears on a document which led to the eventual appointment of Richard Whiting as the next and last Abbot; an appointment which probably suited John as it was likely to result in minimal interference to his occult work.) Frail, ailing old Abbot Whiting, anxious to tread a middle path and lead a quiet, "head down" life hardly seems to have been a likely candidate for taking over the secret order's leadership. Possibly, he did not approve of its activities or comprehend their full extent. There are indications, going by the study of recorded events, that he did not fully trust John. It is documented that he insisted upon the personal supervision of some seemingly mundane, routine business transactions; work which one might reasonably expect to have been left to the Treasurer. Perhaps he felt the latter to be too preoccupied with occult activities to discharge his more down to earth duties efficiently. When appointed, Whiting was as surprised as anyone; a not too fit elderly man quite happy with the unspectacular life of the Abbey's Chamberlain. His desire to lead a quiet life was to be thwarted; his regime terminating with his own death on the Tor.

John Thorne/Arthur, with the ill-fated Roger, his assistant, presumably with the Abbot (who might have been happier NOT knowing about it) would have had knowledge of a secret treasury, which may have been a little more than JUST a treasury, given the comments made by Bligh Bond's Otherworldly informant about the Priesthood's love of subterranean meeting places. This would have rendered the three as comprising an eliteship within the Abbey. If a jealous informant who had somehow found out more than he was supposed to know had "grassed" about their activities to the Reformation commissioners and word of a secret treasury had somehow leaked out, it could explain the historically-documented fact that Cromwell's agents were still trying to prize information from the three victims when the ropes were in position around their necks. One gets the impression that the commissioners never did manage to find their way into that shadowy underground room. As

I was falling asleep one night in 1995 I received a clear, split-second hypno-gogic vision of the approach tunnel leading to a torch-lit, subterranean room, sealed-off by strong iron bars, a room from which a warm, golden glow emanated. On another occasion, I received the impression of a magician-created elemental guardian in the form of a huge black spider; its legs spread across the same iron bars as if they were a part of its web. The spider seems to have been one of the covert order's totemic beasts going by this and other psychically-received material. (We have already discussed the spider's role in the "hidden" aspects of Hampton Court.) It was certainly an apt one, given the group's obvious understanding of the web-like aspects of Terrestrial subtle energies. The members of the order emerge, magically, as quite a "heavy duty" bunch, not too given to half-measures!

"The Priesthood" felt very close to me as I walked in the Abbey grounds on that lovely Autumn afternoon. It was a presence unlike that of an individual; more collective in a sense, like Bond's Company of Watchers. Looking over the hedge into the grounds of Abbey House built long after the Abbey and now used as an Anglican clergy retreat centre, I remembered Bond's received information about a passage located beneath the Dod Lane/Stonehenge ley. The communicant had told Bond that at the time of the transmission, part of it remained; beneath the feathered grasses. Yes, the grasses were still there! A clump of tall, elegant Pampas Grass swayed in the fresh breeze. I wondered how the Abbey House administrators would take to the idea of a forgotten subterranean passage once used by a bunch of monks leading double lives as occultists located under their back lawn. Should I discuss the subject with them? Maybe not. Bond's name had once been mud on the local Anglican scene. Time softens things and hostility has now given way to a degree of tolerance; Bond's findings now being regarded by some as being of minor interest in relation to their curiosity value. Other writers, however, John Michell among them, recognise what I passionately believe to be the importance of Bond's findings.

After a meal in my favourite cafe in the High Street I headed for the Tor. Somehow, a Glastonbury visit feels incomplete for me without a trek up to the summit of a hill which seems to manifest a different quality whenever one focuses upon it. Certainly, the Tor has a special association for me. Some folk might regard repeatedly visiting the place at which one suffered a particularly hideous execution in a former life as being masochistic or dangerous, but for me it is neither. Unlike someone who undergoes a past-life regression session, my experiences and present purpose in Glastonbury, in a former existence context, had been (and would continue to be) revealed to me "bit by bit" as needed. I had, in fact, been told NOT to have a past-life regression possibly due to the sheer volume of the material involved. I had been pointedly told by the Otherworld that there was no point in trying to relive the trauma suffered on the Tor. The REAL point of it all was that I had returned and now, in the 1990's, there were things to DO. These were what I needed to know about; the past providing a contextual framework.

It was a vintage Avalonian sunset; the sky ablaze above the Vale. Visibility was crystal-clear, the dark, distant hills standing out in dramatic silhouette on the skyline. The breeze had become a distinctly chilly wind (as it so often does as one ascends the Tor) in contrast to the warmth felt earlier that day. On the walk up to the summit I passed some notices requesting people to keep to the concrete path due to increased erosion and I saw labourers erecting fences in the fading evening light. When I reached the summit, the Solar disc had dropped below the horizon. Lights were coming on down in the town and on the winding approach highways. A nearly-new Moon hung above me in the rapidly-darkening sky and it was impossible not to be moved by the scene. I shared the summit with just two other people; a couple who had taken to huddling in St. Michael's tower in order to shelter from the force of the wind, which now seemed bent on turning into a hurricane! The Tor wind has a life of its own; it is a living creature. There are some things in Glastonbury which never change!

Chapter 22

Stirrings at the George

Following a brief detour to Stone Down, I strolled down Wellhouse Lane, bound for the town. Darkness had fallen by the time that I had turned into the High Street. The warm, inviting bar of the *George*, that old pilgrim house with so many quest associations, seemed a logical place to visit next. Passing through the double doors I encountered several female staff members emerging from the cellar, laughing and joking. This seemed to present a nicely synchronous opportunity to talk about the underground room to those who experienced it on a daily basis, so I asked the girls why they were in such high spirits. One said: "Oh, we sing when we're down there to keep the monks away". "Bit of a short straw, going down there?" I asked, deciding not to label myself some sort of visiting "nut" by confidentially informing them that they were actually talking to a reincarnated monk from "down there". During a conversation that followed I expressed the desire to see the cellar for myself as I was writing a book on local history. I was accordingly introduced to the manageress, who, to my utter delight, invited me to pop in around 10 a.m. the next day in order to visit the cellar.

Arrangements having been made, I relaxed my way through the evening in the *George*'s welcoming bar; repeatedly staring at the mullioned stained-glass windows in the bay that juts out into the High Street. I reflected upon the fact that my attention always seemed to be drawn back to this end of the bar and remembered my first visit back in January 1994 when I had felt the bay area to be very "charged up" psychically but had no idea as to why. I paced the lagers carefully, as getting over-inebriated and suffering the inevitable hangover the following morning offered few advantages. Subdued music played on the stereo; an audial backdrop to the buzz of conversation in the bar. It was a fairly quiet night; the atmosphere relaxed. Psychic conditions, however, were somewhat more lively and I saw activity around me for much of the time.

The George and Pilgrim's Hotel, Abbot Selwood's Pilgrim's House

At one point, an ill-defined male figure wandered up the bar from the direction of the mullioned windows, casually walking through two girls seated upon replica Glastonbury chairs on the opposite side of the bar to myself. There was nothing self-conscious or spectacular about this manifestation and it took me a few seconds to realise what had actually happened. I had only really been aware of the man's head and hands; the rest of the figure appearing largely invisible. His air had been one of quiet purposefulness -not rushing nor, on the other hand, hanging about. He certainly did not shout out "Hey look, I'm a ghost", rattle chains, shout "Boo" or do any of the other things associated with "ghosts" in popular imagination. So, was this the much-discussed "ghost" said to "haunt" the *George*? Maybe. I was struck by the pathetic inadequacy of the word "ghost"; an umbrella term conveniently used to label a wide range of actually quite different phenomena. No-one else seemed to have noticed the figure but then he was acting in a rather unobtrusive manner, probably not at all interested in creating a spectacle.

For some reason I suddenly remembered Carole Young's impression of a "lady with a French connection" at the *George*. Jo Shrimpton, too, had independently received an impression of a "young woman" who was in some way involved with Brother John and his covert activities. Later in 1995, Doreen Lee, another gifted psychic whose son Tony, a magazine editor and pagan medium is a friend and former questing collaborator of mine, was to telephone me regarding contact which she had inadvertently made with this "lady". This call was quite staggering and a testament to Doreen's very considerable psychic ability. Her "receiving session" commenced with an exterior view of a place which conformed with the *George*'s external appearance in the most amazing detail; all the more impressive due to the fact that Doreen had absolutely no clue as to the inn's actual geographical location. She then experienced the classic vision, seen by both Jo and Carole many times, of a monk absorbed in the task of writing night after night, alone in a dark, damp cellar. This was followed by a picture of the lady who was clad in a deep-blue dress which shone like a stained-glass window. Initially the woman was studying a book, but she slowly raised her head, stared at Doreen and announced that she wished to "make contact with Jack". She then showed the psychic one place which could provide a suitable rendezvous; a place where twilight would be a good time for a meeting. Although Doreen herself had no idea of the location her description left me in no doubt at all. It was Chalice Well gardens! As I thought about Carole's and Jo's impressions I became aware of a female psychic presence lingering in the open bar doorway; the spirit form of a woman who seemed to be looking at me. Again, no fuss - nothing spectacular. I found myself longing to know her name and to learn of her part in that complex chain of events which took place back in the 1530's.

Psychically, the rest of the evening was fairly calm but for repeated whirlpool-like vortices of energy whizzing around the bar just above the carpet. (Oh well, that's Glastonbury for you!) At closing time I returned to my bed and breakfast base. I wrote up notes on the day's events (an essential part of questing routine), drank two mugs of tea and then retired to bed armed with my personal stereo and three tapes: Oysterband's *Holy Bandits*, Wolfestone's *Year of the Dog* and Ketama's crackling first album from 1987, recorded when Joe Boyd's Hannibal label was signing up the cream of Spain's New Flamenco artistes. No, I did NOT listen to any "New Age" music. Following spiritual work or questing in the field, I find that listening to some good, earthy folk-roots/rock music is an excellent grounder. Tea and biscuits are good too.

Around 5. 30 a.m. I was awakened by a curious sound. Upon the realisation of what was actually happening outside I reflected resignedly upon the fact that it could only happen in Glastonbury. Someone in a car equipped with a very powerful sound system was cruising down the High Street playing "New Age" music at full volume; an act unlikely to create any manifestation of the "peace and love and LIIIIGHT" philosophy supposedly to be found behind such music.

At 10. a.m. I reported to the *George* and the eagerly-awaited cellar descent took place at last. To the staff, the cellar is probably a disagreeable, dark, underground alcohol store offering minimal incentive to linger. To me, it was something rather different. The first thing to strike me was the uncanny, unerring accuracy of Jo's psychic work. The place was EXACTLY as she had described it the first time that she psychically saw it back in January 1994. The vaulted roof, the smell of ancient stonework, it was all there. At last, I was standing in John Arthur's secret workplace of 450 years ago. "*The cellars where we worked*", Johannes Bryant had tantalisingly said, during a session with Bond and his psychic in 1908. A throwaway remark; he had said no more on the subject but, nearly a century later, it had not gone unnoticed. The vaulted roof was so low that I could not stand upright with comfort. However, there would certainly have been room for a monk seated at a barrel which served as an improvised writing desk. Tuning in to the situation two months later, Doreen Lee described the solitary writer as a man happy to be involved in this task to which he was so devoted, regardless of the spartan, austere working conditions.

I noticed the bottom of what had once been a second spiral staircase on the opposite side of the cellar to that to which I had just descended, described by Bond in a 1918 archeological report. My attention was then caught by a feature on the wall at the High Street end, immediately below the bay up in the bar. Although the present manageress seemed a little uncertain, I had heard a rumour that the previous manager had unbricked the tunnel entrance which Bond had briefly exposed and then resealed, finding that much of the old passage had collapsed; heaps of bricks being covered in a thick growth of "green stuff" due to the dampness created by seepage of underground water. Whatever the case, a square panel of wood of an appropriate size to cover a crawl tunnel's entrance was bolted to the brickwork in a manner suggestive of removed bricks having not been replaced; the panel perhaps serving as a temporary seal. Taut electric power cables stretched across the panel obviously rendered a casual exploration impossible. Jo had felt, going by presumably symbolic imagery received, that the tunnel STILL contained treasure. As it was to turn out, she was proved right, in a way. As I looked around, I felt that apart from modern beer crates and power cables the place must have experienced few changes since 1539. Going down there was a sensation rather akin to returning home!

The next morning, after returning to London, I rang a Glastonbury contact whom I had missed seeing during my short visit. We had been exchanging collected information with a view to her hoped-for compilation of a booklet containing first-hand accounts of paranormal phenomena experienced in Glastonbury. On a previous occasion, she had told me of some intriguing (and recent) accounts which she had received regarding a dark, menacing, amorphous mass which a number of independent folk had witnessed rising from the Abbot's fishpond and heading for the Abbey. This apparently usually happened at twilight and tended to be witnessed by people who had illicitly climbed over the Abbey's walls after closing time and who had been "scared witless".

My initial impression of the phenomenon was that it could well be a guardian thought form, possibly created by members of the covert order long ago, maybe even by John himself. Such constructs vary considerably in their scope; this one sounding somewhat formidable and probably capable of quite flexible operation, triggered into action by a pre-programmed response. Four and a half centuries would mean little in terms of wear and tear to an entity which functioned mostly in the Otherworld. My friend also had the impression that the dark mass was some sort of guardian or "Watcher". Following the telephone chat, I again studied Carole Young's report on the psychometric work which she had carried out earlier in the year using furniture rubbings and photographs from the *George*. The phrase "transforming base to gold" felt like a direct reference to alchemical activities, as did "the flowering of the soul towards perfection." The mysterious "foreign lady. . . maybe French" returned to my mind. I felt sure that it was SHE whose presence I had felt in the George's bar. Most intriguing of all, perhaps, was the reference to a "secret place" where something had been stored away to "nurture and grow". "Escape. Sunken deep. Running for refuge. Latch key. Let in. Many memories. Murder. A mystery. Fire. White lady." Finally, Carole's impressions had been rounded off with yet another glimpse of the lonely monk, toiling away in the damp cellar, as always, writing.

The references to fire and murder brought to mind Jo's impressions of the ruthless rounding-up of the covert order; fugitives being dragged from their until-then secret subterranean refuges by large, fierce dogs and flushed-out with fire in a manner reminiscent of the defeat of the Warsaw Ghetto uprising by the Third Reich. Jo had seen a monk imprisoned in a dank, filthy cell, so securely chained that he was unable to even scratch a magical sigil on the muddy floor with his fingertip. My impression was that the "authorities" greatly feared the order's power, but they were, it seemed, not the only ones. Jo had also sensed that a betrayer working "on the inside" had been responsible for the wholesale destruction of this magical body on the physical plane. How else would the "opposition" have found out about the secret hiding places briefly referred to by Bond's communicant?

Tony Lee, too, during a psychic session, had sensed the work of a betrayer; one who would try to make reparation by helping out with the work during a reincarnation which took place parallel with my own. Whoever the betrayer was, he certainly knew a lot. John and his group sailed close to the wind, always in or near a potential firing line, as Ian Wicks observed. They were, after all, an elite, which is inevitably true of ANY serious magical body whose work necessitates a degree of secrecy. Reasonably so too, in my view. Magic, after all, is NOT for everybody. A look at the documented history of the Abbey in the 1530's reveals that there was plenty of scope for "ordinary" monks who had nothing to do with the order's activities to "take a pop" at it, let alone some smarting, jealous or discontented personage who was part of it. James Carley points out Henry VIII's astute use of the divide and rule principle in order to create circumstances in which the great monasteries might eat away at their own morale from inside, thus softening them up ready for the end. New measures resulted in an ever-widening divide between abbots and local communities, as well as lower-ranking monks. Carley likens the situation to that of a 20th Century police state. Certainly, there is a Stalinist feel to the manner in which monks were called upon to report on senior colleagues. Such a system could easily become an ideal vehicle for character assassination, maliciousness and petty revenge resulting from grudge-bearing.

Well before the arrests, one reporting monk hinted that Abbot Whiting was siphoning off funds, which should have benefited the community, for his own use. The gradual running-down of the Abbey's education system was another cause for gripe as this facilitated accusations of an elitist ethos which kept the more junior brothers in a state of near-ignorance. Bishops' visitations; a kind of inspection, were occasions when discontent could really make itself felt. One took place in 1538; a year before the storm broke. The "Priesthood" or secret magical order was inherently elitist by its very nature. It is more than likely that some of the Glastonbury brothers were aware of its existence even if they had little knowledge of its actual activities. The forceful Bere, in happier, more stable times, seems to have managed to keep things on an even keel.

Although Whiting's appointment probably suited John in terms of its resulting in minimal interference to his occult activities, things were generally starting to crumble during those last years, with cleverly-engineered pressure from the authorities steadily eroding any solidarity which had once existed. Certainly, the order skated on thin ice. It did not, as we shall see, function in total isolation, but had links with occult groups in other parts of Europe. Given the eclectic nature of the group's activities, it would have been open to accusations of "black magic", "witchcraft", "heresy" and the Goddess knows what else. Even the concealment of Sacred artifacts was fraught with danger, bringing with it the possible charge of hoarding "stolen" treasure for one's own gain. (The Three were, in fact, eventually charged with robbery.) There is a chilling ring about the old prophecy: "*When a Whiting on the Tor is caught, then shall the Abbey come to nought.*"

Michell, Carley and others feel it reasonable to suggest that treasures could still await discovery; if, in Michell's view, the time is right. Dom Aelred Watkins has suggested that one of the surviving manor houses could, for example, house a false wall behind which hidden volumes may one day be found. Such objects will, presumably, end up in museum showcases. Historians have taken no account of the symbol adopted by the Priesthood as their own; one of gestation, fertility and access to other realms of being; a sigilised depiction of the cauldron of rebirth and inspiration which seethes just below Avalon's Holy soil; effectively a symbol of the Holy Grail itself in all its timelessness. To me, and, of course, to many others, the Grail is a number of things, both spiritual and physical, carrying both literal and symbolic meaning. The blue glass bowl, of which more later, is surely one of several physical plane expressions of this Sacred vessel. So, for that matter, is Cerridwen's cauldron in Celtic mythology. It took me a long time to realise that the order's diamond-shaped symbol was, among other things, the Grail, although psychically-received information from Jenni Stather pointed in this direction quite early on. The Grail -surely one might expect a CURVED shape, but then nothing was ever obvious with John's bunch. Such symbols will convey a hidden meaning to those who know and will be seen as pretty decoration to those who do not and thus we return to the subject of magical elitism once more. Being part of an elite, as John and his brothers tragically found out, is not the safest of ways in which to live.

Chapter 23

The Lady

On 1st November, 1995, I had a "chance" meeting with my pagan medium friend Tony Lee. He told me that Doreen, his mother, also a gifted psychic, had recently experienced a vision of an inn which was later identified as, where else but the *George*. Immediately following this she had been shown the familiar (but not, then, to her) picture of the lone monk writing into the small hours in his damp, chilly cellar. Twenty-four hours later, I spoke to Doreen on the telephone. As we chatted, she suddenly began to receive further visions. : "A lady, slim and beautiful in a vivid blue dress. (I had seen an electric-blue pattern unexpectedly during meditation a few days previously.) She wears a belt or chain which rests on her hips. Long hair, very fair. She wears a metal circlet around her head, with an unidentified symbol in the centre at the front. The word 'pilgrims'. This woman was deeply involved in the work. The lady wears a key which dangles from her belt. She will unlock doors for you. It's changing. I think we've come forward in time. I see the outside of an old inn. Coaches roll through the arch beside the bar. Coachmen wear red. Men carry poles over their shoulders with lanterns dangling from the ends. The lady again; in a garden. She wants to meet Jack there. Its an old pagan site, feels like a Goddess site, but its a garden now. Bushes and trees. Much greenery. You can walk in this garden. The evening at twilight would be a good time to meet the lady here Jack. The lady is staring at us. She says she definitely WILL meet Jack. "

On 8th November I felt that I needed to take the initiative myself. I decided, therefore, to undertake a "pathworked" or visualised journey into the *George*'s cellar. At least I now knew what it looked like! The "meat" of the visualisation was preceded by being shown a glowing, diamond-shaped Inguz rune, which I at once used as a portal; stepping through it in the manner previously suggested to me during meditation by a member of the secret order. Once through, I found myself in the *George* and made my way down the worn spiral staircase into that familiar cellar. Entering it, I was startled at suddenly encountering a dazzling purple light. I was told that this

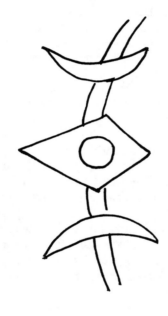

Clive Seymour's psychically-received sketch of the front (forehead section) of a silver circlet worn by Madeleine, April 1997. Doreen Lee also independently saw the same circlet in November 1995 and August 1996

symbolised a sacred key, or component, in the hidden Glastonbury matrix. I felt sure that something missed by Mrs. Bilborough and Bligh Bond STILL lurked in the tunnel. Jo had seen treasure there in early 1994, but I took this to be symbolic imagery, which now seemed to be increasingly likely, particularly in view of the whispered tales of the passage's now poor condition. Whatever it was, I assumed that it was in some way sealed in. Perhaps it was an energy rather than a physical object. It suddenly came to me that "the lady" was acting as a site guardian. I had the intuitive feeling that after death she had opted to remain at the *George*, watching. . . . and waiting. I felt quite certain that her's was the female presence which I had sensed up in the bar back in September. The "gestation" aspect of the Inguz/Ing rune has frequently been commented upon by runic writers. Back in July, Carole Young, whilst psychometrising site photographs, had come up with something "put to rest to nurture and grow". I felt sure that it was here, deep down and somewhere in or close to the now-inaccessible tunnel. "The lady", it seemed, had been keeping an eye on whatever was germinating down here for four and a half centuries.

That night, I was taken back to the cellar just before falling asleep. once more, I saw the radiant, deep-purple light. A new presence seemed to be rapidly increasing its profile. Until then, I had tended to see the secret order as predominantly male (Bond's communicant HAD called it The Priesthood, after all) but this now did not be quite the case. But WHAT was she guarding? I had to find out. On 10th November at 9 a.m. I embarked upon a carefully-planned and structured ritual pathworking during which I intended to return to the cellar and enter the tunnel. This might be a hazardous thing to do on the physical plane, but astrally it presented fewer problems. The journey was prefixed by again stepping through the inguz's rune's diamond portal and petitioning the site guardians for their co-operation. Once these formalities were completed, I concentrated, prior to going "below ground", upon a large, coloured exterior photograph of the *George*. Prior to the meditation, something had urged me to use a craft knife in order to cut out the spaces behind the windows and fill these with flourescent yellow card, thus making a kind of collage.

I soon sensed the presence of a watching guardian behind that elegant, semi-castellated, late-Plantagenet exterior, then sensing the pulsing heartbeat of the "seed", germinating somewhere within. There was an odd feeling of returning home as I saw lights flickering dimly through the windows. I suddenly glimpsed a woman moving about in an upstairs room. At that point,

149

Nick Ashron's splendid psychically-received portrait of Madeleine

the spiritual dynamic radically changed as I felt myself being embraced by a warm tide of emotion; waves of something which I could only, if inadequately, describe as love. Certainly, my heart chakra was buzzing, registering an extremely pleasant, warm glow. Whether this reaction resulted from my final recognition of the lady's existence and her hopes of what I might achieve for the Work now that I was "back" or whether it sprang simply from her regard for me as a person, I did not know. As the meditation continued, the woman's spirit seemed to step in and out of the place spirit of the *George* itself; at times merging with it. I was then told that neither the lady nor her colleagues on site could activate "the seed". It had been the lot of someone to return to the physical plane in order to accomplish this task; to continue the Priesthood's work and to continue what had been started four centuries ago via the use of ritual. For better or worse, that someone, it seemed, was me!

This woman had obviously been deeply involved with the Priesthood's activities. If I WAS a reincarnation of John, she must have been very involved with HIM too and perhaps, had a high regard for him, judging by the warmth of the received emotional response. Hang on, this bloke was a monk, wasn't he? Yes, but obviously not the world's most orthodox monastic. In his portrait, he does not even LOOK like most people's idea of the inhabitant of an early Tudor monastery. I would not, at this point, have been so presumptive as to assume that he had enjoyed a physical relationship with "the lady" although there was no getting away from the warmth and intimacy of her expressed feelings. Maybe it was a platonic relationship; two people working together on a purely spiritual plane. . . . . and maybe not. As the meditation was about to wind up, "the lady" made a curious comment, telling me that I might be able to get a picture of her. After thanking my inner plane contacts and closing down, I pondered upon this remark. Did she mean draw a picture myself? I played around with a pencil for a while but came up with nothing more than a stereotypical picture of an early Tudor period woman. No, she could not have meant this. What then. . . . ?

That evening, Liz returned home from the Healing Arts Exhibition at Victoria and casually mentioned that psychic artist Nick Ashron had turned up at the show and was drawing portraits of people's spirit guides, etc. Nick Ashron! So THIS was what the lady meant. Nick had executed an excellent psychically-received portrait of one of my inner plane contacts the previous May when, unknown to him, I had made a prior arrangement with the "sitter" before approaching the artist. This strongly synchronous piece of information

HAD to be relevant to the curious comment received at the end of the meditation and I decided there and then to approach Nick for a picture the next day; prefixing my request with one to the lady, asking her if she would consent to be in a picture. Due to the fact that he intended to finish early, Nick, at Liz's request, started the picture before I had actually reached the exhibition venue, "tuning in" by hanging one of my hand-made rune pendants which Liz had lent him round his neck. (Liz rang me to let me know that this was happening.)

I reached the Royal Horticultural Hall at about 4 p.m.; my first port of call being the cafe, where I consumed the inevitable cup of tea. I was just leaving my table when Liz entered the room, carrying the completed portrait. Yes, Nick had done it again! There was the lady, rendered in coloured chalk and staring hypnotically from the paper. I noticed sparks of psychic activity on the drawing as it lay on the table (Liz's appearance was a good excuse for more tea) and could feel a strong energy field round it. Nick later told me that a passing exhibition visitor had commented on the energies streaming out of the picture as he drew it, feeling them "hit the back of her neck". The lady had shoulder-length brown, wavy hair; her eyes grey/green. One way and another the portrait was a real cracker and it was good to have some idea of what my past-life magical working partner actually looked like. The portrait, framed, now hangs on my office wall beside the photograph of John's portrait which was kindly provided by one of the fathers from Douai Abbey. I felt that they belonged together.

Chapter 24

Marigold

On 13th November, 1995, I conducted another visualised journey into the remains of the tunnel leading out of the *George*'s cellar. As well as being shown further quantities of purple light, I was also afforded a glimpse of an egg-shaped object which appeared to be concealed among the soil and masonry above the roof of the passage. This image, whether literal or symbolic, was highly relevant to the often-repeated visions of the Inguz rune, with its incubation connotations. The following day, I re-read Jo Shrimpton's psychically-received material from January 1994, when she had "picked up" the presence of the lady, also the name Marigold. Was this the name of the woman drawn by Nick Ashron? I doubted it, particularly if she WAS French, as Carole had felt. The name Magdalene had also been mentioned. Perhaps some research on the history of names at the local library might throw some light on the subject.

Marigold, it turned out, was one of the older flower names adopted for female use in the late 19th and early 20th Centuries. As I suspected, it was not being used as a woman's name in the 1500's and therefore could not have been the lady's name, although Jo must have received it for a good reason. The old English name for this beautiful yellow flower was "Golde"; derived, of course, from its colour. Before the 14th Century the flower had become associated with the Virgin and its name gradually changed to Marygold, which can be found in Shakespeare's work. However, Chris Hedley, a skilled magical herbalist whom I was soon to meet "by chance" told me that he felt the plant to be also associated with Mary Magdalene; a Gnostic figure who may be equated with the Lunar Goddess. The flower was chosen as an apothecary's symbol, still used today by some herbalists. Some nice synchronicities here, as Carole had picked up, at the *George*: "St. Mary. . . the soul's flowering towards perfection. "

In the 1640's, Culpepper wrote of Marigold's use in ointments for lumbago treatment, also its use for treatment of menstrual problems and vaginal discharge when mixed with Mugwort. Back in Ancient Egypt it had been seen as a rejuvenating herb and had also been used for decorating Hindu temples; its culinary properties having been exploited by Persians, Greeks and Arabs. Medical applications seemed endless: a soothing antiseptic ointment for bed sores, varicose veins, leg ulcers and bruises, an infusion to aid digestion, a perspiration stimulant, a post-dental extraction mouthwash, a treatment for chilblains, for conjunctivitis, a healing herbal bath and so on. If infused with yeast, it makes a good face mask! Dying applications also exist. Blonde hair can be brightened with Marigold and textiles coloured with it. Most uses of the plant involve the golden-coloured petals which can provide a colour and flavouring for rice, fish, soups, soft cheese, yoghurt etc. They may also be used in wine making. The leaves can be used in salads and stews.

That night, I stood in my small office at home around 11. 30 p.m., looking at Nick Ashron's picture of the lady which hung on the wall beside John's portrait. Again, I felt warm energy in my heart chakra. I saw repeated sparks of psychic activity on the face of the woman who seemed to have opted to remain at the *George*, watching. As I turned off the light and shut the door, I caught a glimpse of the picture glowing in the darkened room. Stretched in bed and staring up at the ceiling, I watched twinkling psychic sparks playing around the lampshade for a good 5 minutes and was aware that I had been followed into the bedroom by my one-time priestess. I felt her voice calling to me down the misty corridors of time. Where was it all going, I wondered. As I turned over to sleep, I had one last thought. There was an odd synchronicity about the egg-shaped image (presumably symbolic) with which I had been presented in relation to whatever it was that was hidden in or above the tunnel from the George's cellar. The shape is echoed, physically, by the Egg Stone unearthed by Bligh Bond near the Mary Chapel and now almost hidden behind the Abbot's Kitchen; seen by comparatively few. Kathy Jones has expressed the view that as a three-dimensional metaphor of the Goddess' function it deserves to be returned to the chapel. Well, it seemed like a nice thought with which to fall asleep.

On 22nd November 1995, I conducted a solo psychic session aimed, once more, at achieving a "no nonsense" question and answer session. Well, I certainly got some answers! A summary follows. The "egg" is like the Philosophers' Stone of the alchemists. Look at the egg stone up at the Abbey; that, too, is deceptively nondescript-often ignored or unnoticed yet an object of great preciousness. Our "egg" has magical properties and was hidden long

154

ago so that its development could continue unhindered. It is like an egg and contains a force -something which has been incubating -and growing. The "egg" was concealed close to the tunnel as this was an ideal location. It now requires activation by Jack. The "egg" is most precious. It was sought for by the persecutors but they could not find it. Dee knew of its existence but not its hiding place. The egg must be connected to a web. Power will travel. It is an instrument of change and transformation. When the time is right it must be removed from its place of concealment. This activation could be affected via a ritual. The release of the egg will not take place where the egg is concealed but at another location. It has not been harmed by any earth movements or cave-ins over the years.

On 28th November I attended a meeting of the London Earth Mysteries Circle. On this occasion, a highly knowledgeable man named Chris Hedley was giving a talk on magical herbalism. During a casual chat before the talk, I happened to mention the fact that I wished to find out more about Marigold to Debbie, a member of the circle. Unknown to me at that time, Debbie possesses considerable knowledge of herbalism and told me some interesting things about the plant, which she saw as essentially Solar. Just to LOOK at its glowing pigmentation can be healing. It functions, clinically, in a Sun-like, radiant manner, spreading its influence out through the body. There seemed to exist a nice parallel with the possible action of the activated "egg" here.

I then discussed the plan with the evening's speaker; an authority on magical aspects of herbalism and a practising herbalist. He told me that plants which incorporate "Mary" in their names more often than not refer not to the Virgin but to Magdalene; whom he saw as a Christianised form of the Lunar Goddess. Magdalene. . . somehow I felt that name to be more than a little relevant.

The following day I rummaged through the book collection at home, hunting for references to Christ's Bride. I began with Janet and Stuart Farrar's *The Witches Goddess*, which pointed out that the four gospels of the *New Testament* contain conflicting information regarding this mysterious figure. The Farrars feel that in having two Marys (the Virgin and Magdalene) Christian theologians were projecting both fears and fantasies; folk living close to the Earth in a humble manner being provided with dark and light Goddess aspects. Whether condoned or condemned Magdalene seemed to represent the sexual aspect missing from the Virgin's image. Throughout the centuries, repressive male patriarchies have feared the power of woman; sexuality being one of many ways of demonstrating that power. Witches, for instance, who had the power to heal, were hunted down and ruthlessly exterminated. Viewed in a historical context, Christianity has certainly been guilty of its share of female oppression. In the Gnostic gospels, interestingly, Magdalene emerges as an initiate teacher and the wife of Christ. Gnosticism was an esoteric cult with many diverse strands which consisted of a mixture of Christianity, Greek philosophy, Buddhism, Hinduism and Middle-Eastern mysteries. Although a rival to Christianity in some senses, its influence stretched well into the church, and scholars have detected its underground presence in Glastonbury. James Carley sees a hint of Gnostic influence in William of Malmesbury's description of the mysterious geometric patterns once found on the floor of the old church prior to its destruction. Also, Seffrid Pelochin, Abbot from 1120 to 1125 wore a ring emblazoned with a figure of the Gnostic serpent god Abraxas. In Gnosticism, women were more likely to be treated as equals due to a polytheistic emphasis.

The Prieure de Sion took up the notion of Magdalene as Christ's bride in the Middle Ages; their contention being that a subsequent Sacred dynasty was brought to France and that the Merovingian line of French kings who reigned from the 5th to 8th Centuries were descended from this Royal line. Much food for thought here; obviously the figure of Magdalene demanded more detailed study.

Chapter 25

The Bride of Christ

Mary Magdalene appears in France in several contexts, highly relevant to our quest as we shall see. In one legend she and other Christians were set adrift in an open boat and ended up at what is now Marseilles. A better known variant is found at Les Saintes Marie de la Mere, in Provence; a region with a strong history of Magdalene devotion. In this legend Mary the Virgin, Mary Magdalene and Mary Cleopes, accompanied by their black servant Sara, landed in France with the Holy Grail. The shrine of Sara (seen by some as a "demoted" form of Isis) is located in the crypt of the church as Les Saintes and is a major annual focus of pilgrimage for gipsies from all over Europe.

Sara was also called Sara the Egyptian, a name relevant to the notion that the gipsy race may have originated in Egypt or at least been heavily associated with that country; clues such as Sanskrit-related words in the Romany language also hinting at an Indian origin. The annual gipsy pilgrimage became better known outside the area in the 1960's due to touring and recording by various members of the Reyes and Balliardo gipsy clans (French gipsies of Catalan origin). Guitarist Manitas de Plata (Ricardo Balliardo) often referred to the pilgrimage during performances. Younger clan members shot to stardom in the 1980's when they changed their band's name from Los Reyes to The Gipsy Kings and added a rock rhythm section and Latin percussion.

In his enthralling book *The Seventh Sword*, Andrew Collins tells us that St Mary of the Sea's feast day is 22nd July, the eve of the old Isis/Sirius Egyptian festival. Magdalene's feast day falls upon the same date, which may add weight to the notion that she represents a Christianised survival of the Great Goddess Isis. Andrew also links the saints to the Black Virgin cult, stating that theologians trying to comprehend the cult's historical appeal have suggested that the Black Virgin's accessibility as a harlot gave her a popularity suggesting a Magdalene identification. He feels that the Black Virgin embodies an ancient power related to the honouring of Isis as deity of

The Egg Stone

the night sky, which brings us back to comments made to me by herbalist Chris Hedley.

At this point, the weird machinery of synchronicity began to grind again. A new copy of *Isian News*, the journal of the Fellowship of Isis came through my letterbox. In the section detailing new Iseums (working groups) I noticed one dedicated to Mary Magdalene. It transpired that the Iseum's American priestess was being guided and inspired by the Lady. Her view was that Magdalene was an Isian priestess and an initiate of the mysteries, brought up in Magdala; Hellenic Sacred place of the doves. A new book which the Iseum's priestess was engaged upon writing placed Magdalene on an equal footing with Christ, her husband.

Sol and Luna of the alchemists. . . an equation with Christ the Solar God and Magdalene, the Lunar Goddess? Maybe. I became dimly aware of a scenario in which John Thorne represented one and the "lady" sensed at the *George* represented the other; possibly within the context of a sacred marriage rite. Did their alchemical "conjunction" involve "the egg" in as much as it provided the requisite impetus for its fertilisation/ conception; in Mary Caine's oddly haunting words "quickening inert matter"? Did such a rite actually involve a physical sexual union? No slur is intended upon the reputation of Brother John; a brave and honourable man who died in an exemplary fashion with a bravery which amazed his executioners. Psychic work and astrological casting, too, has shown a net gradually tightening around him; one of which he was aware. He did not flee, however, but stayed on to endure what seems to have been an almost inevitable, seemingly sacrificial death. From what we know of John, he was hardly an orthodox Christian. If the Gnostic tradition had covertly survived alongside an alchemical one behind the Abbey's walls, those involved would have needed to operate in strict secrecy to avoid heresy charges.

The similarities between the psychically-seen "egg" beneath the *George* and the Abbey's Egg Stone (apparently made of the local sandstone which constitutes the Tor's cap; such boulders being known as burs) seemed to merit some investigation. In her book *The Goddess in Glastonbury*, Kathy Jones interprets the artifact in Goddess terms, claiming that the menstruating oracle of the Goddess would sit on the depression egg's top surface in ancient times. She also calls the egg an *omphalos*; Greek word referring to the geomantic centre, or navel. Ms. Jones sees some of the markings on the stone as indications of past attempts by the Benedictines to Christianise the egg by

159

using it as the buried foundation of a Calvary cross whose base would have been set into a socket in the stone. Finally, she states that the egg is still very energised and a good place for a menstruating woman to be. As a male I cannot comment upon its properties for menstrual healing but I would strongly agree with her comments about its energy, having found, upon dowsing, that it possesses a powerful field. Bligh Bond's *Archeological Report* for 1913 contains a write-up on the egg's discovery. It was found when a cut was made Eastwards along the line of a water channel running from the cloister's South-East angle. The egg was found a short way along the line, lying in the bank on the Southern side of the drain, irregularly positioned and on its side. One flat side, obviously artificially levelled and found to possess a central cavity, was exposed.

Initially Bond wondered whether the stone had been used as a socket for a post/shaft base, as similar stones had been used as foundations. The stone was found to be covered in markings, some of which, Bond stated, were not natural. These consisted of small circular holes, parallel grooves, convergent "star point" grooves, grooves of an "X" shape and other incised shapes. When the stone was completely unearthed another hole was found, back to back with the first. Bond found traces of grey cement in it, and had the impression that an object once set in the hole had later been roughly pulled out. He further remarked that some markings suggested hieroglyphs. In conclusion, he felt the stone to be natural, but shaped by human hands; possibly used for a range of purposes at various times. As with the famous Tor Bur it is composed of local sandstone rich in mica (muscovite). Like other geomantic writers, Bond commented upon the omphalos or "navel" tradition.

In his book *The Subterranean Kingdom*, Nigel Pennick inclines towards the view that St. Joseph's Well in combination with the Egg Stone may once have played an omphalic role. Frances Howard-Gordon's 1982 book *Glastonbury -Maker of Myths* devotes a surprising amount of space to the subject. She comments upon the strong reactions to it experienced by independent dowsers and also upon the marks cut into its surface. She stresses the feminine aspect of the omphalos and the Aphrodite holes found in other omphaloi around the world; female genital-shaped depressions which tell their own tales. She feels (and I wholeheartedly agree) that the stone is now treated like an embarrassment; tucked away behind the Abbot's kitchen as it is. According to local hearsay, some time after Bond's discovery of it, the stone was "mislaid" (???) temporarily. Perhaps a precious object being treated with seeming indifference by its reluctant custodians is in accord with the old alchemical tradition of priceless treasure veiled behind a nondescript facade; in this case a sandstone boulder. During a talk about the history of psychic questing in Glastonbury delivered at the 1996 Psychic Questing Conference in London, I asked for a show of hands in respect of how many folk present (about 500) had actually seen the Egg Stone; it being a reasonably safe bet that a fair number had at least visited Glastonbury. If dumping it behind the Abbot's carries the hidden agenda of keeping it largely out of sight, then the policy must surely be a successful one, for less than ten hands went up!

On a cold, dark, rainy afternoon in January 1996, when I had just dowsed the stone's subtle energies in pouring rain, I simply stood by this awesome boulder, waiting to see if it wished to communicate anything of itself to me, which it did. I received the following terse communication: "Magdalene Stone. Unnoticed -waits to hatch. Magdalene Stone -Philosophers' Stone. " I had already began to detect the presence of a strong Magdalene current in Glastonbury; a current of an essentially underground nature which seemed in the process of pushing its way back up to the surface after so long. At that point, I had little more than feelings to go on. We did, however, have Magdalene Street and the once-named Chapel of Magdalene now dedicated to St. Margaret, while Bride's Mound, according to local lore, was also once dedicated to Christ's Bride before developing its strong association with St. Bridget. In relation to the Magdalene's role as prostitute, so often used to malign her over the centuries by paranoid, neurotic lovers of patriarchy who lived celibate lives through sheer terror of women's sexual power, (if she WAS a prostitute, I suspect Sacred Prostitute may have been nearer to the truth) Glastonbury once boasted its now conveniently-forgotten "red light" district; old names like Cock Lane and Grope Cunt Lane (a street name found in other parts of Britain also) hinted at a trade once carried on in the Middle Ages under the shadow of St. Benedict's Church.

It was not until I began to give talks "trailering" the release of this book and dealing with its main themes, both in Glastonbury and other places, that I started to get a glimmering of the real power and extent of the surviving Magdalene cult's influence. Several folk told me that they regularly worked with this Lady in a magical/religious context, and they felt sure that there were many others who did too. Nick Ashron's picture of "the lady", whom I subsequently learned was named Madeleine (the old French form of Magdalene; of whom she was a covert priestess) caused startling reactions from people to whom it was shown. One woman resident in Glastonbury High Street felt sure that she had seen Madeleine upstairs in her home on a number of occasions. Another, who lived in my native Greenwich and had only been to Glastonbury once, had experienced repeated dreams and visions of a lady in a dazzling, electric blue dress (as seen by Doreen Lee in November 1996) whose face was identical to that in Nick's portrait, walking among the Abbey ruins. When asked for her name, the lady simply replied "I am Magda".

Several classic paintings of Magdalene show her holding an egg. In the light of the communication received on that wet, dark afternoon in 1996, one is led to wonder whether the Egg Stone was, at one stage in its long career, the physical focus and centre of a cult devoted to Mary Magdalene. Even if it was not, given the apparent increasing strength of this magical/mystical current flowing just beneath the surface in Glastonbury, it could well end up performing such a role in the not too distant future. At this point, it is now time to consider that most sacred of Glastonburian artifacts which seems to be so intimately connected with the wonderful Lady in blue and, according to information psychically received, strongly connected to John's priestess Madeleine herself: The Blue Glass Bowl.

Chapter 26

The Lunar Goddess and the Blue Glass Bowl

In February 1885 Doctor Arthur Goodchild, a North London physician with metaphysical inclinations, found himself working in the North Italian resort of Bordighera, not far from the French border. Looking in the window of a local tailor's shop one day he found his attention rivetted to a glass bowl which bore blue, green and amber floral designs and was decorated with Maltese cross and silver leaf repeat patterns. Upon asking some questions, he found that the bowl had been discovered hidden within a bricked-up compartment in an old vineyard building which was in the process of demolition, built on the site of a very early Christian settlement at nearby Albenga.

Goodchild at once felt there to be something very special about the bowl. Back in Britain, he took it to the *British Museum* for an opinion. The examining curator could find no resemblance to any known example and was also mystified by the totally unfamiliar process with which it had been made, leading him to believe that it was quite ancient. For a while, the artifact was stored in the home of Goodchild's father. In 1897 Goodchild was staying in a Parisian hotel when he suddenly experienced the traumatic sensation of paralysis. An inner voice then told him that he must take the bowl to Bride's Hill at Glastonbury, after the death of his father. He was assured that the bowl would end up in the safe keeping of a young woman. In the Spring of the following year the doctor's father died. By August, Goodchild was on his way to Glastonbury, determined to follow through the bizarre, psychically-received directive which had been briefly accompanied by such alarming physical symptoms.

Early one morning he was told to act and was led by the familiar inner voice to Bride's Well in the Beckery area, about a mile from the Abbey. The well at that time was basically just a muddy sluice. Goodchild hid the artifact in a depression beneath a stone. A subsequent psychic vision showed him three maidens caring for the recovered vessel. In September 1906, Janet and Christine Allen, friends of the Tudor Pole family, were led to search for "something" in Bride's Well during an Avalonian visit. They found the bowl but were so impressed by its sense of sacredness that they replaced it. Subsequently, they synchronously met Dr. Goodchild. Together with Katherine Tudor Pole (sister of Wellesley; Christian psychic and mystic and later founder of the Chalice Well Trust) he recognised them as the triad of maidens seen in his vision. Wellesley, meanwhile, then a young business-man, had been at work in his Bristol office when he suddenly became aware of an image of Bride's Well, pulsating with energy, appearing on the wall. A brilliant light was seen on the portion of a map displayed on the wall in which Bride's Well was located.

Following a meeting with Goodchild, Katherine Tudor Pole went alone to Glastonbury. On 1st October, she waded into the mud and recovered the bowl. Cold and wet but exhilarated, she returned to Bristol with the precious artifact. Back at the house which she shared with her brother in Royal York Crescent, an upstairs room became an oratory; a sacred space in which the bowl was the central feature, placed in a casket set upon an altar. People were invited in for healing and meditation and there were tales of visions, revelations and healing miracles taking place in the room. The vessel became a focus for the expression of female spirituality. Services were conducted which, while still reflecting a fairly orthodox Christian ethos, were radical at the time as women played a large part in conducting them. These unordained females even officiated at communion services, where the bowl, or cup, as they called it, was filled with consecrated wine.

So was it the Grail? Janet Allen was sure that it was. In 1907, the vessel was exhibited before an audience of psychics and academics. One psychic felt that it dated back to 1000 B. C. The Theosophist Annie Besant felt it to be magnetised, acting as an aerial for Otherworldly contact. A. E. Waite felt it to be a physical symbolic image rather than the actual grail. Archdeacon Wilberforce, a progressive Anglican cleric, felt that it WAS the Grail, although he later modified this opinion, probably due to ecclesiastical pressure. Cardinal Gasquet, the Roman Catholic historian, was sceptical, feeling there to be no hard evidence for a historical grail presence in Glastonbury or for the presence of Joseph of Arimathea there. The press got it wrong at a subsequent conference which was addressed by Wellesley Tudor Pole; an *Express* headline announcing *"Finder believes it to be the*

Holy Grail", which "WTP" had certainly NEVER said. For the record, as stated before, I personally believe the Grail to be many things, including a spirit and a symbol. If one looks for a physical plane representative, then it seems to me that the blue glass bowl is as good a contender for the role as any artifact.

Dr. Goodchild died in 1914. WTP eventually saw the bowl as a symbol. It certainly seems to have served as a catalyst, both for feminine spirituality and for the psychic questing spirit in Glastonbury. Between 1947 and 1956, WTP's associate Margaret Thornley took the bowl to places dedicated to St. Michael all over Europe, with the intention of awakening these sacred sites to a new spiritual impulse. As John Michell later pointed out in *Twelve Tribe Nations*, she more or less followed the course of the European St. Michael alignment, about which little seems to have been spoken or written at that time, although the French geomant Jean Richer was soon to be documenting the Greek portion. A prayer wheel marked with names and locations of the Michael sites visited may be seen in the lounge at Little St. Michael. The bowl passed into the care of the the Chalice Well Trust.

WTP made various intriguing statements about the bowl, or cup. Although he experienced some clear visions of episodes from the life of Christ, he never explicitly claimed that he had seen the bowl in use at the Last Supper. He did, however, report that he had seen a vessel of identical shape. (The bowl, or cup, is shaped like a saucer.) This vessel, he stated, was passed around so that folk might drink from it. On these occasions, it was lifted off the glass stem or support upon which it rested when not in use, when it would have looked more like an ordinary chalice. WTP also stated that the bowl had its own built-in psychic protection and could never be put to negative use if it fell into the hands of power seekers. He also stated that it had periods of activity and inactivity; an interesting comment. The bowl seems to have had (and HAS) a gentle but profound magical effect upon many who have experienced contact with it, if only via a photograph or just hearing about it. In 1905 Christine Allen experienced a vision of a saucer-like sacred object at Bride's Hill and being offered clear water to drink from it. Maidencroft Lane (whose junction with Stone Down Lane is in the path of the Mary band as it sweeps in from Edmund's Hill) was where she experienced a voice which described its source as the Mother of Life. (Virgin Mary or the Goddess - does it matter?) The voice told her to make her way back via Paradise Lane; surely one of Glastonbury's most magical and inspiring places, where throngs of invisible presences are often sensed.

In January 1907 WTP took the bowl to a psychic living at Notting Hill; Miss Humphries. She felt that the bowl as made around 1000 B. C. in India; then seeing visions of the Last Supper and Christ's crucifixion before having to "switch off" as she was becoming overcome with the bowl's power. During the session, she saw a female figure close to the bowl as others had done; both kneeling and standing with veiled face. My own intuitions tell me that this was Magdalene. Annie Besant foresaw unpredictable developments focussed upon the bowl in the future, involving strange combinations of people and circumstances. Miss Humphries also saw an old manuscript which told the bowl's story. Miss Moore, a South African psychic, was aware of documents detailing the cup's history concealed under a stone slab in Constantinople, close to the Seraglio Palace. WTP was thus inspired to make a visit but the war with Armenia made such a questing trip difficult and dangerous. He came home leaving one Mr. Bryant to keep an eye on matters and hopefully recruit a local digging team. Miss Moore, however, felt Bryant not to be trusted, and vulnerable to bribing from Rome, which could have meant that any manuscript found would have vanished behind the Vatican's doors. WTP was also warned that a return visit could be fraught with danger.

Being a thorough psychic, Miss Moore provided some details of the hidden documents, which were apparently dictated to Polycarp by John of Patmos, author of *The Book of Revelation*. John had provided (on mica plates) information regarding the bowl's early years. Although the bowl had been taken to Rome it had then been moved to the Seraglio Palace area as part of the Emperor Constantine's library. Despite warnings, a disguised WTP returned to the quest, finding that Bryant's locally-recruited men had found markings on a stone slab which matched those seen psychically by Miss Moore, but a further search proved fruitless; a later search financed by paper baron Sir David Russell (a close friend of WTP) also yielding nothing. People seldom refer to the bowl's companion: a platter. This item was found with the bowl at Albenga in 1885 and was sent by Goodchild to a member of the Garibaldi family, according to psychically-received instructions. The platter exhibited a gold mosaic; the bowl being decorated with silver; maybe solar/lunar references. The account above perhaps illustrates the lengths which people may go to for the sake of the bowl/cup. Its power is such that several people who only heard me TALKING about it during lectures began to receive psychic information on the subject. At the 1996 Psychic Questing Conference I gave a lecture on the history of questing in Glastonbury. On this occasion a photograph of the bowl in a book illustration which had been turned into a transparency was projected onto a large screen; the saucer-like

166

object being blown-up to the size of a small house! The effect upon several audience members was profound; two people actually FEELING the bowl in the air in front of them!

During a stay at Little St. Michael in April 1996, I received some psychic information from Madeleine, John's priestess, which put the bowl's 1885 discovery at Albenga into a kind of perspective. It transpired that John had requested Madeleine to secretly take the bowl with her when she returned to Provence after her stay in Avalon during which the Marigold energy was created. The vessel was regarded as being SO sacred that even concealing it deep below ground seemed too risky. Madeleine took the bowl, but, due to the work of an informer, certain other interested agencies sent men across the channel in pursuit, bent on getting the vessel back. Getting wind of this, however, the Magdalene priestess crossed the border into Northern Italy; not travelling far before reaching Albenga, where a safe house was found. The rest is recorded history.

In January 1996 I gave a talk on the history of questing in Glastonbury to a group at Ealing, at which a Druid astrologer friend of mine was present. She afterwards told me that the bowl made her think of Mary Magdalene and also of the great cathedral at Chartres. She saw the intense blue of the cathedral's windows as exhibiting an alchemical significance, given that the process involved had included a mixing of glass and metal in order to facilitate staining. Many folk, she told me, see Magdalene's "unofficial" role in the Chartres context as priestess of Isis, the vivid blue of the windows on the cathedral's left-hand side being "Isis blue", the deeper blue on the opposite side signifying Mary the Virgin.

Glastonbury's Magdalene Street was also once known as Spital Street (from the word hospital). The name Magdalene is derived from the 1251 erection of the Mary Magdalene Hospital, complete with a statue of the saint. This institution once existed on the North side of St. John's Church. Some sources state that the name Magdalene Street replaced Spital Street in the 15th Century, but Prof. Rahtz is of the opinion that evidence supports the name having been used since the 13th Century when the hospital (later an almshouse) was built, complete with its own chapel, now called the Chapel of St. Margaret.

So what of Beckery? John Michell describes the area as being one of the seven island which, when map plotted, create a shape mirroring that of the

167

constellation of the Great Bear, which he reasonably equates with Arthur. Kathy Jones pertinently writes of the area as being forgotten. About a mile South-West of the Abbey, the place is now partially covered by a sewage plant. Bride's Mound itself has a sad, desolate air; a truly forgotten site of sacredness, but I am pleased to report that moves are thankfully afoot in Glastonbury to remedy this situation. With the River Brue looping round it, Beckery certainly was an island on occasions in times past. The 13th Century High History of the Holy Grail combines with archeological research to indicate that a community of women once lived here, bringing to mind the bowl's role (it was concealed here) in the revival of feminine participation in the Christian mysteries. Excavation has yielded up the remains of an early chapel on the site which, in Glastonbury tradition, was dedicated to Magdalene. Kathy Jones recognises Magdalene as the unnoticed dark aspect of the triple Mary Goddess and suggests that a Magdalene hermitage and chapel once occupied this site. Such a chapel figures in Glastonbury's old legend of Arthur receiving a crystal cross from the Virgin Mary. Kathy Jones' book *The Goddess in Glastonbury* has an illustration of a Magdalene statue from Rennes-le-Chateau, showing the Lady as archetypal death Goddess, holding a cup of anointing oil with which to anoint the one chosen to die and with a skull at her feet.

St. Bridget came to Becekery from Ireland on a visit in 488, and it seems that a church dedicated to St. Mary Magdalene was subsequently rededicated to the Irish saint. John Michell focuses upon the seven key islands found within the area occupied by the original Twelve Hides of Glastonbury: Avalon, Beckery, Godney, Martinsea (Marchey), Meare, Panborough and Nyland. Michell draws our attention to the fact that the shape made by the islands on a map echoes that of the constellation of the Great Bear. (This is independent of Katherine Maltwood's Zodiac.) The star group was anciently associated with King Arthur, Arth Fawr actually being derived from the Great Bear. In the *Avalonians* Patrick Benham comes up with another wonderful slice of Glastonbury lore. He writes of an ancient local belief in the obscure Great Salmon of Beckery. (The salmon, as readers may know, was a major Celtic sacred animal which was associated with wisdom.) Dr. Goodchild was aware of a local belief in an immense salmon figure in the landscape. Benham reproduces a 1909 letter to *The Spectator* in which a Mr. F. G. Powell of Christchurch discusses the Salmon. Bride's Well, it seems, represents the eye of the fish. Mr. Powell describes the salmon, whose shape is outlined by landscape features, as being 300 feet long, reaching from the Isle of Beckery towards the Abbey, skirting Wearyall Hill and "swimming" away from the town. (Mrs. Maltwood, like Mary Caine, felt that Wearyall Hill WAS the Salmon, and so the two landscape figures do not exactly agree.) Powell states than an outline made by richer grass could still be seen (in 1909) in evening sunlight if one stood on the now long-vanished railway station platform. Mr. Powell also referred to the celebrated "Women's Quarters" once located at the salmon's eye/ Bride's Well.

It will be seen from the above that the landscape to which Dr. Goodchild was psychically ordered to take the bowl was a magical one indeed. In August and September 1906, Goodchild experienced two very pertinent visions. On 26th August at 5 p.m. he became aware of a sword poised in the Eastern sky. On 3rd September at 5. 43 p.m. another vision occurred; a cup suspended in the Western sky and accompanied by five balls of light. The sword, as Patrick Benham tells us, was seen on a Sunday (the day of the Sun) and the cup was seen on Monday (the Moon's day). We have here obvious male/female, Solar/Lunar symbolism. Third degree Wiccan readers will certainly be aware of the sword and Chalice symbolism, as will other readers of a magical/pagan bent. The sword and chalice configuration, as Miller and Broadhurst have demonstrated, is also echoed by the pattern made by the Michael and Mary bands on the Tor, and was no doubt more than a little relevant to the shadowy, half-remembered rite carried out by John and his priestess Madeleine upstairs at the *George* so long ago, when Marigold was created.

In conclusion, WTP once expressed the view that as Christianity evolved it seemed possible that the chalice would replace the Calvary cross as its key symbol. For it do so would surely reflect a more balanced Christianity which more actively recognised the role of the divine feminine. Personally, I hope he was right.

Chapter 27

Priestess of Magdalene

The article on Mary Magdalene which had come through my letterbox in an oddly synchronous manner proved to be well worth a read. (*Aromatherapy Quarterly*, No. 47.) Victoria Edwards, a practising aromatherapist, teacher and researcher, had written an article entitled *Catching the Fragrance of Spikenard*, which was a scarce, expensive substance used by Magdalene, in some gospel accounts, for the anointing of Christ. It is apparently derived from Indian Nard oil. Edwards states that the first time that she experienced its unique perfume it evoked images of ancient tombs. The source plant, *Nardostachys Jaumans*, grows on high mountain ranges above the sacred rivers Ganges and Jumna. It was harvested annually and brought to the lowlands for trading. Spikenard is clinically noted for its relaxing, harmonising, balancing effects. In John's Gospel we read about Mary anointing Christ's feet, wiping them with her hair. Luke's Gospel also mentions her as the sister of Lazurus who sat and listened at Christ's feet.

The Alexandrian theologian Origen (C. E. 185-254) equated Magdalene with the Bride in Solomon's *Song of Songs*. Historically, extracts from the canticle were read on 22nd July, her feast day. The 6th Century Benedictine Pope Gregory identified Luke's woman referred to as "a sinner" with John's woman named Mary and with the woman in Mark's gospel from whom Christ cast out seven devils. Edwards likens Christ's anointing by Mary to anointing rituals performed by sacred prostitute priestesses in the Roman Goddess cults and to the old practise of a king's anointing by his royal bride, again taking us back to the imagery of the Song of Songs. The *Gnostic Gospel of Philip* portrays Mary Magdalene as Christ's consort, with Jesus often kissing her "on the mouth" to the consternation of his disciples. Edwards feels Mary to have been more bride than prostitute and wishes to set the record straight, for while the gospels of Mark, Luke, John and Matthew do not tell us that Christ was married, neither do they tell us that he was single or celibate. The Gnostic *Gospel of Mary* portrays Magdalene as an initiate of Christ's mysteries, while a 4th Century Gnostic text "*The Dialogue of the Saviour"* (literally unearthed in 1945) calls her *"The woman who knew the all. "*

In his book *Gnosticism -Its History and Influence* (1983), B. Walker tells us that some scholars interpret Magdalene as a Greek rendering of the Aramaic word *Megadella*, meaning "hairdresser". Jews at the time might have seen a woman of this occupation as being one of easy virtue, hence the prostitution association. Maybe the name could, of course, also derive from an origin at Magdala, on the Sea of Galilee. Walker, too, sees links between Luke's "sinner", Mark's Woman of Bethany and John's Mary of Bethany. Victoria Edwards highlights ground-breaking work carried out by Margaret Starbird, whose 1993 book *The Woman with the Alabaster Jar* took many years to research and write; a dedicated study on the part of a Catholic scholar who, initially setting out to disprove notions of Magdalene as Christ's bride, ended up seeing her as occupying just that role and pleading for the return of the suppressed feminine principle to male-dominated Christian theology. This amazing book traces the survival of a hidden Magdalene cult, relating it to the Cathars, the Grail and the Tarot! For anyone seriously interested in Glastonbury's hidden saint it is required reading. The book ends with a beautiful, moving and sensual poem in which the Magdalene, wrinkled, aged and seemingly having given up hope still vainly waits in her arid, barren garden, longing for the return of her bridegroom. And he returns at last, realising, after centuries of separation, that he is incomplete without her.

On the evening of 3oth December 1995, I sat down with a copy of Margaret Starbird's book. As I opened it I was aware of the inner voice of John's priestess telling me "I'm with you. Just read this book". The "French connection" picked-up by Carole hovering at the back of my mind, I read on. A bulb seemed to light up in my head as I read about the Magdalene cult which once flourished in Provence and the number of sacred places dedicated to her still to be found in this part of France. Of course! Provence! THIS was where my lady came from! "A lady. . . French. . . " Carole had said.

Right back in December 1993, she had received the terse, one-word communication "France" whilst standing at the Motherstone fountain in Greenwich Park. Starbird sees Joseph of Arimathea's flowering staff as an essentially male symbol, while, to her, Magdalene IS the Grail; a living receptacle who, fleeing from abroad whilst pregnant with the child fathered by Christ, WAS the sacred vessel carrying a royal dynastic bloodline. John as the flowering staff and Madeleine (as I later learned that his priestess was named) as the Grail thus paralleled the configuration of the Michael and Mary bands on the Tor.

In terms of our quest, Madeleine's nationality suggested that the covert order had links stretching far beyond Glaston's confines; links with other groups in Europe. Madeleine, belonging to a secret group in Provence who still honoured Magdalene, was a member of one such order. Putting the book down after an hour's reading, I made for the kitchen and filled the kettle. As I made the tea, I suddenly felt a tide of powerful emotion sweep over me. It seemed that Madeleine had been truly recognised by me at last and was briefly allowing ME to experience the emotions which SHE had felt for so long. "Brew-up" accomplished I read on, finally retiring around midnight. Madeleine seemed close that night; psychic lights hovering just below the bedroom ceiling until I fell asleep. The following day, I returned to Starbird's book.

According to legend, the bloodline of the anointed messiah/king/prophet was covertly taken to Western Europe. Initially, Egypt would have provided a safe haven. Alexandria already housed some Jewish communities. Some years later, the royal fugitives set sail and landed at what is now Les Saintes Maries de la Mere where each year Sara the Egyptian is honoured by gypsies; Sara -Kali -The Black Queen. In the Middle Ages the July festival was thought to honour a dark Egyptian child who accompanied Magdalene who, with Lazurus and Martha would have landed in roughly 42 C. E. In Hebrew, Sarah means queen or princess. According to legend the child who came ashore in Provence was about 12 years old; the age which the child of Christ and Magdalene would have been then. In Hebrew lore black symbolised "the unrecognised in the streets" to quote the *Book of Lamentations.* The colour may, then, have been symbolic rather than literal; the hidden child of a secret union.

European women had little status in the Middle Ages -except in Provence. By the time of the crusades the area had boasted a Magdalene cult for centuries; chapels, wells and fountains being dedicated to the Lady. She became the patron saint of gardens and vineyards (the blue glass bowl slept in a vineyard building for three hundred years); like an old Goddess a saint of fertility and joy. Good on her! The "Holy" Inquisition was originally convened with the specific intention of destroying the heretics of Provence. Many Templars came from the region, which also spawned the Cathars.

172

Again, I read until I kept nodding off in the chair and finally gave up the ghost. Once in bed, however, I suddenly developed a "second wind" and felt ready to ponder upon the mysteries once more. How about an astral journey or a bit of lucid dreaming? Why not. The *George* never seemed far away during the dark hours despite its geographical distance. Relaxing mind and body, I framed a magical statement of intent, briefly held a vision of the Pilgrims' Inn in my mind's eye and then freewheeled.

As Greenwich and Blackheath slept, I journeyed to Avalon; roaming cold, dark, mysterious little streets in the shadows of St. Benedict's Church, threading the old-time red light district. Eventually I crossed Magdalene Street and approached the *George*. A superficially-incongruous yet oddly "right-feeling" piece of music played as an audial backdrop: The Rolling Stones performing Dylan's *Like a Rolling Stone*, which I had seen them doing recently in a film called *The Stones Stripped*, in which they played in a number of smaller than usual venues. The *George* glowed like a welcoming lighthouse in the chill December night. Through mullioned windows lamps flickered; conversation buzzed. I entered the warm, inviting building which seemed to beckon me in, as if pleased to see me returning again. A montage of images floated past my closed lids: ill-defined glimpses of the Abbey in its pre-Reformation glory -soaring arches and Gothic windows of dazzling beauty. I zoomed in on one such window, seeing a crystal-clear image of a bearded man standing in a central space. The stained-glass image (whom I took to be Christ) seemed to come alive; turning to face me and then stepping out of the window. A chain of Ing runes followed; familiar stuff. The runes were followed by an image of a large black spider. After this, I saw repeated images of a skull. I would stress that these impressions may have been stark but they were essentially non-threatening. I remembered Jo's comment about human remains lingering in the vicinity of the *George*'s tunnel. Had John's dismembered body parts been unobtrusively reassembled and laid to rest in the place which he loved so much? Perhaps.

And so back to images of the *George* and repeated sensations of warm heart energy and a sense of belonging; of oneness with the place. I felt aware of the presence of my woman from France. I was gently told: "Do not search. Be relaxed and you WILL find me". This remark was followed by a flower-like image of a sun surrounded by a circle of stars, rather reminiscent of the starry bracelet surrounding the cosmic lovers Sol and Luna in old alchemical illustrations. I climbed the worn, spiral staircase, opened a first-floor door and entered a room. Mixed, dimly remembered images swept through my consciousness - a high magic ritual working space illuminated by flickering candles - a blending of the energies of King Sol and Queen Luna (it subsequently occurred to me that any form of "marriage" ritual at the *George* would have been carried out upstairs, where the rooms are sufficiently spacious. The cellars, although useful for a private writing and meeting area, would have been unsatisfactory for ceremonial purposes as it is difficult to stand upright down there) -a fleeting memory of a night spent together afterwards -the joy of being together -the pain of parting. The impressions gently faded and I found myself lying in bed, staring up at the ceiling and listening to the wind whistling outside. I turned over and drifted into sleep, still aware, at the back of my mind, of something which had been started. . . and something which had to be continued.

Chapter 28

Avalon in the Rain

On 4th January 1996 I returned to Glastonbury for a "one nighter" in order to check out a few things in the field. The trip hardly exhibited a promising start, as I awoke that morning with a splitting migraine headache which worsened as the day progressed. On this occasion I would be staying in a house in Benedict Street whose chief attraction was the fact that the Stonehenge/Dod Lane ley passed through the living room! Christmas decorations still strung out across the High Street looked sadly redundant now. Rain began to pour down as I walked away from the bus stop; rain which was still falling when I left the following day. My first port of call was the Egg Stone, which I dowsed in the torrential rain and found to be exhibiting a strong energy field. A freezing wind was now blowing which sliced through my imitation Barbour coat like a knife. I was no fair weather quester and it was not going to stop me. "No work, no wage" one of Bond's communicants had said and, puritanical though it may sound, in magic and in questing it seems to be spot on. After a wander round the windswept Abbey I made for the calm of St. Margaret's Chapel in Magdalene Street; a chapel once dedicated to Magdalene herself. Sitting there, taking in the calm atmosphere, it struck me that Glastonbury seemed bent on "glossing over" Magdalene's presence, what with the re-dedication of this chapel and Bride's Mound now being chiefly associated with St. Bridget in popular imagination. Maybe, but if Magdalene was dead, she certainly was not lying down! Later that afternoon, I took shelter in a bookshop where I found a book on Magdalene which reproduced a painting of her from the Magdalene Cathedral in Jerusalem, in which the Lady holds an egg! (I had previously received the words "Magdalene Stone" whilst standing by the Egg Stone in the rain and gloom.)

I arrived at the *George* later that evening, synchronously reaching the bar just in time to see a group of visitors being shown a priest's hole at the far end. The man-sized hiding place was cleverly hidden behind dark wood panelling and the discovery set me thinking. Abbot de Selwood seems to be chiefly

The bar of the George and Pilgrim's Hotel, looking towards the bay window remembered for building this pilgrims' inn. Ripley was very active at exactly the same time. Was it, from the start, intended to double as a pilgrims' resting place and a secret venue for "Priesthood" activities? If the tunnel dates from the building's erection then this would quite likely have been the case; it following that Selwood himself was "in" on things and that the secret group was well established when John came along. Or were things like the priest's hole and the tunnel put in later?

During the evening, I chatted to a barmaid who told me that the "strange atmosphere" down in the cellar had increased during the last few months. This was hardly surprising due to the amount of magical attention which it had received from me in the form of visualised exploratory journeys. I slept well that night; my head resting in the path of the Stonehenge ley. Upon waking around 7.30 I was dismayed to find my headache still much in evidence, but predictably it was to clear completely once I got out on the sacred hills in that wild, elemental weather.

Leaving the house, I found St. Benedict's Church to be open. This delighted me as I had often felt a "buzz" around Abbot Bere's edifice. Later that year (in August) I was to briefly glimpse this gentleman standing in the doorway. This also pleased me as I have the distinct impression that the two of us (privately) were good mates when I was around in early Tudor days. There was definitely a psychic "buzz" inside the church. I found two Glastonbury chairs. Examining them I was struck by a design feature not noticed before. The number 8 was obviously important to the secret order, judging by the octagonal shapes often psychically shown to me and the repeated spider imagery. Only the day before I had psychically glimpsed an octagonal magical working space. And here, in St. Benedict's, I saw, on a chair back, the Priesthood "diamond" set in the centre of an eight-pointed star! The chair back front exhibited the usual squared circle set in a figure with 24 points (3x8). Left alone in the church when the cleaner had departed I contemplated meditation but was forcefully told: "DON'T try to tune in, it'll only bring your headache back. Just relax and keep on the move. You'll get more that way!" I did not argue; suddenly realising that my headache had all but gone.

Walking down Benedict Street I began the trek to Bride's Mound; a locally-produced walkers' map getting soggier by the minute in my hand. I soon found myself leaving the town behind me and heading out into the rainswept Somerset Levels. Travelling alone through the open countryside in fierce wind and pelting rain was an exhilarating experience and I suddenly felt close to Katherine Tudor Pole for it was on just such a day that she made the same journey in order to find the bowl in the early years of the aging Century. Reaching Cradle Bridge I turned left, following the bank of the swollen Brue. The map's "footpath" seemed largely non-existent and I was soon smothered in mud but, of course, this is part and parcel of outdoor questing. At last, I saw it, way across the fields; a mysterious, muddy little mound covered with sheep and securely tucked away behind an entanglement of rusty barbed wire which looked like a relic of the Battle of the Somme. As I approached, the sheep bolted, heading for the mound's crown. I made no attempt to cross the wire. As I stood in silent meditation in the rain I sensed the presence of the site guardian, whom I greeted, then saluting Mary Magdalene; Goddess, archetype and forgotten saint.

Finally taking my leave of Bride's Mound I continued along the bank until I reached Pomparles Bridge where, according to local legend, Sir Bedivere returned Excalibur to the waters. Crossing back over the Brue, I made for Wearyall Hill. Less obviously "up front" than the Tor, Wearyall has much to offer. Today, it had a fiery, elemental feel. Pausing at the Holy Thorn I sensed a tall, masculine Otherworldly presence on the opposite side of the tree. I saluted the guardian, wishing him well and introducing myself. I was answered by several flashes of light among the thorn's branches. Margaret Starbird has written of the essentially male nature of Joseph's staff sprouting like an ejaculation here on this Holy hill and it seemed very in keeping with the strongly male character of the site's watcher. A week later I learned that my friend Debbie; a Londoner who grew up in the West Country, had also experienced this guardian entity in much the same way when alone on the hill.

After a change of footwear I walked up Chilkwell Street, pausing to study the carvings above the Abbey House gate, once the Eastern gateway to the Abbey. The carving on the left shows a pelican pecking open its breast in order to feed its young with its own blood. In purely Christian symbolism this device signifies Christ's sacrifice at the crucifixion; in some paintings the pelican has been depicted perching atop the cross of Calvary. Similarly, the device has a parallel significance in the alchemical tradition. "Pelican" was the name of a piece of alchemical equipment in the Middle Ages which actually resembled the shape of the bird when caught in this self-sacrificial act.

The pelican was intended to foster digestion of substances via a long steeping in heated fluid, the goal being essence extraction. The process worked via reflux distillation. When a substance was boiled, vapour condensing on the vessel's glass head would flow back, caught up in the circulation process. A 16th Century alchemical treatise shows King Sol and Queen Luna climbing out of a well which is reddened by the pelican's blood sacrifice of death and rebirth. The phoenix (located by Caine and Maltwood at the Glastonbury Zodiac's Aquarius point (its presence here on the ecliptic justified by historical astrological research) was also a classical sacrificial motif in Christian tradition; the archetypal solar symbol which flies into the flames, burns to ashes and then rises again.

Progress up the Dod Lane ley track beyond the stile was slow. Due to soaked, leaking boots, I had changed into my only other footwear; a pair of worn Doc Martens shoes. I had not anticipated the muddiness of Bushey Combe and nearly slipped over with every step! The pathway up the Tor from the Stonedown side is concreted throughout its length, so this HAD to be my route today, given the inappropriate nature of my shoes. Looking up as I approached, I saw St. Michael's tower frequently vanishing in the low clouds sweeping across the holy hill.

The Tor positively crackled with psychic energy. I just had to go up there today! Once at the summit, I took out my pendulum. The famed view had all but vanished; a misty grey nothingness in its place. I announced myself to the hill's guardian using a suitably dramatic manner as befitted the "charged-up" atmosphere. (Well, why not? In magic there's nothing like really going for it and "hamming it up". I always feel compelled to use my best "magician's voice" at full volume if alone on the Tor. It was Pete Carrol, I believe, who once committed himself to the statement that in magic, nothing succeeds like excess. How right he was!) I told the guardian that I, who had been killed and dismembered on this summit, had now returned. Psychic lights sparkled continually around me. Far from being tiring, the climb up through rain, wind and mist had been exhilarating in the extreme. I found myself riding on the fierce, elemental waves of energy, feeling supercharged and glowing with life. The headache and fatigue had completely gone. I felt great!

I programmed the pendulum to respond positively when my right foot came into contact with the spot upon which John had been executed as I wished to check map dowsing performed at home with a similar exercise carried out in the field. This done, I walked down the path to the Coursing Batch side of the tower concentrating upon my pendulum, my feet and nothing else. At length, it whirled clockwise; a positive response. Yes, it did not gently rotate; it whirled round like an aircraft propeller. It always does; why I do not know. On occasions it has flown out of my hand, which can be a bit "dodgy", like the time that it almost broke a window whilst map dowsing in the kitchen at Little St. Michael! On another occasion it flew off into a barley field while I was dowsing two crop circles in a Herefordshire field. Finding it again was a miracle. Looking round, I realised this to be the exact spot found on the map, within the outline of Miller and Broadhurst's giant Michael phallus and its point of entry into Mary's chalice/vagina. Turning, I saw the tower's dark shape looming through the drifting mist and reflected upon the fact this view of St. Michael's would have been one of the last things seen by John before he left the physical plane in 1539. An inner voice told me "But life goes on". It sure does. I was back, this time, in the body and mundane personality of Jack Gale. . . and there was work to be continued. The way could only be forward.

On the way down, I was overcome with the need to urinate. In the absence of other visitors I relieved myself beside the path, telling the guardian that I intended no disrespect and bearing in mind the fact that Saxon inhabitants of the monastic building once perched on the summit must have done much the same thing. My comment was answered by a bright flash of spirit light on the hillside above me. Reaching Chilkwell Street I still felt gloriously energised and healed. I popped into Chalice Well gardens for some water and then collected my bags. Before catching the bus, I dropped in on some friends in the Avalon Library (a fabulous and so worthwhile institution) where we checked out Jimmy Goddard's "leys" which he felt passed through the Dod Lane site using a ruler and a large-scale Ordnance Survey map. Yes, it all seemed to make sense. Several lines, including a portion of the Mere Road, did indeed line up with the shelf on the hill above the stile. Darkness falling, I caught the Bristol bus. It had been a short but enlightening stay, if slightly wet!

Chapter 29

Of Sacred Marriages and Spiders

On January 18th, 1996, hovering between sleeping and waking, I caught a vivid glimpse of a subterranean room viewed from the passage leading to it. Flickering candles burned within, seen through a closed wrought iron gate and small, high window grilles. If the "secret treasury" of local legend ever existed, then what I was seeing seemed a likely candidate for being just that. I was shown, superimposed upon the room, the Othala rune, echoing clan and priesthood connections which stretched through incarnations. Then, dimly, I saw a huge spider, stretched across the bars of the gate as if on guard. This arachnid, I felt, must surely relate to the octagons which I was being frequently shown in a psychic context. It also seemed relevant to the concept of a geomantic web; a web which was not only relevant to physical space and the arrangement of sacred sites but also a web of time, space and destiny as in the Northern Tradition concept of The Web of Wyrd, and the weaving of the Norns.

In April 1992 the magazine *Pagan News* published a splendid article by Chrys Livings on the lore of Spider Woman. This ancient Goddess seemed to be a good starting point for some arachnid lore investigation. Livings describes Spider Woman as spinning in both time AND space; a tricky concept. Spider Woman. . . a Lunar deity. The writer cites the Norns in this context. She sees the web as relating to time, procreation and dissolution; forces continually cancelling each other out -the web being both a fatal trap and a nest. Behind a veil we find Kali, to whom the noose (John relevance here) is sacred; likening the immobilising force of spider thread to the Thugge's killing cord. Livings also reminds us of lx Chel; ancient, claw-equipped Mayan Lunar Goddess and her aspect as lx Ch'up or lx Tab, deity of snares and ropes who receives the souls of the self-hung. South American tradition views the web as a vehicle for travelling between upper and lower worlds, likened by Livings to "ballooning" tricks employed by some arachnid

The author's impression of a chair in Little St. Michael's Upper Room species enabling a climb of thousands of feet into the sky. For the Chibcu indians, the web is a boat in which to cross the lake of death.

Odin MUST crop up here. Sleipnir, his steed, has, of course, 8 legs. In the Northern Tradition. This mount carries the shaman God around the 9 worlds and Odin is also gallows God and a conductor of the dead.

As February came and went, I received psychic intuition which convinced me that the name of the priestess from Provence was Madeleine; the old French derivation of Magdalene. An open, stated request for confirmation of this had been rewarded by a brilliant flash of psychic light beside that name on a page in a book on the history of names in the *British Library*. During the same visit to that institution I came across some sparse fragments of additional griffin law, relevant to guardian creatures seen by independent psychics in the Abbey vicinity and also to the odd creatures on the chair in Little St. Michael's Upper Room. This mythical beast was associated with the Sun, and represented the divine and human elements in Christ, while also being Sacred to another Solar God, Apollo. Traditionally, the griffin guards gold, hence a Dunstan connection. In its pure form the griffin has a lion's legs and body, an eagle's head and wings.

Perhaps my most important discovery at that time was a book called *Secrets of the German Sex Magicians* (now called *Secrets of Sex Magic*) by one Frater U. D. The volume's Egyptian-born author, a well-travelled and resourced gentleman, is a highly-experienced occultist who studied at Bonn and Lisbon Universities. The book ends with a chapter entitled *The Chymical Hierogamy*; a term borrowed from the Alchemical tradition referring to the Holy Alchemical Marriage portrayed in the famous text *The Chymical Marriage of Christian Rosencreutz -Anno 1459*, probably written by Johann Valentin Andeae and published in 1616. Frater U. D. feels the Chymical Marriage to embody Western sex mysticism, although, as he tells us, Andreae's script contains only allegorical allusions. U. D. 's book gives the outlines of two possible rituals which can be adapted for those wishing to have a go. He does not state explicitly whether these are his own inventions or are based upon existing rites which may have survived over the years. It does not matter; what DOES matter is that to me, the partner version which he gives totally sums up the spirit (and quite likely the actual procedure) of what happened on that night upstairs at the *George*.

The rituals contain imagery which would be familiar to Wiccans in relation to their own "Great Rite" of Third Degree initiation. The reader will imagine my excitement at discovering these written outlines which were considered so important to Frater U. D. that he made them the culmination of his book. Unlike most magic, U. D. stresses that the ceremony does not involve any pragmatic acts of will aimed at creating magical changes in the material world via the casting of sigils or charging of talismans, etc. The rite aims rather at the achievement of a transcendent state beyond male/female polarity where birth is given to one in an inner sense; the birth of a mental/spiritual androgyne; a hermaphroditic inner state where Solar and Lunar energies fuse in one being. Here, perhaps, U. D. 's ritual and that of John and Madeleine part company, at least in terms of purpose. Rather than being an end in itself, the 1530's rite seems to have been aimed at the conception of something which needed to incubate and then subsequently be released.

In the partner form of the ritual as supplied by Frater U.D., the male magician identifies with the Solar God; the female magician with the Lunar Goddess. During a calendar month's preparation, the male invokes Solar energy, meditates on male aspects, wears golden jewellery steeps himself in Solar matters and charges his ritual dagger. Similarly, his partner meditates on female aspects, wears white clothes and silver jewellery, soaks herself in Lunar energy and charges her ritual cup. U. D. describes the setting-up of an altar and a protective circle which will accommodate the partners plus a bed, which, of course, again brings back that night at the *George*. After cleansing and banishing the ritual begins in earnest. Lunar energy is invoked into the "Goddess", Solar energy into the "God", then cup and dagger are consecrated with the relevant energies. A symbolic fusion of cup and dagger energies (back to Mary and Michael on the Tor again!) takes place, followed by an energy exchange on the part of the priest and priestess. The rite ends with thanksgiving and banishing.

After examining Ripley's Wheel, Ian Freer expressed the view that there could be something very sexual well hidden below the layers of weirdness. Certainly, U. D. 's script, devoid of the bewildering camouflage so loved by old George and other alchemists, feels much in accord with the spirit of their writings in that it translates the mind-numbing complexities of ancient charts and verses into direct physical and spiritual action. A 17th Century alchemical print really sums it up; a naked King Sol and Queen Luna hovering in space on each side of a huge terrestrial globe surrounded by a bracelet of stars while, superimposed upon the globe, we see an equilateral triangle which contains a square within which is inscribed a circle -the mystical union of opposites.

In early February I carried out a meditation with my green, apple-scented candle burning and a copy of Nick Ashron's portrait of Madeleine on the table before me. "Relax and it'll come easy", I was told. "Much of what you need you already have. " There was an emphasis on my need to "get back to your maps". I was told that the maps concerned were, predictably, those showing the Isle of Avalon; my task being to make a detailed dowsed study of the path of the Michael and Mary bands, putting in the details which Miller and Broadhurst missed from *The Sun and the Serpent*. Other comments came through. "The web. Spreads out. The Grail. Michael and Mary. Chalice Hill. Wearyall Hill. The Fish Pond. The Circle and the Square are keys. You need to meditate on the rising Gemini figure. The union births a child. The *George* is a nursery - a nest. Use your maps - it WILL come, like automatic writing. . . . "

Given the above comments, I felt that it was high time to get stuck into the maps again. What was I doing, after all, but tracing the outline of the geomantic counterpart of the Chymical Marriage in the sacred landscape of Avalon? Miller and Broadhurst had found that following its nodal crossover and symbolic copulation on the Tor, the Mary band went through the Fair Field and then into Chalice Well gardens at Arthur's Court. Following the water line up through the Lion's Mouth to the wellhead, it heads over Chalice Hill towards the town, crossing Chilkwell Street en route for the Abbey's axis, with which it lines up. From the well to the Abbey seemed like a largely uncharted, crucial stretch. The room in which I dowsed soon became very "charged-up". Psychic energy sparks frequently appeared on the map and elsewhere in the room; Madeleine's penetrating eyes staring down at me from the wall as if her picture had almost "come alive".

I found that Mary does not head straight for the Abbey but loops and meanders in a manner far from aimless, as we shall see. The pattern traced out over Chalice Hill almost resembles two female breasts; appropriate for a Goddess hill. Crossing the Bushey Combe/Dod Lane footpath it reaches Jimmy Goddard's forgotten sacred site above the stile; looping round the seat and then making an "S" bend to go back through the fence and through the mysterious and lovely seven beeches. The band plunges downhill through the Southern end of the garden of Chalice Hill House, keeping clear of the Dod Lane stile. Taking a North-Westerly path it reaches the junction of Chilkwell

Street and Dod Lane, from whence it passes into the grounds of Abbey House close to the gate but not through it. Passing through the house it aligns with the Abbey axis and is crossed by Michael at the high altar. Miller and Broadhurst observe that when it reaches Arthur's tomb it temporarily splits and then rejoins, oddly repeating this procedure a little further down the axis at a seemingly unremarkable spot felt by the dowsers to conceal some secret. Leaving the Abbey's Western end, Mary takes a Southerly course, passing close to the Abbot's Kitchen and then plunging into the fish pond which it leaves in a South-Easterly direction. Outside Abbey precincts, Mary crosses Bere Lane and makes for the Abbey Barn. Leaving at the North-Eastern end. Travelling on through Hood close, Mary goes to Edgarley, passing through St. Dunstan's Well on the way. According to local lore, a chapel once dedicated to Dunstan formerly stood on this site; converted to a barn after the Reformation.

The following day, I visited a local garden superstore in order to buy some trellis. Whilst wandering round, I decided to buy some Calendula seeds as it seemed appropriate to have a go at growing some Marigold plants at home. As I held a seed packet I at once experienced a very strong "left hand tingle" and knew that certain systems were being switched on. Several things suddenly snapped into place. I already knew that Marigold was definitely NOT the name of John's priestess. It was a coded encapsulation of the nature of the magical operation set in motion by John and Madeleine. A study of Marigold's clinical properties from the herbalist's viewpoint gave some idea of how our "Marigold" was intended to function, indeed WOULD function, once released after four centuries of incubation.

Mary's Gold was how the plant would have been named in Tudor times. "Gold" and Mary". . . so telling. Gold was, too, an indication of the operation's alchemical aspects; a metaphorical form of gold being an end-product. My friend Debbie, the herbalist, had spoken of Marigold's radiant, Sun-like clinical effects and I now knew that OUR Marigold, when released, was intended to radiate out from its encapsulating egg case; golden, glowing power spreading along the threads of the subtle terrestrial web and this was, so I was told, where the strong relevance of Michael and Mary came in as they were to act as the carriers.

That evening, I returned to my maps. As I worked, Madeleine, seemingly in vocal mood, commented as follows as my pencil hovered above the part of my map at which *The George* was located: "This is the divine alchemy, the seed that turns to gold, the seed that was planted and fertilised. Rejuvenating, glowing healing power. " I completed the suggested dowse, plotting Mary's course from the cemetery at Edmund Hill. The St. Michael band, Miller and Broadhurst have written, after leaving the Tor, passes through the junction of Stonedown Lane and Basketfield Lane before heading downhill to the glorious old Gog and Magog Oaks. Later that year, I checked out the Oaks in the field, spending a few days in the magical and truly inspiring environment of the little camp site which lies just behind them.

Standing back to look at the completed dowsed diagram, I felt its implications to be quite profound. As well as being enacted ritually, the alchemical marriage also took place in the landscape. Where, on the map, was the focal point from which Marigold's energies were to stream out, once I had figured out how to "lift" them from under the *George* and how to release them into the energy matrix? Would the "release" birth an entity with an intelligence and life-force of its own? Strong stuff. Looking up, I saw Madeleine's eyes staring down at me from the wall. I knew that her co-operation had led me to carry out the dowsing sessions and to ponder upon those matters which now occupied me. I knew, too, that I would be working with her much more from now on.

Chapter 30

The Launch

On the evening of 10th February 1996 I sat down in my office holding a pen and staring at a blank A4 sheet, waiting for something to happen. "Just relax" Madeleine had previously urged me. True, most of the really profound stuff was now coming when I was drinking tea, dozing in the armchair or even sitting on the loo! I took her point, adopting a "laid back" mode rather than my customary formal meditation, which was prefaced by candle lighting, breathing exercises, etc. I was suddenly shown an image of the glowing Marigold energy accompanied by the words: "Spreading -radiant -golden - glowing -warm -quicksilver -pulse -alive -arteries. . . Dundon's Child rises -a promise. " After this I saw the intersection of the Michael and Mary bands at Arthur's Court which, out of the blue, one of the previous wardens had asked me to dowse, two years previously. "THIS is the place" I was told; having hoped for some guidance as to where the Marigold power should be released. "The energy will spread in four directions, up and down both lines. . . . " Being androgynous, I knew that the energy would be at home with both male and female currents. Miller and Broadhurst had reported the fact that they had found both Michael and Mary to function with alternating currents, each band comprising a number of sub-bands which flowed consecutively in alternating directions.

The Marigold current's androgynous nature is illustrated by its name; Mary being associated with Lunar/female properties and Gold indicative of a Solar, male aspect. I hoped that any earthbound watchers, Madeleine included, would be released when the launch had taken place. There was still much to be divined. On 13th February I used a calendar in an attempt to dowse the relevant date for Marigold's release. Going through the months without really looking at them I received a positive from one which I found, upon checking, to be June. O. K. , so now, what time? Checking through tabulated hours and minutes from midnight to midnight, I received a positive response at midday. But if June, upon WHICH day? What else, but the 21st -the Solstice!

The Solstice was 5 days after New Moon; a waxing condition which seemed absolutely ideal. Th Solstice itself, at midday, also seemed ideal; a great Solar orgasm with the Sun at the height of its powers and giving the launch exactly the sort of "oomph" which it would need. From the practical viewpoint Arthur's Court seemed like an ideal venue; nicely secluded and one of the points at which Michael and Mary intersected, insuring a four-way flow. The Court, at midday, WOULD be open to the public, so to some extent, this ruled out any sort of "all systems go" robed, High Magic ritual in the physical sense. However, there would be ample opportunities to carry out a "virtual magic" ritual on site; in other words one which is visualised but no less powerful for that, having the advantage that it LOOKS as if the magician is simply sitting there meditating, which folk do in Glastonbury all the time!

There was still a lot to check out, but a relaxed pace seemed likely to get me a lot further than a feverish rushing about. I had to find out how to transfer Marigold from its secure nursery beneath the *George* to some sort of physical carrier which could transport it to Arthur's Court where it could, like a carrier pigeon, be then released. A crystal came to mind as the obvious carrying vehicle. Although the New Age folk pay much attention to crystals, their use as "spirit traps", as has been pointed out by Phil Hine and others, has been largely ignored by all but the more "heavy duty" magical crowd. Such a crystal could be placed in the gently tumbling waters of the Red Spring at a strategic place, where it could "hatch". Whist thumbing through an alchemical textbook I synchronously encountered the word "citrine". Citrine? maybe the ideal carrier, once I had worked out HOW to get the Marigold energy into it. Citrine is a form of quartz; iron contamination accounting for its golden tinge. As it happened, a piece of citrine which had been bought from the shop at the Horniman Museum back in 1990 lived on the shelf in my bedroom. Research shows that genuine citrine is hard to find; a citrine-like effect often being produced by heating. This piece FELT like "the real thing". Opaque, milky white quartz has a feminine quality while clear quartz is often seen as stimulating and male. Citrine has both - perfect! The clear, golden tips merged subtly into a milky whiteness -Solar God and Lunar Goddess in one androgynous stone.

I read up on Citrine. In crystal healing it is used to purge toxins and improve circulation, which seemed totally in sympathy with Marigold's intended effects, parallelling them in a microcosmic way. Citrine aids tissue regeneration, improves communication and projects wishes. Yes, citrine definitely seemed to be the right one to use! The Marigold energy itself seemed to exhibit a Grail-like quality, perhaps even being an aspect of the Grail itself, passed down via the Magdalene current. Frequently in the past, both in writing and during talks, I had heavily criticised New Agers who force "land healing" onto sites without first asking them if they need it. Such "healing" MAY take the form of haphazard burial of crystals in a landscape whose energy matrix may be seriously thrown out of gear as a result. Yet here was I about to release a potent, long-incubated energy whose purpose I but vaguely comprehended into the subtle terrestrial matrix at a powerful and sacred place. My mind went back to alchemy and I delved into various treatises in the hope of finding information about the hoped-for properties of the legendary Philosophers' Stone which seemed to parallel Marigold. What was gold which was alchemically derived supposed to do? I, after all, was operating with the "Gold of Mary".

Gold was often alchemically seen as a form of medication; a prolonger of healthy life. In Chinese alchemy it was seen as an elixir which brought youth and energy. In the Middle Ages it was also seen as an elixir and a stone to perfect other, inferior metals. Red elixir produced gold, white produced silver. C. G. Jung expresses the view that the REAL alchemists strove for a spiritual gold and used riddles (like Ripley) to conceal their true purpose, also stressing the hermaphroditic nature of the final product.

Like other writers, Jung dwelt upon the relevance of the word redemption. This word occurs frequently in ancient and modern alchemical texts. The late New Age prophet Sir George Trevelyan wrote a book called *Operation Redemption* in which he discussed the idea of the ley system acting as a carrier for a new high-frequency, transformative energy. Although not always on the same "wavelength" as Sir George despite respecting the man (with whom I had some contact in the early 1990's) I now seemed to be contemplating something rather similar. In the magazine Ambix for October 1960, George Heym reviewed T. Burchkhardt's book *Alchemy*, commenting on the alchemical myth of King Gold; the Sun who must be killed and buried in order to awaken to fulfilment, when he transcends the seven rulers (planets). Rising above seven consciousness phases the Red Lion would emerge; the transformative elixir. Jung equates the Philosophers' Stone with Christ's redemptive power. He sees a redemptive phase as representing the Self's transcendence of ego consciousness which, occultly, could be conceived as the Higher (reincarnating) Self transcending the mundane personality, to use a Dion Fortune-ism.

The sacred hermaphrodite often occurs in old alchemical texts. The marriage between King Sol and Queen Luna is also represented as the union of sulphur and mercury, but not in literal terms. A hermaphrodite was, in mythology, originally birthed as a result of the union of Hermes and Aphrodite and the androgynous theme is echoed in Gnostic and Hermetic texts. An important aspect of the androgyne is its ability to impregnate and therefore multiply itself. In the 17th Century Rosarium (Rose Garden of the philosophers) Sol and Luna merge in an alchemical bath and the resulting hermaphrodite is a triumphant figure; a redemption stone to cleanse from all impurities. In many ways, the squared circle sums all this up; a symbol of a new being/order created by reconciled opposites.

Between 1947 and 1956 Wellesley Tudor Pole's colleague Margaret Thornley took the Blue Glass Bowl on a tour of the Michael shrines of Europe. As John Michell has pointed out, she travelled much of the length of the European Michael line although she never explicitly referred to this great alignment. Pole saw this tour as the fostering of a new spiritual impulse. By taking an essentially feminine artifact to these essentially masculine sites Margaret Thornley was, perhaps, parallelling the creation of the Marigold energy. Questions regarding Marigold's post-launch passage inevitably formed in my head. Would it travel to the North Sea in one direction and, simultaneously, to the Atlantic in the Other one? At Shepton Mallet, Miller and Broadhurst found the Michael Band to be 22 paces wide, containing 280 channels each containing 64 streams a fraction of an inch apart, flowing in alternating directions. I knew that one end of the configuration went into the sea at Hopton, East Anglia, while the other ended up at St. Michael's Mount, where it crossed the European Michael Line. Inevitably, I began to wonder whether it went further. . .

Initially, I had thought of Marigold's possible effects in a largely localised, Avalonian context, particularly in the light of ancient prophecies. But if the Michael Line continues on around the globe, where might the unleashed energy end up? I had heard rumours that Hamish Miller had (with dowsing rods) picked up the Michael and Mary bands in Russia under twelve feet of snow and I had also heard that after leaving English soil at Hopton they crossed the North Sea and then came ashore and passed through St. Petersburg in the Netherlands. I had been psychically told that this androgynous energy would be able to self-replicate at junctions. Would it, therefore, shoot off up other web strands encountered at node points? Maybe. The whole subject of global alignments is a tricky one. The "ley hunter" who draws a straight line across a map of England and then continues the same line on around the world at once betrays an ignorance of the crucial subject of spherical geometry. Any map projection attempting to depict our spherical Earth on a flat surface inherently involves a degree of distortion. There seems to be some debate among global geomancy folk about whether major global alignments consist of great circles (circles whose planes pass through the Earth's centre) or rhumb lines (lines on the globe whose planes do NOT pass through the Earth's centre) represented by a straight line on a Mercator-type projection. This does not mean, of course, that global alignments, energy bands, or whatever, cannot exist. Writers, in the past, as diverse as Rudolph Steiner and Dion Fortune have invested belief in the concept.

Glastonbury is often referred to (especially there) as the Heart Chakra of Britain and also of the world. This may initially come over as fanciful New Age bullshit. However, Tiphareth (the "heart" station of the Qabalistic Tree of Life) imagery had repeatedly come through in my own work. My psychic questing colleague and Glastonbury resident Paul Weston has referred to Glastonbury as Tiphareth during lectures, suggesting a model in which the Michael alignment becomes the spine of the giant Albion, different locations up the line equating with various stations on the macrocosmic/microcosmic Tree. As Paul has pointed out, the Thelemic writer Kenneth Grant, hardly noted for his "fluffy bunny" New Age views has described Glaston as representing a planetary heart chakra (in his book *The Magical Revival*; 1972) and if it's good enough for him it's good enough for me. There are implications here, of course, for it follows that an energy dropped into the local matrix at Glastonbury could be pumped all over the planet via the Heart mechanism, assuming that one adopts this paradigm for a moment. Was all this just a symptom of me going "over the top"? I was not sure but one thing WAS certain, in the face of such profound implications I needed to stay grounded and maintain a sense of humour. It was vital not to get carried away, as it were.

On the afternoon of 11th March 1996, I had a long telephone chat with a friend, Julia Day. During our conversation she suddenly mentioned a psychic communication which she had recently received. The material came from an entity which identified itself in no-nonsense terms as the Archangel Michael. The angels appearance in my friend's living room had been accompanied by powerful waves of psychic energy and a considerable "buzz" in the spiritual atmosphere. Being a pagan with little interest in this particular archetype, my friend's initial reaction was to say "But you're Christian, aren't you?"

Consistently to the point, the angel replied "Yes, but I was something else before that." This male figure appeared in a blaze of warm, golden light, visible as a muscular, well-proportioned man with short, curly hair. This description tallied uncannily with with many accounts of classic Michael visions experienced by various folk over the centuries and commented upon by Miller and Broadhurst. I was reminded, too, of a vision experienced by the French geomant Jean Richer, immediately prior to his discovery of the European Michael line. The visitant communicated two key words which seemed to refer to qualities: "love" and "strength". (Occultists among the readership may be reminded here of the balancing and fortifying, protective power of the Qabalistic Cross ritual.) It subsequently dawned on me that the relating of this experience by Julia to me was highly synchronous, as I had been longing for some indication of the quality of the energy which, as an act of faith, I planned to drop into the local subtle energy matrix at Glastonbury at the coming Solstice. Love and strength. . . . well, it did not sound too bad. Tudor Pole had talked prophetically of a new spiritual impulse related to Michaelic energy which was coming. I hoped that he was watching from out there, for it would be good to have him "on the case". By another odd piece of synchronicity, the vision took place at around the time that Hamish Miller and Paul Broadhurst were preparing to set off on the next leg of their survey of the European Michael line. Clearly, something was going on.

On a subsequent occasion, Julia saw Michael approaching an immense dragon, armed with a lance. Upon reaching the beast, Michael had hesitated, realising that he had no need to KILL it. Instead, he plunged the lance point deep into the Earth. As he did so, an image of a woman rose from the ground. (Mary Magdalene?) I was prompted to remember Paddy Slade's lovely book *Seasonal Magic*. Ms. Slade is the only pagan writer of whom I know who includes the festival of Michaelmas on her wheel of the year. In an enlightened and inspiring pathworking, she leads the participant through an experience in which she/he becomes both Michael AND the dragon, thus fostering balance. Personally, I have never been entirely happy with the notion pedalled by some New Agers (and extensively written of in the late Sir George Trevelyan's Operation Redemption) that Michael will bring down the heavenly fire and sweep away all darkness. Such a view, I feel, is unhealthy, unbalanced and essentially patriarchal; devaluing, as it does, the feminine quality of darkness -the darkness in the Earth -the darkness in the nurturing environment of the womb -the darkness under which the seed may germinate and the refreshing darkness which enables us to recharge our bodies and minds with sleep. Surely, the ideal is for Michael's Solar Light

193

energies to fuse with those of the Dark Goddess of the Earth, doing a deal with them. This matter preoccupied me to such an extent that I eventually produced a painting which depicted Michael, having descended from above and made his way down into the Tor's crystal cave, making love to the Dark Earth Goddess; his sword plunged into the cavern floor in an act of cosmic union. The picture was later made into a card which sold well in Glastonbury and was dubbed "the snogging angel" by one retailer who (staggeringly) felt it to be too risque for her shop.

Chapter 31

Equinox

At some point just prior to the 1996 Spring Equinox it occurred to me that the citrine carrier should be exposed to both direct Solar and Lunar rays in addition to a preparatory cleansing and dedication rite. One Sunday afternoon I sat in my office, staring at the chunk of citrine which was placed by a window through which sunlight streamed. As I watched, a haze formed around the stone, like a mist. Sparks of psychic energy danced around the stone continuously, obviously activated by the Sun. It was as if a legion of tiny nature spirits had suddenly been filled with a manic energy. The mist condensed into a spiral, rising above the citrine, about a foot in height. I reflected upon the time which had been given for the Marigold launch: midday on the Summer Solstice. Obviously Solar effects were more than a little relevant.

March 19th, a day before the calendric Equinox, seemed a good day upon which to make an Avalonian return visit. That night, Fred and Colleen, Chalice Well's new wardens, now called Resident Guardians, were hosting the site's first open ceremony. Reaching Glastonbury early in the afternoon I found it to be buzzing with equinoctial power, despite the cold. Wandering round the Lady Chapel I experienced a curious "time slip", hearing a male voice choir singing and, for a moment, where the piped music was coming from. I then there realised that there WAS no audio playing equipment, at which the sound gradually faded. As I stood there I was psychically told that "Others" had also returned from 1539. At that time, I had no clue as to their identities as I had not yet met them.

A "chance" meeting in November was to introduce me to a Lancashire business man a month younger than myself who was quite obviously one of the "Others", given the insights, impressions and feelings that he had long experienced with regard to Glastonbury and the *George* in particular! In the same month I also met a young woman who was quite clearly in the same situation, having experienced a previous incarnation as a young monk who

195

was a member of John's "inner" group. She could not bear to look at a photograph of the *George*'s staircase which I showed to her; dimly recalling a horrible event which seemed to have taken place there during the order's destruction phase. Another young woman wrote to me telling me of a dim remembrance of being woken around 2 a.m., being dragged from the monks' sleeping quarters and taken to a small outbuilding where she was beaten to death. She, too, had "odd" feelings about the *George*'s staircase.

But it was not only "our side" that were back. On December 30th I was to have a great surprise when an old friend who had shared a meal and a drink with Liz and myself happened to spot the Madeleine portrait on my wall and suddenly came out with a stream of psychic impressions which amazed HIM, let alone me. The curious knowledge of Madeleine's circumstances which he revealed strongly indicated that he had been one of the "opposition" who had pursued her into France. It was good to meet up with former members of "the mob" as, for a long time, I had been experiencing a growing suspicion that I could not possibly be the only one who was "back". One senses that the Reformation agents and maybe even Thomas Cromwell himself were pawns who were being used by a very powerful and extremely secret organisation which saw the secret order within the Abbey as a rival not to be tolerated. Cromwell himself was to go to the block a few years later when, presumably, his usefulness had been outlived. The dissolution events provided this faceless group with an umbrella beneath which they could operate, successfully carrying out a bizarre execution on the Tor which bore all the hallmarks of a mock passion play, covertly wiping out every last member of the group which seemed to threaten them and, one suspects, desecrating the Abbey fabric, again under the pretext of serving the Reformation and the King. One cannot but wonder whether even Henry himself was unknowingly under their influence to some degree.

Glastonbury was certainly well "vibed-up" that afternoon. Whist visiting Jimmy Goddard's forgotten site close to the seven beeches on the shoulder of Chalice Hill I met a little smoke-blue elemental which seemed rather intrigued by me; following me almost to the Tor. Looking up at the tower, St. Michael crossed my mind. A pale blue flame shot high into the air above the tower, to be followed by a rising column of energy. Michael seemed well in evidence! Reaching Chalice Well at 8 p.m. I found Colleen and Fred, the new guardians, welcoming in a steady stream of pilgrims. It was heart-warming to see the dark gardens illuminated by countless tiny flames. The ceremony simply involved lighting a candle and being quiet with it anywhere in the gardens between 8 and 10 p.m.; a low-key, non-sectarian format which resulted in pentagram-wearing pagans and local churchgoers rubbing shoulders in a calm but powerful ecumenical get together devoid of any threatening sectarianism.

The event acknowledged the Equinox and new Moon and also signalled remembrance of Wellesley Tudor Pole's concept of a light burning on the physical plane which also produces an inner light able to link with others in an act of gentle magic. There was a subdued but discernable buzz in the air; a feeling that we were taking part in a new beginning; something bigger than any of us could fully comprehend at that point. If WTP was there (he surely MUST have been), then I am sure that he was a happy man by the end of the evening. In some intangible way it all seemed linked to the Michaelic energy which meant so much to Tudor Pole. I remained in the gardens until 9.30, by which time the cold had made its point and I felt a need to thaw out. It had been a magical hour and a half; surely one of the most magical times of my entire life. I left the garden still filled with pilgrims and still lit by the gentle glow of their candles and the few garden flares which Colleen and Fred had provided. The sight of the well head ringed with burning candles on that still, cold but magical night will stay with me for a long time.

In the course of the following morning, a friend asked me if I had ever tried mixing the waters of the Red and White Springs for the purpose of ritual, ceremony or whatever. This fusion of male and female potencies in order to create an androgynous compound sounded highly alchemical and an intriguing parallel to the creation of the Marigold energy. This was definitely something to do upon returning to London, as a mixture of the two waters would provide the ideal cleansing fluid for the citrine block. Arthur's Court just HAD to be the most suitable place for the release of Marigold. Not only Michael and Mary intersect at the waterfall but Miller and Broadhurst suggest that the Red and White Springs may once have merged here, sending an androgynous flow down to the Abbey. Later that year, Nick Mann's splendid book *The Isle of Avalon* would be released in Britain; a book which focuses upon the profound implications of the fusion of the Red and the White and their need to once more flow together, also upon the curious devaluing of the White Spring at Glastonbury in more recent history.

Back home, I prepared the citrine block for its task. In view of the teeming nature spirit activity which I had seen around the stone on that sunny Sunday afternoon, it seemed a good idea to approach the citrine's guardians and ask

197

for their co-operation. With the house quiet, I lit candles for Sol and Luna and began a meditation. After a while, I found myself drastically reduced in size and standing before the crystal, politely requesting access. The citrine's bulk loomed above me like some spectacular crystalline cliff. When I had announced my identity and purpose a door in the crystal swung open and I walked forward down a long, low passageway, roughly cut from the milk-white Goddess quartz. The floor of the tunnel felt dry and brittle beneath my feet and I seemed to be entering a timeless vacuum. At length I came to a spiral stairway and began to ascend. Here and there, fragments of clear, sun-coloured quartz were discernable in the white walls. The incidence of these fragments increased the higher I went until I found myself climbing stairs fashioned from smooth, shiny, amber-coloured crystal; hard, cold and sharp. I fleetingly glimpsed the odd pair of eyes watching me curiously from within the depths of the walls but the nature spirits were generally keeping a low profile.

The top of the staircase led directly to the main chamber. I was in a wondrous cavern; the floor composed of white, Goddess crystal but the upper walls and soaring, vaulted ceiling fashioned from fiery, dark orange quartz which glowed like the Sun. I had expected to find a guardian whom I would address and was therefore surprised to discover TWO thrones standing in the chamber's centre. Of course; a King and a Queen. It made sense in a stone reflecting Solar and Lunar properties. The thrones' occupants were vague and ill-defined, obscured by the blaze of diffused light issuing from both figures; gold and pure white respectively. Bowing low, I greeted the two rulers, introduced myself and asked for their co-operation in the work to come. The king told me that he would be honoured to take part in the Marigold transfer; the queen, too, seeming happy with the idea. (Just as well!) Bowing again I thanked them, wished them and their crystalline domain well and made my way back down the spiral staircase and the low tunnel. Once I was outside the block, the door closed and vanished. Mission accomplished, it seemed. Having returned to "normal size" I thanked the citrine again and was answered by a spark of golden psychic energy.

The following day I ritually blended Red and White Spring water in a bath in which the citrine block would be placed; the covered receptacle to be then hidden away in a wooden box for seven days. The ceremony took place in a previously cleansed working space in which a Lesser Banishing Ritual had been carried out. After consideration, I decided to opt for a "grand manner", High Magic-type ritual in which the Archangels were called upon at the four quarters, as this seemed appropriate to the task in hand and its historical background. What to do with the dogs constituted a slight problem. As the ritual needed some space I had decided to turn the living room into a temple for the occasion, tidying and cleaning it and then ritually banishing the area, taking care to return it to its living room identity at the end. (This is very important if one performs such operations in a room also used for more mundane day to day activities.) The dogs were asleep on the settee. I knew that if I shut them out of the room they were likely to bark on the other side of the door; not over-conducive to an undisturbed ritual although one can normally rise above such things. Why move them anyway? I decided to leave them where they were; their settee coming within the area defined by a cast magic circle. As it happened, they slumbered right through the working!

I was aware of the radiation of great power when the waters of the Red and White springs merged; psychic energy sparkling above the surface of the clear liquid. As the crystal was immersed in the blended waters, I visualised it performing its task and was taken off on a "journey", watching changes and events which would take place within the citrine block. I was shown a hollow space being created within the crystal and the Marigold energy in the form of a glowing egg resting in this newly-created cavity on an ornate four-poster bed equipped with cloth of gold curtains!

Michael continued to "come up in the mix" and a few days later I read a copy of John Michell and Christine Rhone's book *Twelve Tribe Nations*. A section of the book deals with Europe's Michael line. Michell and Rhone describe the typical Michael sites: sacred rocks, island hills, places of initiation and burial. They explain how the Christianised Earth spirit became identified with a poisonous serpent or dragon and how, by piercing it, a Solar hero was believed to fix its power at one spot. Michael, wielding spear or golden sword, also carries a balance, and became heir to caverns such as the Tor's crystal cave. He is a multi-faceted angel, initiating, protecting, watching over pilgrims and souls at death, usually found at Western island mounts within which cavities are concealed and upon which beacon fires blaze.

The gradual Christianisation of the European line spread eastwards from the Irish island monastery of Skellig St. Michael where the strange, beehive cells of Celtic monks may still be seen. Michell and Rhone suggest that Templars travelled the line (which eventually passes through Mount Carmel) as they escorted pilgrims to the Holy Land. The line's bearing is given as 60 degrees West of North and it passes through many sites where Michaelic visions have been experienced. The authors quote Jean Richer's proposition that the line is not a great circle but a rhumb line as it intersects all Longitude meridians on a Mercator projection at the same angle. Robert Forrest's exhaustive mathematical investigations support this view. I read about the line with much interest as it seemed likely that the Marigold energy, if able to self-replicate at junctions, would do so at the English Michael line's intersection with its European counterpart at St. Michael's Mount, its power shooting off to Skellig St. Michael in one direction and to (eventually) Mount Carmel in the other. The energy was certainly going to get around!

Chapter 32

Countdown

The citrine block having been submerged for seven days, it was brought out and placed in a position inside a South-facing window where it could experience maximum exposure to Solar and Lunar rays. This done, I began to plan the practical details of the Solstice launch. This work, however, was interrupted by the sudden need to sit down and commit the following passage to paper. I do not claim it to be "automatic writing" or "direct past-life recall" (if such a thing exists) or anything else, but it is reproduced here due to the strong need to write it which I experienced. Its tone also illustrates the reason why I felt that I owed it to those who had gone before to "see through" the Marigold launch.

How I longed to cast aside my monk' habit, dress as an ordinary man and take ship for France with Madeleine, where I might melt into the warm countryside of Provence. But how could it be? Honour, if nothing else, demanded that I remain at Glastonbury. There was much left to be done: sacred treasures still to be concealed before they fell into the hands of the King's greedy commissioners. . . and the others. And Abbot Richard Whiting - how could I desert that poor, frail, confused old man? I knew that my superior, were he to be honest, would have preferred some other brother for his treasurer and for me to be many miles away. He would happily have remained ignorant of my covert activities and thoroughly disapproved of my preoccupation with the Great Work. It was all too much for him; he who had never sought to be abbot in the first place, content with the quiet life of a chamberlain, supervising the abbey's dormitories, wardrobe and toilets and the accounts from the pilgrims' inn. To lead a quiet life was all He desired; to tread a middle path and run an orderly, efficient house. How our ambitions evade us on occasions!

Madeleine, too, had a mission to accomplish. Among the baggage with which she returned to France was an artifact even more precious than those which we would soon be hiding; an object so sacred and powerful that it could only be safe on the other side of the Channel: the Blue Glass Bowl. Even in Provence English agents might seek for it but our contacts abroad had given us, as a last resort, a hiding place over the border in Northern Italy where any pursuers would not dare to follow.

These and other thoughts occupied my mind as sleepless, I lay in bed upstairs at Abbot Selwood's Pilgrims' Inn as our last night together neared its end. I felt the soft warmth of my beloved's peacefully sleeping body close to me and it seemed hard to believe that by this time the following day she would be far away. My recent nightly absences were probably now of little concern to Father Abbot when compared to the imminent crisis which faced us all. Madeleine had journeyed here in order to accomplish, with me, the creation of a living force which would subsequently be released into the lifeblood of the land. Our ritual mating had been successful. That which had been conceived was now securely and secretly tucked away above the tunnel which linked the pilgrims' house with the abbey; buried like a germinating seed. We had, however, reckoned without one thing: we had fallen in love.

I knew dawn to be upon us, for the plaintive chirping of a small bird could be heard somewhere beyond the mullioned window. Today, the dawn was both unwelcoming and unfriendly, ushering in an early September day at the start of which we would have to part. Following some unaccountable impulse, I gently detached myself from Madeleine's arms and slipped out of bed, crossing to the window. Looking out, I saw, beyond the low buildings across the High Street, the towers of the great abbey which had been my life delicately washed with the pink light of sunrise. I had, I felt, served the place as honourably as I could over the years, dividing my time between my treasurer's duties, my woodwork and the Great Work which now meant so much to me. The Work - that strange, indescribable force which drove me ceaselessly on and on, questing to the limits and beyond.

It had been an unforgettable night. We had made love passionately and urgently as if the following day had no existence. The curtains had remained open so that I might see something to remember for ever: the body of my lover, priestess of the Moon and Mary Magdalene, bathed in the soft Lunar rays. Silently, she rose and stood close to me. We did not speak for there were no words, but suddenly held each other as tightly as a drowning man might clasp a floating beam. Still in silence, we dressed, holding each other once more before the door opened. Halfway down the dark, winding staircase we briefly halted and our lips met for the last time. Was anyone about? Could

I be seen? I felt past caring now. Madeleine's carriage awaited her at the rear of the inn. Reaching the foot of the stairs she turned right, bound for her conveyance. For both of us the pain of parting was almost unbearable for we knew that we would not see each other again in this life. I would have memories. Madeleine, too, would have memories, and possibly a child who would represent the fruit of our union in human form. To prolong things would have been too cruel. Without a backward glance I turned left, leaving the pilgrims' house and crossing the High Street as I headed for the abbey.

Leaves fell and the landscape around me gently died in a blaze of glory. In the days that followed I busied myself with the final tasks to be accomplished before the full force of the storm broke. At night I threw myself into writing up the Great Work. The cellar was a dark, damp, cheerless place, reached by an arduous, backbreaking crawl along an inhospitable tunnel. Yet, to me, that to which I diligently applied myself there was everything. I was at no time happier than when my pen was in my hand; alone and undisturbed. Sometimes, as I wrote, I seemed to feel Madeleine close to me. Southern France was far away but her love was not. Thus, I worked on, knowing the end to be close.

A formally choreographed, robed ritual seemed to be out of the question in Arthur's Court at midday, when many members of the public could quite reasonably be around. A "virtual magic" (visualised ritual) approach, however, would work well enough as people are often to be found meditating in various parts of the Chalice Well gardens. The only vital physical act was the placing of the citrine at the centre of Michael and Mary's crossing at the waterfall and, again, people are often seen doing such things. In a place as charged and sacred as Arthur's Court, casting a circle might seem an almost redundant act anyway, and banishing it could come over as positively inappropriate. During a meditation my colleagues on the inner planes who had been, and were, members of the "Priesthood", stressed that this was a joint effort and that I would NOT be working alone. I still found myself wondering about the properties possessed by the energy which I planned to release. The words "Love" and "Strength" had been received by my friend via the Archangel Michael and I had a strong conviction that they were supposed to be passed on to me. Was Marigold, then, to act as some sort of catalyst which would initiate a further evolutionary stage? As I pondered this issue I felt a delicious golden, glowing heart energy; a strong yet very gentle healing force. (I often experience such a feeling when Madeleine is around.) In a flash, I was told that THIS was what Marigold was really about -LOVE!

The gateway to Arthur's Court, Chalice Well gardens

Love -that word so glibly over-used so endlessly in New Age circles. So what? Did it matter? No, it did not. At the end of the day that glorious heart chakra sensation was real enough and nice, too, so why fight it just to hang on to a security-providing image of oneself which exhibits a safe degree of cynicism. Why be ashamed of the word love? It seemed better to use it with pride.

A visit to the *George* in April 1996 had prompted me to adopt a new course of action with regard to the energy transfer. I found the hotel's ground floor to have a Gents' toilet which boasted but one cubicle and this with a fair-sized gap between door bottom and floor. Given that a full-blown robed ritual would be somewhat out of place in the *George*'s bar I had originally planned to conduct some sort of visualisation working in the toilet which would build up the energy needed to shift the Marigold force. However, with only one cubicle one at once had visions of trying to concentrate on the working while an irate bar user waited impatiently to evacuate his bowels! Clearly this was not on and I would have to embark upon a strategy which could work under its own steam without needing any help from me. In other words, I would HAVE to create an elemental, or what is sometimes known these days as a servitor. John, of course, had been a dab hand at such things. His methods were fine for him but I was living in the 1990's and needed to use methodology which worked for ME. I had learned to create such entities some years previously for such purposes as healing, protection, etc.

A servitor is essentially an astral robot. Such magician-created entities vary from single, one-task specific elementals to larger, more powerful thought-forms with a higher degree of flexibility. The latter variety should be created only after considerable thought, as they have a reputation for taking on a will of their own and becoming awkward, a little like the sorcerer's apprentice's broomstick. It is considered good magical practise to dismantle such elementals when they are no longer of any use, as to leave them to wander in an unemployed state is to add yet more debris to the astral plane. As an alternative to recalling and absorbing them (they are, after all, a projection of a magician's own consciousness) they can be pre-programmed with a self-destruct mechanism which is built into the elemental's core intent statement. It should go without saying that servitor creation is usually something turned to when no other methods are suitable. In his book *Condensed Chaos* and in his now out of print (and wonderful) booklet on servitors, Phil Hine has described the use of servitors which may be activated via a dab of essential oil of an appropriate variety on the elemental's material base (for example, its core sigil drawn on paper). This seemed wonderfully appropriate to my task; a bottle of Calendula oil infusion from Starchild at Glastonbury seeming just the right fluid to use. Once the servitor had been designed, programmed to react to the Calendula stimulus and then fired off into the astral, I was ready for the job, which I planned to execute in two stages on two consecutive days: loading Marigold into the citrine on 20th June and releasing it into the landscape on the 21st at midday.

Just under a week before my departure for the above operation, I learned of a significant event due to take place at the same time via the Druid network. This was a call from Arvol Looking Horse, 19th generation keeper of the Sacred White Buffalo Calf Pipe for the Lakota, Dakota and Lakota nations. (The pipe is a sacred Native American artifact of an importance comparable to that of the Holy Grail or certainly the Blue Bowl.) The call stated that tribal knowledge and prophecy gave 21st June 1996 as a day upon which ALL nations should journey to their sacred sites to pray for global healing and peace. This was Marigold's release day! It really did seem as if the secret Glastonbury order and certain Native American shamans had been getting together somewhere "out there"! On May 3rd a group of "indigenous people" had started a horseback pilgrimage from Saskatchewan (Canada) to Grey Horn Butte; a sacred site in the Black Hills of Wyoming where, at 10 a.m. (South Dakota Mountain Time) their trek would culminate in a ritual and prayers for world peace. The U.N. had been told of their intention and spiritual groups all over the world were asked to participate in this last-ditch attempt to repair a sacred hoop which was in the process of disintegration. Clearly, these people were "the real thing", NOT a bunch of well-healed, white, New Agers pretending to be "native" people or "shamans". The date's synchronicity was, frankly, staggering.

As a result of the call my friend Philip Shalcrass, joint head of the British Druid Order, had organised a ceremony by the Gorsedd of Bards of Caer Abiri (of which I am a member) to take place at Avebury on 21st June at 5.30 p.m., synchronised to occur simultaneously with the event in Wyoming. A representative of the Sioux Nation was present at the ceremony and took part. I found that many of my friends on the London scene knew nothing about the "call" but were keen to join in. After a few days' networking telephone calls we ended up with many folk pledged to "plug in" at 5. 30 to this wonderfully ecumenical current for global healing and peace, both in groups and individually. Several London pagans took part in ceremonies while others took place in Coventry, Berkshire and the Welsh mountains. Unaware of all

206

this, Carole Young suddenly heard (psychically) Native American music and felt a powerful Amerindian presence during a train journey to Cornwall on the day!

Well, the time had come round at last. Equipped with a holdall containing Calendula oil infusion, the citrine block, some hastily-produced fliers informing people of the 5.30 Amerindian link-up on the 21st and the usual items such as torch, pendulum, etc, I headed for Glastonbury.

Chapter 33

D -Day

After booking in at a bed and breakfast close to mysterious Wick Hollow, I ran around the town distributing my fliers. I soon ended up with a number on display in shops, the Assembly Rooms, etc. Most people were sympathetic to the idea and keen to help in the spreading of the word. I was a little surprised when a lady in the church told me that a flier could not be displayed in that building due to the fact that this initiative had nothing to do with Christ or Christianity. I endeavoured to explain that world peace and healing was surely for us all, Christians included, and that Arvol Looking Horse's call was meant to transcend any form of sectarianism. I was simply told that there were more than enough "alternative" outlets up and down the High Street and that display space in church MUST only be reserved for explicitly Christian material. It seemed sad, in a way, but fair enough, it was her gig.

Visiting Arthur's Court, I dowsed the intersection point of Michael and Mary (which may be subject to seasonal and other changes in terms of EXACT location) and selected a strategic point for the positioning of the citrine block at the foot of the waterfall. A Tor trip followed. Although the Solstice was two days away travellers and others were already gathering in large numbers; some with bed rolls spread out close to the tower -bedding destined to be soaked in the pelting rain which fell in the early hours of the next morning. And so to the *George* for drinks and memories; a good way to end a day. The next morning I went out carrying the citrine block in a Safeways carrier bag. Finding the Chapel of Bridget in the Glastonbury Experience courtyard open I rested there for a while, finding its atmosphere very conducive to meditation. I contacted my Otherworldly colleagues and asked them to bless the day's endeavours, lending any help deemed appropriate. I had taken little notice of the chapel before but suddenly realised that I had been missing out on something a bit special. A leaflet provided states that the chapel is situated on the Abbey's boundary wall and houses a concealed doorway into the Abbey. The fireplace is said to date from Abbot Bere's day, it being conjectured that this dynamic figure once occupied rooms on the site. A recent visitor had suggested that the hearth might contain a spring. What a place!

At 11. 05 a.m. I entered the Gents' toilet at the *George*. Locking the door, I took out the servitor's material base, a golden coloured sigil made from holographic card, and stood it on the cistern. Opening the Starchild bottle, I applied a dab of Calendula infusion to the base in order to instruct the astral robot to get on with its job. I was at once psychically told to dab some oil on the citrine also, which I did. I had a mental picture of the servitor wandering down the long corridor that leads to the *George*'s front door and then plunging into the ground; entering the tunnel, absorbing Marigold energy and then rising again; bulging with a precious cargo to be pumped into the citrine. This done, I adjourned to the bar where I ordered a pot of tea. Settling myself close to the bay window I placed the carrier bag containing the citrine block on the floor directly above the tunnel entrance in the cellar below, and just let things happen. I was soon aware of a powerful energy close by. Initially I assumed that the energy transfer was still going on but it soon dawned on me that the task had been accomplished very quickly and what I was feeling was, in fact, the energy now stored in the citrine block. Taking my leave of the *George* I headed back up Bovetown. I felt like someone carrying a powerstation in a supermarket plastic bag, for the radiation from the crystal was unbelievable.

Back in my bedroom at the bed and breakfast I destroyed the servitor's elaborate material base, placed the loaded citrine in my travelling holdall and sank into an armchair. I could see a huge, mobile aura around the bag as if Marigold's contained energy threatened to burst out at any moment. At times, the field took the form of an open funnel which teemed with dancing psychic energy sparks. At other times it resembled distant heatwaves dancing over a Summer landscape. Eventually, things calmed down a bit as Marigold gradually adjusted to her/his very temporary home.

After lunch I dozed for a while and then decided to take an afternoon stroll, heading for the Gog/Magog Oaks via Paradise Lane and Wick Hollow. An unhurried stroll seemed a good antidote to the tensions of the morning's admittedly successful operation and I knew that the Marigold energy would be safe in my room. Wick Hollow was dark, dripping and mysterious. I was fascinated by this natural, eroded cleft through which a road had been driven. I knew the top of Paradise Lane to be close and reflected upon the fact that Katherine Tudor Pole and her friends once returned to the town from the Tor

Chalice Well

via this route, treating it almost as a sacred processional way. It was in nearby Maidencroft Lane, too, that the voice of the Great Mother had been heard in those far-off Avalonian days. I might be coming at things from a quite different angle but I felt a great sense of kinship with these questers from the early years of the century; a sense of shared purpose and continuity. The wet countryside smelled wonderful; the fresh, vital scent of nature having a strongly rejuvenating effect.

Passing the Tor I headed on down Stonedown Lane, turning left at the bottom. Reaching the wide sloping field through which Paradise Lane passed I halted. I was aware of the field being filled with spirit presences of a very welcoming character. Clearly, this was a special place and it was not hard to see why Katherine Tudor Pole found it attractive. The oaks, wonderful though these gnarled trees are, seemed almost an anticlimax after this! An assembly had gathered on the Tor by nightfall. I was tempted to join them but the need for single-pointedness won through and I spent the evening in the bed and breakfast's comfortable lounge. I knew that if I went up to the summit I would inevitably join with the dancing, singing and general energy expenditure which would go on until dawn. I had, however, come to Glastonbury to do a job which would need every ounce of my energy and concentration the next day and so a Tor trip was not really an option. I suddenly became aware of the awesome, profound nature of that which involved me but I knew that getting "freaked-out" by it would help no-one, least of all me, so I turned on the television and watched a European Cup game!

The Solstice dawned cold, wet and misty. By breakfast time the Tor, from which drumming and singing had resounded all night, had fallen silent. When I reached the town I decided to make for Bridget's Chapel. I could do some preparatory meditation here AND it was dry! Seated in the chapel's Glastonbury chair my thoughts turned to Abbot Richard Bere, whose dwellings, some say, were once to be found on the site of the present Bridget's Chapel. Almost at once I saw a brilliant light on the far side of the room and became aware of the presence of a tall, conventionally handsome, charismatic-looking middle-aged man of whose identity I had no doubt. Here he was; the man whom John seems to have succeeded as head of the secret order; the dynamic, radical, intellectual foreign traveller and diplomat. In many ways he was Whiting's absolute opposite; displaying boundless energy, a thirst for heightening the Abbey's profile via building programmes and an enthusiasm for filling the institution's coffers as a result of fostering a Joseph cult centred upon the awkwardly-excavated crypt. Bere's charm and diplomatic skills made him the natural envoy, hence the trips to Italy, which he obviously loved as much as Whiting would probably have hated them. The feeling was one of a couple of mates meeting up after a long absence. I greeted the Abbot, remarking on how good it was to meet an old friend and colleague. Obviously not lacking a sense of humour, the lively Bere commented: "AND I was your boss!", which he certainly was, until his death. John had been very much Bere's man; a personal friend as well as a subordinate. This may help to explain the distrust of John which Whiting seems to have exhibited according to the archives. Bere was around for a while; leaving unobtrusively. After one last link-up with Otherworldly colleagues I rose from my chair, intent upon heading for Arthur's Court. As I did so an inner voice told me: "Don't start rushing about. You'll do it. Take your time."

Reaching the Chalice Well gardens, I first popped into the toilet. The morning's tea intake was making its presence felt and once I had "bagged" a seat in Arthur's Court I would be stuck to it for over an hour. A brimming bladder would be the last thing I would need! As I headed up the broad lawn towards the Court I caught sight of sparks of psychic energy through its open gateway and knew that the "company" were already there and waiting for me. I had the brief mental picture of Madeleine accompanied by black-robed figures. Unlike myself they had not had to walk up Chilkwell Street from the town, taking a somewhat quicker route as those without physical bodies are able to do.

At 11.55 a.m. (BST) I took temporary possession of the Court's only single seat, carrying it over the stream of Red Spring water to the shelter of a tree, beneath which I placed it in a position which enabled me to look straight at the point at which the citrine would be placed in the centre of the intersecting bands. The chair was drenched with rain, so I covered the seat with opened magazines, Folk Roots and Avalon which I took from my holdall. I placed the bag on the wet stonework beside me, unzipped, with citrine at the ready, also a large-dialled alarm clock for timing the countdown. I then settled myself on the seat; the launch an hour away. It had been imperative to get there early in order to claim a seat and to experience the gradual build-up to the Sun's meridian transit; the point at which Marigold would receive the requisite "oomph" to send it out into the matrix delineated by Mary and Michael. Now in position I could relax a little and take time to greet my Otherworldly companions with whom I was to work. Greeting Madeleine

212

was quite an emotional experience. Together, long ago, we had fused our Lunar and Solar energies in order to conceive Marigold; an energy characterised by the words Love and Strength. The "Gold of Mary" was, in fact, an androgynous force which bore a strong resemblance to the hoped-for goal of the old alchemists. In the process of doing this, Madeleine and myself had become lovers and loved each other. We had been equal magical working partners who had also enjoyed a few great times together during Madeleine's stay at the *George*, where our sacred marriage had taken place.

When one studies the one surviving portrait of John the eyes betray a feint twinkle indicative of a man whom, despite a deep involvement in things esoteric had a good capacity for the enjoyment of those things which are here to enjoy and good luck to him! Madeleine had returned to France, as we have seen, taking the Blue Glass Bowl with her; pursuing agents eventually necessitating the crossing of the border into Italy where a safe house was found at Albenga; a place where the sacred vessel could rest in its bricked-up compartment until 1885 when the sheltering building was demolished and the bowl found its way to the tailor's shop at nearby Bordighera where Goodchild found it, subsequently being told to return it to Glastonbury. With Madeleine back abroad, I had lived out a persona which in alchemical and magical terms I had assumed, dying as one who had assumed the role of the sacrificed Solar God, executed and dismembered but returning in the "it all comes round again" spirit of old George's wheel where King Sol and the sacrificed Christ (to whom Madeleine had played Mary Magdalene) are identified as one; paying the price for "quickening inert matter" as Mary Caine puts it. The covert designs of a mysterious, faceless organisation with considerable power and influence, taking advantage of the Reformation in order to act under its "umbrella" to destroy what they saw as a competing or threatening order had helped to bring about John's oddly ritualistic execution. (One is reminded of the manner in which the Nazi party relentlessly persecuted any practitioners of occultism who were not found to be numbered among their own ranks.)

Four and a half centuries later I had returned to finish the job; to effect the fruition of that which had been conceived by the magical union of my French priestess and myself. I did not let the profundity run away with me, however. I was in control and HAD to stay that way. I was, in effect, acting as a midwife, in at the birth of something in whose conception I had already played my part. On the physical plane, too, there had been results, for we have been psychically told that Madeleine gave birth to a baby girl after returning home. It is just possible that in present-day France (or somewhere else) there is someone going around who is actually their very distant descendant. The dripping garden looked wonderful and smelled even better. The continual sound of cascading water just in front of me was very sleep-inducing. This combined with the audial backdrop of birdsong and the intoxicating scent arising from rain-washed greenery and the rich Avalonian soil made a very pleasant environment indeed. Again, I reflected upon the absurdity of anyone considering doing a banishing ritual as a prelude to magical work in this sacred place. By about 12.20 I had become gradually aware of the intersecting Michael and Mary bands teeming with energy which travelled simultaneously in four directions. At 12. 30 I psychically saw that a depression was beginning to form at the place where I intended to place the citrine. The bands had an intelligence of their own, knew of my plan and were demonstrating a willingness to co-operate. They were hollowing out a socket into which they invited me to plug the loaded crystal.

As the Sun crept closer to the Meridian the Marigold energy began to pulse in the citrine block; its frequency increasing in direct correspondence with the decreasing time from transit. By 12.50 the frequency had speeded up to such an extent that a pulse was no longer detectable, replaced by a continuous, dazzling glow. The Michael and Mary bands, too, gathered momentum as midday drew closer. By 12.52 Marigold had blossomed into a towering, egg-shaped mass of light. Two women who had been sitting quite close to me in the Court rose from their seats and unobtrusively wandered away as if some polite request had been made by the Otherworld to the effect that I needed to be alone for a few minutes. 12.55. . . I rose from my seat and plugged the citrine into the socket which Mary and Michael had prepared for it, placing it in the tumbling waters of the famed Blood Spring. The company came closer and we linked hands and wills, forming a circle around Marigold, now but minutes from its birth. Ten seconds from 1 p.m. (midday BST) we started a countdown: 10. . . 9. . . 8. . . By 7 I had a mental image of myself staring into the eyepiece of a Victorian meridian transit telescope like the ones on show in the old Royal Observatory at Greenwich. I saw the Sun's limb swim into the field of view. As it did so I was aware of fragments of Marigold's blazing energy breaking off and hurtling away, riding on the now almost orgasmic power of the Michael and Mary bands.

BLAST OFF! Marigold seemed to explode in a blinding burst of radiant light which shot off in four directions. I then visualised it hurtling through Glastonbury, round the Tor, through the Abbey, over Edmund's Hill, behind the *George*, along the spine of Wearyall Hill. . . on and on through Avebury, into East Anglia, plunging into the sea at Hopton's caravan site, streaking towards the Cornish coast in the opposite direction where it met the European Michael alignment and Miller and Broadhurst's Apollo and Athene bands at St. Michael's Mount; at once self-replicating and flying off to Skellig St. Michael in one direction and heading, in the other, for Monte Gargano, Athens, Delos, Delphi, Rhodes, Mount Carmel and Nazareth. Marigold was on its way, released into the Terrestrial energy matrix at last.

I felt the company unwind; relaxing and collapsing as much as people without physical bodies can do these things. We'd done it! We'd bloody done it! I "shook hands" with my brothers and "kissed" Madeleine. There was a feeling of warmth and togetherness; a sense of mutual achievement. After closing my psychic centres I stamped my feet upon the Court's wet paving in order to ground myself. I was brought down with a bump when I saw that the magazines which I had spread over the seat had glued themselves to it. Taking a face flannel from my bag I soaked it in the Sacred water trickling past at my feet and then used it to clean the seat. I was in the process of packing up when, without warning, I was suddenly engulfed in a wave of unconditional love. It was a great feeling, as if I was receiving thanks for the effort which I had invested in the launch. I felt a glowing, inner warmth impossible to describe. The sensation of joy was so overwhelming that I wanted to run round the gardens and hug people; to jump in the air. I did not, however, as here in reserved Britain such things seldom happen and in any case there was no-one else in sight.

As I made for the town I encountered the last, bleary-eyed revellers struggling down from their night on the Tor. I paused at the baker's shop to buy some sandwiches and then caught the Bristol bus. Four hours later I was back at home, watching a Rolling Stones video as a final grounder. The mission had been accomplished!

Epilogue

I had come a long way since those early psychically-received messages about a Tudor monastic past-life. With Marigold released from the confines of its nursery in the *George*'s cellar tunnel, it was tempting to wonder if I had got to the end of the road, Glastonbury-wise. Madeleine, however, had told me that all this was a beginning rather than an end and as I write this, nine months after the 1996 Summer Solstice, I realise what she meant, already being off on the "next leg"! Perhaps there IS no end. Indisputably, things are happening. I now, incredibly, know three members of the secret order who have reincarnated and who are "back". When I started to give talks in Glastonbury "trailering" this book I was amazed by the number of people who had been psychically picking up material relating to several of The *Circle and the Square*'s thematic strands. Similarly, I was pleasantly surprised by the number of other folk who were apparently picking up on Mary Magdalene's return to our consciousness. As in the words of Fairport Convention's anthemic song *Meet on the Ledge* "It all comes round again. "

What of Marigold? Are its effects quantifyable and if so, by what criteria? Magicians often use the term "lust of result"; words which, as far as I know, originated in Crowley's *Book of the Law*. In simplified terms, this means getting so obsessed with gaining a result from a magical working that one sets up a resistance which disastrously intervenes in the workings of magical currents set in motion, preventing them from doing their job unhindered. I had received vague indications as to the quality of that which I released into the subtle energy matrix. To a large extent, this release HAD to be an act of faith on my part. If it was good enough for "the company" with whom I worked then it was good enough for me. I feel it more important to just let Marigold get on with its job than to worry about the long or short term effects and how to measure them.

Magic, essentially, involves DOING, after all. And the Citrine? After the release at Arthur's Court, I found that a residue of the energy remained in the crystal; an unexpected "perk" of the task. Initially, the crystal rested on a shelf in a shrine-like context, but I soon found that it had no wish to rest; quite the contrary, in fact. I used it for a few room cleansing operations, to which it seemed well-suited. Subsequently, after contacting the crystal's resident guardian spirit for permission, I detached a few crystals from the block in order that a friend could wear them around her neck in a small bag as she was suffering from severe health problems at that time. I still felt, however, that the main block was suffering from inactivity. On 3rd February 1997 I gave a *Circle and the Square* talk (presenting a much cut-down version of the contents of this book) for a private healing group run by Liz. At the end of the talk, the block was handed round so that the assembled company might take turns at holding it. Several folk present were aware of the strong, positive interaction which resulted; the citrine being very "vibed-up" indeed. I decided, therefore, that the block should, from then on, "live" in the room in which Liz carries out her work as a counsellor, reflexologist and healer, where it would be free to "join in" when it felt so inclined. Liz liked the idea, and judging by its radiant state at the end of a day's healing work, so did the block!

Does this book's material throw new light upon the manner of the executions of The Three in 1539? I believe that it does. As Geoffrey Ashe pointed out, (in *King Arthur's Avalon*) the notion of dragging men spreadeagled on hurdles up the Tor, pulled by heavy horses on a cold, late Autumn day when the mud and general conditions must have rendered the task a very difficult one, seems strange indeed; almost insane, I would add. The town would surely have been a more effective place at which to demonstrate the fate of those accused of going against the royal will. Psychic work on the part of myself and others has indicated that a faceless, sinister and very powerful covert magical order seems to have been exploiting the situation and operating under the umbrella of Reformation; one consequence of which may well have been the sacrificial nature of the executions. This order obviously saw John's "mob" (as I now affectionately call this intrepid bunch of psychonauts, to use a term coined by Pete Carroll) as a serious threat; as competition; hence the covert wiping-out of certain monks which does not seem to have been recorded anywhere. Similarly, one has to examine the correspondence between Cromwell and his commissioners in the field to find any mention of the hangings which took place on Wearyall Hill the same day as those of the Three. The victims were found guilty of "rape and burglary" but, at present, we do not know with any certainty whether these charges were manufactured to cover up something quite different.

Similarly, we do not know why "the felon Capon" was reprieved at the last minute. This was upon Cromwell's direct instructions; the letter in which they were given having, sad to say, vanished over the centuries. It seems unlikely that Cromwell and his "three stooges" in Glastonbury were actually members of the secret group which seems to have taken advantage of the prevailing religious/political climate although they were certainly used by it; Cromwell being executed himself the following year; fallen from royal favour and, I suspect, having outlived his usefulness to the the hidden manipulators. We can only guess at the forms of blackmail and coercion that the latter may have used in order to get what they wanted. The fact that the covert murders picked up by various independent psychics were not officially recorded anywhere as far as we can tell strongly indicates that the perpetrators took good care to cover their tracks.

The wiping-out of John's order WAS a savage affair; yet it only succeeded in destroying "the mob" on the physical plane, for they have obviously never stopped working on the inner planes and to work with them now, as I have been honoured and privileged to do, is to experience a wonderful sense of solidarity. As stated above, three other members have now reincarnated and are back; amazing though it may seem and perhaps they are only the ones I know of.

The affair of the bones identified as those of Abbot Whiting is a matter yet to be fully resolved. Given that this identification came through a psychic (Captain Bartlett) in 1908 and was relayed to Bligh Bond; a figure of controversy to this day, one wonders WHAT it will take to persuade the Roman Catholic Church to officially recognise these human remains and bury them in the Sacred soil of Glastonbury Abbey; the ground which poor old Richard Whiting longed to visit one last time as he was taken from Wells to his execution site on the Tor. His request was callously denied. During a psychic session with me in late March, 1995, the Abbot expressed a desire for his earthly remains to return to the place which he loved so much. He also implied that some sort of general recognition of the Three and their tragic deaths was also overdue. Well, we now have the yearly Tor remembrance ceremony and, at the time of writing, a play about the Glastonbury Three is actually scheduled for performance in the Abbey ruins at the Summer Solstice; one year after Marigold's launch!

Things have obviously been moving at Prinknash, where the bones, still trapped in a limbo-esque "Catch 22" situation now rest. Although they spent years languishing in a locked cupboard wrapped up in brown paper they are now kept in a reliquary; each surviving bone individually wrapped in cloth. The remains are available for viewing by visitors although they cannot be unwrapped. Modern science could assist with identification as a pathologist could surely tell whether the bones had all come from the same, once-dismembered corpse and such an expert would also have some idea of their age. We are, of course, dealing with ecclesiastical politics here, given that the Abbey now comes under the jurisdiction of the Anglican Church and the bones are held in a Roman Catholic Abbey. Such problems, though, are surely not impossible to sort out and, as I wrote earlier in this volume, I, for one, will feel that the affair is finally "sorted" when Abbot Whiting's skeleton is finally laid to rest beneath the green turf of Glastonbury Abbey. If the publication of this book in any way promotes the debate and consideration of this issue in a wider context, then it will have been worthwhile if for that reason alone.

Bibliography

Aswynn, F. *Leaves of Yggdrasil.* 1988.

Ashe, G. *King Arthur's Avalon.* 1957.

Benham, P. *The Avalonians.* 1993.

Bond, F. B. B. *The Gate of Remembrance.* 1918.

Bond, F. B. B. *The Company of Avalon.* 1924.

Broadhurst, P. and Miller, H. *The Sun and the Serpent.* 1989.

Caine, M. *The Glastonbury Zodiac.* 1978.

Carley, J. *Glastonbury Abbey.* 1988.

Collins, A. *The Seventh Sword.* 1991.

Collinson, J. *The History and Antiquities of Somerset.* 1791.

Coon, R. *The Glastonbury Zodiac.* 1993.

Coon, R. *The Revelation of the Glastonbury Zodiac.* Pisces. 1995.

Farrar, J. and S. *The Witches' Goddess.* 1987.

Frater U. D. *Secrets of the German Sex Magicians.* 1991.

Frater U. D. *Secrets of Sex Magic.* 1995.

Fortune, D. *Avalon of the Heart.* 1934.

Gale, J. *Goddesses, Guardians and Groves.* 1996.

Gundarsson, K. *Teutonic Magic.* 1990.

Haeffner, M. *The Dictionary of Alchemy.* 1991.

Hine, P. *Condensed Chaos.* 1995.

Kenawell. *The Quest in Glastonbury.* 1965.

Lee, D. *The Cyberzoo. Chaos International,* number 17.

Maltwood, K. *The Enchantments of Britain.* 1982.

Maltwood, K. *A Guide to Glastonbury's Temple of the Stars.* 1929.

Matthews, J. and C. *The Western Way.* 1986.

Michell, J. *The View over Atlantis.* 1969.

Michell, J. *City of Revelation.* 1972.

Michell, J. *The New View over Atlantis.* 1984.

Michell, J. *New Light on the Ancient Mysteries of Glastonbury.* 1990.

Michell, J. and Rhone, C. *Twelve Tribe Nations.* 1990.

Nichols, R. *The Book of Druidry.* 1990.

Pennick, Nigel and Jackson, Nigel, *The New Celtic Oracle.* 1997

Phelps, W. *The History and Antiquities of Somersetshire.* 1832.

Pole, W. T. and Lehman, R. *A Man Seen from Afar.* 1965.

Pole, W. T. *The Silent Road.* 1960.

Pole, W. T. *Writing on the Ground*. 1968.

Rahtz. *Glastonbury*. 1993.

Richardson, A. *Earth God Rising*. 1990.

Richardson, A. and Hughes, G. *Ancient Magicks for a New Age*. 1989.

Ripley, G. *The Compound of Alchemy*. Various editions.

Scott-Holmes, T. *Glastonbury and Wells*. 1898.

Slade, Paddy, *Seasonal Magic - Diary of a Village Witch*. 1997.

Starbird, M. *The Woman with the Alabaster Jar*. 1995.

Thorsson, E. *Northern Magic*. 1992.

Weston, P. *Avalonian Aeon*.

Weston, P. *The Michael Line, the Qabalah and the Tarot*.

Weston, P. *War in Heaven*.

The above three entries are all taped lectures delivered at the Isle of Avalon Foundation in 1995.

FREE DETAILED CATALOGUE

A detailed illustrated catalogue is available on request, SAE or International Postal Coupon appreciated. Titles are available direct from Capall Bann, post free in the UK (cheque or PO with order) or from good bookshops and specialist outlets. Titles currently available include:

Animals, Mind Body Spirit & Folklore
Angels and Goddesses - Celtic Christianity & Paganism by Michael Howard
Arthur - The Legend Unveiled by C Johnson & E Lung
Auguries and Omens - The Magical Lore of Birds by Yvonne Aburrow
Book of the Veil The by Peter Paddon
Caer Sidhe - Celtic Astrology and Astronomy by Michael Bayley
Call of the Horned Piper by Nigel Jackson
Cats' Company by Ann Walker
Celtic Lore & Druidic Ritual by Rhiannon Ryall
Compleat Vampyre - The Vampyre Shaman: Werewolves & Witchery by Nigel Jackson
Crystal Clear - A Guide to Quartz Crystal by Jennifer Dent
Earth Dance - A Year of Pagan Rituals by Jan Brodie
Earth Harmony - Places of Power, Holiness and Healing by Nigel Pennick
Earth Magic by Margaret McArthur
Enchanted Forest - The Magical Lore of Trees by Yvonne Aburrow
Familiars - Animal Powers of Britain by Anna Franklin
Healing Homes by Jennifer Dent
Herbcraft - Shamanic & Ritual Use of Herbs by Susan Lavender & Anna Franklin
In Search of Herne the Hunter by Eric Fitch
Inner Space Workbook - Developing Counselling & Magical Skills Through the Tarot
Kecks, Keddles & Kesh by Michael Bayley
Living Tarot by Ann Walker
Magical Incenses and Perfumes by Jan Brodie
Magical Lore of Cats by Marion Davies
Magical Lore of Herbs by Marion Davies
Masks of Misrule - The Horned God & His Cult in Europe by Nigel Jackson
Mysteries of the Runes by Michael Howard
Oracle of Geomancy by Nigel Pennick
Patchwork of Magic by Julia Day
Pathworking - A Practical Book of Guided Meditations by Pete Jennings
Pickingill Papers - The Origins of Gardnerian Wicca by Michael Howard
Psychic Animals by Dennis Bardens
Psychic Self Defence - Real Solutions by Jan Brodie
Runic Astrology by Nigel Pennick
Sacred Animals by Gordon MacLellan
Sacred Grove - The Mysteries of the Forest by Yvonne Aburrow
Sacred Geometry by Nigel Pennick
Sacred Lore of Horses The by Marion Davies
Sacred Ring - Pagan Origins British Folk Festivals & Customs by Michael Howard
Seasonal Magic - Diary of a Village Witch by Paddy Slade
Secret Places of the Goddess by Philip Heselton
Talking to the Earth by Gordon Maclellan
Taming the Wolf - Full Moon Meditations by Steve Hounsome
The Goddess Year by Nigel Pennick & Helen Field
West Country Wicca by Rhiannon Ryall
Witches of Oz The by Matthew & Julia Phillips

Capall Bann is owned and run by people actively involved in many of the areas in which we publish. Our list is expanding rapidly so do contact us for details on the latest releases.

Capall Bann Publishing, Freshfields, Chieveley, Berks, RG20 8TF